D1075011

DOING ACCOUNTING HISTORY
CONTRIBUTIONS TO THE DEVELOPMENT OF ACCOUNTING THOUGHT

STUDIES IN THE DEVELOPMENT OF ACCOUNTING THOUGHT

Series Editors: Gary John Previts and Robert J. Bricker

Recent volumes:

STUDIES IN THE DEVELOPMENT OF ACCOUNTING THOUGHT
VOLUME 6

DOING ACCOUNTING HISTORY

CONTRIBUTIONS TO THE DEVELOPMENT OF ACCOUNTING THOUGHT

EDITED BY

RICHARD K. FLEISCHMAN

John Carroll University, Cleveland, USA

VAUGHAN S. RADCLIFFE

Case Western Reserve University, Cleveland, USA

PAUL A. SHOEMAKER

University of Nebraska, Lincoln, Nebraska, USA

2003

JAI
An imprint of Elsevier Science

Amsterdam – Boston – London – New York – Oxford – Paris
San Diego – San Francisco – Singapore – Sydney – Tokyo

ELSEVIER SCIENCE Ltd
The Boulevard, Langford Lane
Kidlington, Oxford OX5 1GB, UK

First edition 2003

Library of Congress Cataloging in Publication Data
A catalogue record from the British Library has been applied for.

ISBN: 0-7623-0983-0
ISSN: 1479-3504 (Series)

⊗ The paper used in this publication meets the requirements of ANSI/NISO Z39.48-1992 (Permanence of Paper).
Printed in The Netherlands.

CONTENTS

PREFACE

Accounting historians have had a hard road to travel in the U.S. For nearly two decades now, history articles have not been welcomed by journals of the perceived highest echelon. Lacking empirical bases, for the most part, history has received short shrift from the *Accounting Review*, the *Journal of Accounting Research*, and the *Journal of Accounting and Economics*. Relatedly, history scholarship is frequently regarded as of secondary importance even when appearing in top-rank journals published abroad, such as *Abacus*; *Accounting and Business Research*; *Accounting, Organizations and Society*; and *Contemporary Accounting Research*. At many universities, accounting history studies must be supplemented by work of a more contemporary genre lest their authors be discriminated against in tenure and promotion decisions. While a broad portfolio of work might indeed be more desirable, an academic would scarcely fail with a publications list that included nothing but capital-market or agency-theory research.

The discrimination does not seem as prevalent in other venues around the globe where accounting academics have more well-rounded educational backgrounds and interests. Perhaps the difference lies in the frequency with which history is a component of university curricula, either as a course or as a feasible dissertation topic. In the U.S., there are only a handful of doctoral-granting institutions that would allow an accounting history dissertation.

Accounting historians, as a community of scholars, have few options. We can complain bitterly about the shortsightedness of U.S. academe; we can write articles in which we argue the contemporary relevance of history in terms of understanding accounting practice. These approaches have been tried and seem to have fallen upon increasingly deaf ears. Maybe the only solution is for us to write more and better history.

It is with this hope in mind that the Academy of Accounting Historians some years ago commissioned this manual on doing accounting history. Originally the idea of Paul Miranti and Paul Shoemaker, the plan was to solicit chapters on various topics in accounting history methodology from leading scholars in the field. However, the project languished because certain designated authors did not deliver their chapters in timely fashion. Subsequently, Professor Miranti ascended to an administrative position, leaving him insufficient time to complete the effort. Professors Fleischman and Radcliffe joined Professor Shoemaker to bring the project to fruition. The lengthy publication delay has mandated that some of the authors herein represented have had to expend considerable efforts updating submissions made years ago. The editors are grateful to these authors who have undertaken revisions with universally good grace. It is service to the discipline above and beyond the call of duty. Likewise, the Academy is accorded high marks for not allowing the project to lapse.

Precedent to a brief synopsis of the articles comprising this book's contents, the editors would like to say a word about its appropriateness for a series entitled "Studies in the Development of Accounting Thought." It is the obligation of accounting historians to research the context in which the great thinkers of the profession have moved its theory forward, much in the same way that the Financial Accounting Standards Board has promulgated its concepts project to rationalize the standard-setting process. Furthermore, accounting historians are charged with bringing together information that has heretofore been disjointed and isolated. This focus on past theoretical offerings and/or practical applications can be either horizontal, as in drawing together the thought and times of a distinguished accountant through biography, or vertical, as in the analysis of an aspect of accounting's development over a longer time horizon. A classic example of the horizontal would be the inaugural volume in this series, Stephen Zeff's exhaustive biography of Henry Rand Hatfield. David Solomon's *Studies in Costing* (1952) exemplifies a vertical rendering of one of accounting's important theoretical and practical components over extended time.

Accounting historians of the next generation need to know how these essential contributions have been conceived, formulated, and presented. While it might be suggested that these essays do not constitute the "development of accounting thought" per se, the editors represent that accounting thought would be severely fragmented were it not for the organizational and presentational talents of the discipline's historians. It is to communicate this vital art that this primer stands testament.

The opening article of the collection is by two of its coeditors, Richard Fleischman and Vaughan Radcliffe, commissioned before they became editors. It is a broad, historiographic survey of the many approaches that contribute to the richness of accounting history. Featured are the dichotomization of the field into traditional and critical scholarship, the old and new accounting history, and modernism/postmodernism. The theoretical underpinnings of the major paradigmatic schools (Neoclassicism, Foucauldianism, Marxism/labor process) are discussed, along with critiques of each. The authors urge a softening of the lines of demarcation that divide these groups in order to take advantage of the positive synergies and additive knowledge forthcoming from interaction and mutual respect.

There follows thereafter three chapters that deal with various aspects of archival research. Richard Fleischman and Thomas Tyson attempt to justify the importance of primary source utilization, as well as to provide helpful hints for doing archival research and for accessing archival collections in the U.S. and the U.K. Gloria Vollmers writes of her experiences in doing archaeological research where the archives are more typically physical rather than written. She tells of the pitfalls associated with this variety of historical research and reviews the literature of studies done on ancient cultures. Finally, Professor Fleischman returns again to consider how archival research is necessary for unraveling episodes in cost accounting history when theory/practice schisms apparently occurred. Using the British Industrial Revolution and the age of Taylor and scientific management as case studies, Fleischman cautions that a misunderstanding of these formative periods has resulted from the tendency of historians to accept the amount and sophistication of the accounting reflected in the literature as a surrogate for the techniques actually in practice.

The next section features two articles dealing with specific approaches to historical research that transcend the archival methodologies described above. Theresa Hammond discusses the importance of studying underrepresented groups in U.S. accounting history, specifically African Americans and women. She emphasizes the value of oral history in work she has done, but supplements that technique with other innovative methods to compile as complete a story as possible. Dale and Tonya Flesher have had long and distinguished careers in the art of biography. Their article explores their methodology in depth, while providing valuable insights into how information about historical figures can be secured from the government, typically after an onerous process.

Articles by Paul Miranti, Daniel Jensen, and Edward Coffman (Miranti et al.) and by Robert Bricker and Nandini Chandar narrate how accounting historians can secure important allies in doing accounting history. Miranti et al. analyzes the immense theoretical and practical contribution business and economic historians have made to what we do. Since their discipline is significantly older and more mature than ours, it is most helpful if we take some of our methodological cues from their time-honored work. The Bricker and Chandar article demonstrates the synergies that exist between accounting history and what must be considered mainstream accounting research in the U.S. Historical perspectives provide enhancement to empirical research in such areas as capital-markets and agency-theory studies. Illustrating another important avenue of support, Richard Vangermeersch draws upon his vast experience working with practitioners' organizations to furnish ideas as to how their participation in historical projects can be encouraged. Vangermeersch takes us step-by-step through the publication of the "Encyclopedia," an historical reference of significant appeal to the practice community.

The concluding section of the book is comprised of two articles that point the way forward for accounting history in the 21st century. Leonard Goodman and Dan Palmon's article demonstrates the state of the art as far as the Internet is concerned. The authors tell us chapter and verse what is available out there in cyberspace, as well as caution us to beware the pitfall of an overdependence upon this resource. The book concludes with an article by Francisco Badua, Gary Previts, and Miklos Vasarhelyi (Badua et al.) that explores the attributes of the *Accounting Research Database*, a classificatory taxonomy of the contents of the *Accounting Historians Journal* and of the citations contained therein. The paper indicates the value of such media for historical research and prognosticates how their refinement will expand the potential for the extended use of historical materials by students and scholars, policy makers, and practitioners.

It is the editors' fervent desire that this collection of essays will contribute to the art of accounting history research. We thank the Academy of Accounting Historians for its foresight in encouraging this project.

Richard K. Fleischman
Vaughan J. Radcliffe
Paul A. Shoemaker

Editors

DIVERGENT STREAMS OF ACCOUNTING HISTORY: A REVIEW AND CALL FOR CONFLUENCE

Richard K. Fleischman and Vaughan S. Radcliffe

INTRODUCTION

Accounting history is an established and growing body of research, marked by differing streams of thought, a tremendous opportunity for the study of primary source material, and an energetic and internationally diverse academic group. The purpose of this piece is to review recent developments in accounting history, to describe the main bodies of work, and to narrate the positions of the various historiographical divisions in relation to one another. While ostensibly working in the same subject area, accounting historians have of late perhaps overemphasized the philosophical and tactical differences between approaches. We use the opportunity of this discussion to call for a confluence of these streams of thought, if not in the rather unlikely outcome of unanimity of view, then at least in mutual learning and exchange.

The remainder of the paper is organized as follows. The move to contextualize accounting practice is examined first as providing the underpinnings of "new" or "critical" accounting history. Key areas of inquiry that have been characteristic of this body of research are developed to illustrate the particular concerns of this work. This is followed with a direct comparison of critical and traditional accounting histories, a discussion that is further refined through attention to the characteristics of the Neoclassical, Foucauldian, and Marxist/labor-process paradigms as they have developed in recent accounting history. Further comparison of "new" and

Doing Accounting History: Contributions to the Development of Accounting Thought
Studies in the Development of Accounting Thought, Volume 6, 1–29
ISSN: 1479-3504/PII: S1479350402060015

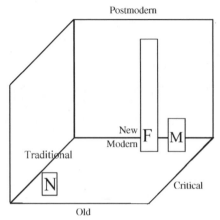

Fig. 1.

Historical Research Paradigms. *Key:* N = Neoclassicism; F = Foucauldianism; M = Marxism. *Note:* Figure 1 is a diagram without specific scale, but ordinal in nature. It shows the relationship of three research paradigms within three dichotomous research approaches, or perspectives. The three paradigms, Neoclassicism, Foucauldianism, and Marxism, are social contextualizations used as interpretive styles. The three dichotomous approaches, old/new, traditional/critical, and modern/postmodern are value systems applied to the paradigms. At nearly opposite ends of the spectrum are Foucauldianism and Neoclassicism where Foucauldianism interprets history from a critical, new, and postmodern value system; Neoclassicism uses a traditional, old, and modern approach. Marxism more closely resembles the Foucauldian interpretive style using critical and new value systems, but more closely resembles Neoclassicism in its application of the modern perspective.

(The authors thank Paul Shoemaker for the design of Fig. 1.)

"old" accounting history is followed by a discussion of modern and postmodern influences. We conclude with a call for accounting historians to improve their craft, irrespective of their chosen paradigm or approach, through mutual learning and exchange (Fig. 1).

THE MOVE TO CONTEXTUALIZATION

In the last 15 years, there has been an increasing focus on the history of accounting among more theoretically driven researchers, encouraged in part by a growing interest in accounting practice. Attention has been paid to the circumstances surrounding the emergence and development of accounting practices, often with the aim of uncovering relations between accounting and society (Burchell et al., 1980, 1985; Hopwood, 1988). In what has been termed the "new accounting history" (Miller et al., 1991), researchers have analyzed social influences, sometimes known as contextual factors, on the development of accounting techniques, such as value-added accounting (Burchell et al., 1985), cost accounting (Loft, 1986), bookkeeping (Hoskin & Macve, 1986), inflation accounting (Robson, 1994), budgeting systems (Preston et al., 1992), and efficiency auditing (Radcliffe, 1998). Much of this research was initially stimulated by Tinker et al.'s (1982) historical work in tracing what was argued as the normative origins of positive theory.

Analysis of relations between accounting and the social world can help in understanding how accounting and auditing practices are developed. It can also aid in providing a more detailed understanding of the processes involved in the interaction between accounting and the social. Researchers have come to consider how ideas, often pre-existing, are taken up and given specific shape (Burchell et al., 1985; Hoskin & Macve, 1986). Burchell et al. (1985, p. 382) stated the research problem succinctly in arguing that the relationship of accounting, auditing, and the social world has tended to be stated and presumed, rather than explicitly described and analyzed by reference to practice. Indeed, in recurring editorials in *Accounting, Organizations and Society*, Hopwood called for an attention to practice that focused more on studies of accounting as a discipline rather than *in* accounting, in the sense of working within the discipline to refine extant technical knowledge. As Hopwood (1978, p. 94) put it, in calling for an analysis of the way that accounting problems were defined and positioned for "solution" in practice:

> The derivation of such descriptive appreciations of accounting in action and the process of accounting change might not be welcomed by many practitioners however. Whilst there might be demands for technical assistance there are few, if any, signs of interest in studies, which question the formal roles served by accounting information, the negotiated and political nature of technical accounting solutions and the way in which design options are constrained and shaped. For such studies *of* accounting rather than *in* accounting, where accounting itself is regarded as a problematic organizational and social process influenced by, and in turn influencing many vital elements of the wider context in which it operates, are quite obviously capable of challenging the status quo by providing a basis on which to question what has not been questioned and what some would prefer not to be questioned (emphasis in original).

It was with this stance of reconceptualizing present practice through a lens provided in the uncertainties of the past that accounting history was used to contextualize accounting practice, an approach that Hopwood presciently observed would inevitably present a challenge to the authority of contemporary practice.

CRITICAL ACCOUNTING RESEARCH AND THE DEVELOPMENT OF PRACTICES

The development of different branches of research presents problems of classification. While some write of "alternative" accounting research (Broadbent &

Guthrie, 1992), others refer to the "new accounting history" (Miller et al., 1991), "critical" or "radical" accounting (Chua, 1986; Moore, 1991), or the "new accounting research" (Morgan & Willmott, 1993). While each brings different nuances, there is general agreement as to the body of work that is referenced. For consistency, we use the term "critical accounting research" in the remainder of the text. As Morgan and Willmott (1993, p. 3) suggested, critical accounting research has broadly been concerned to be "self-consciously attentive to the social character of accounting theory and practice." It has involved a questioning of the consequences of accounting and skepticism of the roles of accounting in society (Burchell et al., 1980). Calls for an accounting to improve corporate governance, to establish the "facts" of costs, to link corporations with capital markets, and to enable the state's orchestration of both private and public enterprises have all been predicated given the view of accounting as a largely calculative, objective, and socially neutral activity. Such calls involve a vision of accounting as a means to an end, a way of taking moral objectives and turning them into activities and facts (Miller & O'Leary, 1993, p. 189). Critical accounting research seeks to resist such presumed facticity as part of an ongoing questioning of practice.

In line with Hopwood's call for studies *of* accounting, the new accounting research problematized and placed at the center of its concerns the presentation of accounting as an objective practice. One of the key means of destabilizing this claimed objectivity, and undermining technocratic representations of accounting, has been an analysis of the social and historical constitution of specific branches of accounting practice. To illustrate the specific concerns of this work, we now examine a leading example of such analysis, presented by Burchell et al. (1985) to review certain of the conceptual and theoretical concerns that developed as part of an attention to accounting change. Significantly, Burchell et al. (1985, pp. 399–401) described their work as a genealogy, informed by Foucault's theoretical analysis:

> Notions of efficiency and participation did not exist as a pair of pre-given, disembodied categories .... Nor did the debates and discussions concerning them simply consist of a series of words and statements, lacking any historical or contextual specification save that of the dates between which they occurred. In our discussion of the three arenas we have attempted to outline a three-branched genealogy (Foucault, 1977) of the specific social space within which value added appeared and developed. As a consequence of tracing this genealogy, the space which the value added event occupied is seen to be comprised of a very particular field of relations which existed between certain institutions, economic and administrative processes, bodies of knowledge, systems of norms and measurement, and classification techniques. We have called such a field an accounting constellation ....
>
> It is this idea of an accounting constellation, along with the processes of its formation, modification and dissolution, which now appears as our prime object of interest.

To Burchell et al., the conditions of accounting change were objects in themselves to be studied as part of efforts to understand relations between accounting, organizations, and society. Their work presents a powerful and early statement of these concerns, concerns that have been addressed in an ongoing stream of research (Morgan & Willmott, 1993).

In contrast to traditional bodies of historical research, the "facts" of the development of an interest in value-added accounting in the U.K. in the 1970s were rather subsidiary to the social processes that they illustrated. In this sense, the "story" of value added was of analytic importance less for the particularities of the case and more for its resemblance to other events in the development of accounting practice. In tracking the development of value-added accounting through what they termed three "arenas," Burchell et al. examined the influence of concerns with accounting standards, macro-economic management, industrial relations, and information disclosure. But beyond the specific terms of this debate, a broader interest in the functioning of accounting is revealed. It is in challenging an essential or predetermined characterization of accounting practice that critical researchers turned to history, as Burchell et al. (1985, p. 409) described their interest in conclusion:

> We have . . . adopted a historical, genealogical approach as a device to avoid the assumption that accounting has some essential role or function. Our working principle in this has been that 'the cause of the origin of a thing and its eventual unity, its actual employment and place in a system of purposes are worlds apart' (Nietzsche, 1969, p. 77, quoted in Minson, 1980). It has been suggested elsewhere that the organization of our concepts and the philosophical difficulties that arise from them have to do with their historical origins. When there occurs a transformation of ideas, whatever made the transformation possible leaves its mark on subsequent reasoning. It is as if concepts have memories (Hacking, 1981) . . . we have attempted to indicate how the processes underlying the value added event determined the character of the discourse bearing the category value added.

As a prime example of Foucauldian-influenced research in accounting, Burchell et al.'s work was important in locating the potential contributions of a concern with accounting development and change, as well as in indicating the theoretical potential of Foucault's work in accounting. We discuss this further below, but we would note for now that their writing was broadly contemporaneous with other work similarly influenced by postmodern or post-structuralist inquiry (Sarup, 1989), that questioned the rhetorical structures of research and practice (Arrington & Francis, 1989; Boland, 1989), re-interpreted the history of accounting (Miller & O'Leary, 1987), and further elaborated processes of accounting change (Radcliffe et al., 1994; Robson, 1991).

TRADITIONAL AND CRITICAL

Traditional Historiography

The dichotomy between "traditional" and "critical" accounting researchers is difficult to explore because there have been two distinct strands of traditionalism in the recent past, while critical research has stood consistently in opposition to both. The critical school became prominent in the 1980s, partly in protestation against the U.S. accounting research mainstream, a body of research that in actuality has lost very little of its privileged position in the past two decades. Drawing inspiration from natural sciences methodology, traditional research sought to discover the natural laws of accounting. Positivists took rationality for granted, found comfort in their objectivity, and felt they were discovering and describing the one true way (Lodh & Gaffikin, 1997, pp. 438–439). The research investigations of the mainstream, particularly into capital markets and agency theory, were highly quantitative (Baker & Bettner, 1997, p. 293), conservative in defense of the status quo (Gallhofer & Haslam, 1997, p. 78), and confident in the "reflection of a technical reality" (Covaleski & Dirsmith, 1988, p. 20). Particularly galling to critical theorists was positivism's insistence upon its own neutrality, that "what is" could be explored uncritically without questioning the role of vested interests in giving birth, sustaining, and legitimizing the purported reality of the status quo (Hines, 1988, p. 259). Baker and Bettner (1997, p. 303) drew up a bill of particulars against "mainstream" research by identifying five underlying assumptions briefly summarized as:

• Cause and effect relationships exist between initial conditions and outcomes.
• These connections are determinable and can be used to predict outcomes with certainty.
• Relevant human behavior is governed by cause and effect (no free will).
• All economic activities can be quantified.
• All humans have equal access to systems within which economic activities are undertaken.

It would be comforting to think that the philosophical differences between traditionalists and critical researchers would engender lively discourse and dialogue, but, unfortunately, the debate has been one-sided in that the mainstream has refused to become engaged. What debate has occurred has included charges of exclusion from journals based solely upon research prospective, the discounting of critical research in personnel actions at leading U.S. universities, and a continuing questioning of conventional modes of analysis. Over time a number of important institutions have developed, including scholarly journals (*Accounting, Organizations and Society*; *Accounting, Auditing and Accountability Journal*; *Critical Perspectives on Accounting*) and conferences dedicated to the publication of critical research.

Fortunately, a second contretemps between traditional and critical researchers has been waged in more civilized fashion, albeit far distant from those U.S. journals typically ranked highest in terms of prestige and scholarship. Here the participants are accounting historians per se. While some of the issues are similar, at least in the U.S., there is no privileged position as all accounting historians, whether traditional or critical, have been cast into the same hell (perhaps purgatory) by colleagues doing contemporary research with little or no grounding in the past. They understand little more about history's value than the average practitioner, leaving all historians as outcasts. Yet, we soldier on, perhaps intellectually praying that we could teach at a British or Australian university, but at the same time willing to accept a North American professor's remuneration.

Perhaps a good starting point for discussion is the "traditional" accounting historian caricature Carnegie and Napier (1996, p. 8) attributed to a "new" accounting historian. Depicted is an historian who "decontextualizes accounting," "subtly denigrates the past" by measuring it in terms of the present, deploys neoclassical economics as a sole explanatory paradigm, and is embarked on a "treasure hunt" to locate origins and precedents for present-day practices and technologies that are revered as representing linear progress from former darkness. While untrue collectively, these attributes have all been raised individually in critical historiography attacking the traditionalist position.

We have seen earlier how contextual expansion to include political, cultural, and societal parameters to complement traditionally privileged economic factors has been a feature of critical research (Hopwood, 1987; Loft, 1986). As will be discussed in the succeeding section, most accounting historians who bear the "traditionalist" label subscribe to the economic-rationalist paradigm wherein accounting developments are explained in terms of rational, cost-beneficial deci-sions on the part of entrepreneurs within the context of a neoclassical, transactions-based theory of the firm. Indeed, given this theoretical grounding, a charge of economic reductionism, frequently deserved, has been leveled against much his-torical research of this genre. While Marxism as a predominant, critical-research paradigm has likewise been so accused, the "vulgar" Marxism of earlier times, with its focus on economic determinism and dialectical materialism, has given way to a more eclectic "labor-process" orientation that encompasses a variety of disciplines and perspectives. Similarly, economic rationalism, the "traditionalist" paradigm, has not suffered having its theoretical underpinnings undermined by expanded investigations, including the gamut of contexts espoused by critical scholars.

Traditional and critical accounting historians have substantial disagreements about issues such as objectivity, facticity in history, and the significance of primary source material. Traditionalists have tended to think themselves the neutral reporters of information they have gleaned from the past through archival investigation. These data are seen as reflective of an historical reality. In this sense, traditionalists believe that the figures of the past should speak for themselves. The historian acts as an intermediary by bringing to light primary source materials that serve as the medium by which the past communicates an historical reality. Critical historians, primarily postmodernists, have significant difficulties with this interpretation of the historian's craft. First of all, the possibility for an historian to provide an objective narrative is problematic. On this there is agreement; even traditionalists concede that the mere selection of which pieces of information to report from the larger archive is itself subjective (Fleischman & Tyson, 1997). Related to the objectivity issue is the question of historical facticity. Most traditionalists would argue, as did Tyson (1995), that facts transcend mere perception and should be viewed as representative of reality. This position has no place in postmodernism, particularly in Derridian deconstructionism, where an historical text is subject to as many different interpretations as readers. Funnell (1996, p. 48) put the traditionalist position well, observing that many were comfortable with interpretation and theorizing but that it should "be tethered in its wandering to a spike of facts."

Critical historians are also willing to debate the traditionalists' emphasis on primary sources as the medium through which the past speaks. There are two central issues here. First, the documents themselves achieve neither neutrality nor objective reality. The Marxist commentary has been particularly focused on this point. Accounting functions that economic rationalists take for granted (such as striving for efficiency and cost reduction) have "conflictual underpinnings" (Tinker & Neimark, 1988; Tinker et al., 1991). Accounting ranges from a method "to bolster particular interest groups" (Tinker et al., 1982, p. 167) to an "ideological weapon" in the class struggle over wealth distribution (Tinker et al., 1991, p. 37). Second, there are the numerous categories of people who because of economic or social position have no access to an historical accounting archive. Consequently, the voices of the past speaking to us through primary sources are severely limited. Hammond and Sikka (1996, p. 79), in urging oral history as a mechanism to give voice to suppressed groups, have argued, "traditional historians elide the complexity of accounting change and ignore the impact on and the contribution of ordinary people's struggles in checking, advancing, facilitating and resisting accounting developments."

Several aspects of the Carnegie-Napier caricature concern the traditional historian's perception of how the present impacts his/her efforts to narrate the past. We are not sure that very many accounting historians, as distinct from mainstream positivists, subscribe to the Whig interpretation of history; namely, that the present is the end result of progress and continuous improvement from the past. Famous economic rationalists Johnson and Kaplan (1987) did not subscribe to the idea that the present constitutes best practice when they declared that all then-contemporary managerial accounting techniques had been devised by 1925 and had subsequently lost their relevance.

A more significant issue was the charge leveled by Miller and Napier (1993, p. 639) when they wrote of traditional historiography, "within the traditional evolutionary model, the now is always present, if only *in utero*, in the then." Although the comment was reduced in intensity to "a warning against using the past as a shadow of the present" (Carnegie & Napier, 1996, p. 16), the points raised by Fleischman and Tyson (1997, pp. 93–96) still stand. It is not realistic to think that historians can so envelop themselves in the past that contemporary biases and agendas can be precluded from intrusion upon the analysis. Moreover, by establishing linkages between past and present, the historian is able to engage the reader more fully into the reading and comprehension of the narrative.

Critical Historiography

It would be an injustice to critical research to claim that a major priority was to debunk the efforts of traditionalists. Such a limited and unfruitful purpose is belied by the variety of analytical perspectives critical scholars have employed in the study of accounting's past, present, and future. Perhaps a good starting place for the following summary pages would be Laughlin's (1999, p. 73) recent definition of critical accounting to be:

> A critical understanding of the role of accounting processes and practices and the account-
> ing profession in the functioning of society and organisations with an intention to use that
> understanding to engage (where appropriate) in changing these processes, practices and the
> profession.

In relation to history specifically, Laughlin (1987, p. 482) argued that the past provides critical research with insights that help forge the "methodological tools" to change the future. One can immediately see in these descriptions the proactive orientation of critical accounting research, whether or not it is realistic to expect that academicians can influence change. While Laughlin (1999, pp. 74, 77–78) believed that the critical engagement could precipitate meaningful change, he conceded that this parameter of critical research is its weakest heretofore and wondered if it is not the case that too many of his colleagues feel that their "job" is to expose injustices rather than to participate actively in seeking remedies.

The diversity of the critical-research project is investigated by Lodh and Gaffikin (1997, pp. 437–438) in which the authors identified 10 alternative theoretical approaches under the critical umbrella. Marxism (labor process) and Foucauldian-ism, as pervasive paradigms in contemporary historiography, will be discussed at length in the next section. Jürgen Habermas of the German critical school represents the transition of critical theory into postmodernism as "the theorist who best articulates a sense of the commingling of the modern and the post-modern" (Arrington, 1997, p. 4). Habermas' methodological approach underscored the centrality of language and communication as necessary prerequisites for non-violent change to occur (Habermas, 1990, p. 9; Laughlin, 1987, p. 485). Habermas was also influential in moderating Derridian deconstructionism. Deconstructionism, as a fourth critical perspective, is distinctly postmodern in its skepticism about the hermeneutic "fusion of horizons" wherein participants in dialogue unite their differences in understanding. Arrington and Francis (1989, p. 3) observed, "the purpose of deconstruction, then, is to subvert the attempt to get closure around knowledge production – the attempt to silence other voices by illicitly claiming to possess a superior awareness of 'truth.' " Habermas, by contrast, urged a critical hermeneutics that constrains total democracy of interpretation lest closure be unattainable. Arrington and Puxty (1991, p. 52) questioned the Habermasian views that "consensus was the objective of social discourse" and that, in dialogue, "rationally motivated agreement must be reachable" (Habermas, 1990, p. 105).

Other alternative perspectives include Gramsci's concept of hegemony wherein accounting's role is examined in relation to strategies developed by conflicting interest groups of people aligned on the basis of belief rather than economics (Richardson, 1987); "symbolic interactionism and ethnomethodology," typified by Covaleski and Dirsmith's (1988, p. 20) view that accounting is perhaps more reflective of a social rather than a technical reality; and Armstrong's (1991, pp. 1, 9–10) "critical structuralist" vision that whereas the traditional agency theorist is concerned only with a monitoring and incentive system that socializes agents into an organizational structure to allow for top-down control, a radical focus would be on how the contradictions and tensions of conflicting interests would impact agency relationships within a capitalist system. The reader is referred to the Lodh and Gaffikin article for the other strains of critical scholarship.

Critical accounting's agenda presents a grand design. Its task does not end by describing the world; it suggests a duty to change it (Cooper, 1997, p. 15, referencing Neimark, 1990). An "overwhelming priority" is to deal proactively with questions of justice (Arrington, 1997, p. 13), and to wade in on those occasions where the public interest demands (Bebbington et al., 1999, p. 50). Prominent in critical action is the power of accounting as an enabler, "to act as a force for radical emancipatory social change through making things visible and comprehensible and helping engender dialogue and action towards emancipatory change" (Gallhofer & Haslam, 1997, p. 82). As discussed, part of the enabling task of accounting is to give voice to suppressed groups who historically have had no voice; including women (Kirkham & Loft, 1993), ethnic minorities (Annisette, 1999; Fleischman & Tyson, 2000; Gaffney et al., 1995; Hammond & Streeter, 1994), the poor, indigenous populations (Neu, 1999), post-colonial societies (Arnold & Hammond,

1994; Catchpowle & Cooper, 1999; Elad, 1998; Hoogvelt & Tinker, 1978), and even perhaps the more obscure participants in the accounting function (Cooper, 1997). At times, amid a certain self-pity, it may seem that critical researchers would have themselves added to the list of the disadvantaged given their perception of "accounting's repressive tendencies" (Gallhofer & Haslam, 1997, p. 77) and the marginalization that critical researchers perceive arising out of their stance against the status quo and their advocacy of changes to the prevailing system (Baker & Bettner, 1997, p. 307).

We would conclude this section by urging that the gulf between traditional and critical accounting historians is not as wide as much of the literature would suggest. Critical research has vouchsafed to traditional studies a diversity that should be "celebrated" (Merino, 1998, p. 603). We doubt that many traditionalists would not agree that the recontextualizing and reinterpretation of revealed archival materials is as valuable an exercise as the discovery of new ones (Merino, 1998, p. 607). Napier (1998, p. 696), who has had feet in both the traditionalist and critical camps, identified common ground:

> Rather than being rivals, traditional and genealogical approaches to accounting history complement each other. However, genealogical approaches, by explicitly aiming to understand accounting in the (historical) contexts in which it operates, provide a broader basis for determining the ways in which accounting ideas and practices emerge and influence (often in subtle and indirect ways) the operations and activities of wide elements of society.

Our feeling is that this greater contextualism has been a feature of critical historical research in accounting, but that the best of traditional historiography embraces wider parameters and perspectives as well. It has also been the case that critical researchers have tended to be more combative in staking out their place in the sun, though some traditionalists have taken up the cudgels strongly when under attack. In the case of accounting history, however, unlike with the battle against mainstream positivism, there is a common enemy – the substantial numbers of academics and practitioners who devalue and marginalize history.

PREDOMINANT PARADIGMS IN ACCOUNTING HISTORY

Much of the investigation of the origins of accounting practices, as well as the processes of change through history, has been done within the context of a number of prevailing paradigms in the past two decades. Arthur (1999, pp. 17–18) has suggested that the search for paradigms only began with Kuhn's (1970) identification of the role of paradigms in the natural sciences. In Arthur's view, the application of paradigmatic posturing in accounting reflected "a lack of confidence" in the traditional view of what for the discipline was obvious and rational. However, as Peasnell and Laughlin have observed, Kuhn's theory is not applicable to accounting (Cushing, 1989, pp. 6–7). The term does not even seem to fit. For Kuhn, a paradigm is what the members of a discipline share at a point in time, while the divergence into separate "schools" occurs when a community of researchers approaches an issue from "incompatible viewpoints" (Cushing, 1989, pp. 11–12).

The prevalence of paradigmatic accounting historiography of late has precipitated discomfort in certain quarters. Tyson (1993, p. 13) was concerned that writing history from a "doctrinaire perspective" causes the historian to lose objectivity by way of seeking out only confirming evidence. Funnell (1996, p. 41) pointed out that no single research paradigm could serve as the "repository of enlightenment" in explaining all historical events or time periods.

The hope has been expressed (Fleischman et al., 1996; Funnell, 1996, 1998; Merino, 1998; Merino & Mayper, 1993) by traditional and critical researchers alike that the gulf between and among the various paradigms is not so wide that dialogue, minimally, and perhaps joint venturing can take place. This chapter echoes those pleas for conciliation and mutual respect. Research has already begun in hopes that the differing viewpoints can contribute additively and synergistically to enhance our knowledge of important events in accounting's history (Fleischman, 2000; Fleischman et al., 1995; Fleischman & Macve, 2002). We also underscore our conviction that accounting historians overtly disclose to their readers their paradigmatic predispositions (Fleischman & Tyson, 1997; Merino, 1998). Furthermore, much paradigm-based historiography has depended upon the philosophy of past great theorists such as Marx, Foucault, Habermas, Derrida, etc. Laughlin (1999, p. 75) pointed out that we must not become totally dependent upon these "giants" as the sole repository for our insights, but that we add to them with insights of our own.

Recently published writing on the history of accounting generally has focused attention on three major research paradigms or "worldviews." For many years the Neoclassical or economic-rationalist perspective has dominated as the mainstream, traditional approach. More recently, this privileged position has come under challenge from critical theorists whose voices are now being forcefully heard. The schools represented here are the Marxist/labor process, from a tradition older even than Neoclassicism, and the Foucauldian, a product in the first instance of French postmodernism. It has been recognized previously that critical historiography is vastly wider than these two, but Marxism and Foucauldianism have been the most prominent. We are also mindful of potential problems inherent in categorizing research under particular paradigms, including a lack of full understanding and the attribution of one classification to studies that in fact draw upon multiple perspectives. In this trichotomization exercise we will attempt a thumbnail sketch of the basic tenets of the paradigm, as well as a statement of directions taken in the critique of each.

Neoclassicism

Traditional explanations have linked accounting developments since the 18th century to the aspirations of entrepreneurs to improve efficiency. Chandler (1977), employing a time-honored metaphor, dated the emergence of the modern business enterprise from the point when firms could function more profitably with a managerial hierarchy rather than market mechanisms. At this point the "visible hand" of managerial decision making replaced the "invisible hand" of the market. Accounting was the managers' ally. Chandler credited managers of the large American railroads with devising nearly all the basic techniques of modern accounting. Williamson (1985) extended Chandler's vision from business history to organizational theory. He described conditions under which forms and practices of internal organizations become more efficient than markets. Transaction-cost theory was Williamson's essential contribution. The "main purpose" of capitalism's economic institutions was to economize on transaction costs.

Building upon the economic theory of Williamson and the economic history of Chandler, Johnson has formed the bridge to accounting history. Cost accounting, he argued, developed as a rational business response to opportunities involving new technologies and markets. The economic-rationalist position was most prominently promoted with the publication of *Relevance Lost* (Johnson & Kaplan, 1987). Though the conclusion that perceived efficiency gains drive accounting change is not universally accepted by scholars, it might be conceded, as did leading Foucauldians, that the book "moved accounting's history centre-stage" (Ezzamel et al., 1990, p. 157).

The ranks of traditional accounting historians are quite extensive partly because no theoretical declaration is required for membership. Critical historians, by contrast, proclaim their paradigmatic heritage more overtly as they theoretically ground their critiques of accounting theory and practices. Consequently, traditionalism includes those researchers who decline overt paradigmatic statement. Sometimes these historians are unjustly labeled "antiquarians" (Hopper & Armstrong, 1991, p. 405; Napier, 1989, p. 241; Stewart, 1992, p. 58), a term suggestive of an innocuous but somewhat eccentric hobby. We would suggest, however, that there is rather more here, a suggestion born out by the vigor of the various critiques that have developed.

Much of the critique of traditional historiography has been directed against groups of academics from which contemporary accounting historians are supposedly descended – Chicago neoclassical economists and the Rochester school of accounting positivists. This legacy has been variously described as positive rather than normative, narrow in focus, ahistorical, abstract, esoteric, and distant from the realities of practice (McCloskey, 1983; Whitley, 1986, 1988). Smith et al. (1988) identified factors that receive scant attention in "positive framework" research – political aspects of management, power relations, organizational past actions, alternative perspectives of social sciences research paradigms, and the legitimacy of practices. Tinker (1988) portrayed transaction cost and agency theory as ideology that protected the interests of the status quo. Shiozawa (1999), in a recent critique, pointed out the failure of Neoclassicism's rational-choice theory in which economic agents calculate future courses of action without either information or memories inherited from the past.

Economic-rationalist historians have come under fire for a number of basic assumptions. We have already seen how Marxist theorists in particular have criticized the neutrality traditionalists find embedded in primary source materials. Similarly, Neoclassicists stand accused of the "economic fallacy," a "privileged position" accorded economic activities (Mills, 1993, p. 802). Recent work has attempted to broaden the context to avoid this charge of economic reductionism (Boyns et al., 1997; Fleischman & Parker, 1997; Williams, 1997). Miller and Napier (1993, p. 639) cautioned against the traditionalist (Edwards, 1989; Edwards & Boyns, 1992; Edwards et al., 1990; Fleischman & Parker, 1990, 1991) tendency to use modern "notions" in discussing and evaluating periods during which contemporary nomenclature and concepts did not exist.

At a higher theoretical level, the basic assumptions of economic rationalism have been challenged. Neimark and Tinker (1987) argued that capital accumulation (profitability and growth) appears more central from a managerial perspective than efficiency. Hoskin and Macve (1988), in questioning the link between technology and accounting innovations, doubted whether economically rational managers would have constructed the systems that prevailed in the early U.S. environment. Johnson and Kaplan (1987) and Fleischman and Parker (1990, 1991) have assumed a link between cost accounting and "effective management" without definitive evidence of that relationship. Ezzamel et al. (1990) contended that the mere existence of cost accounting is insufficient evidence to assume its utilization for management control and decision making.

Foucauldianism

The French philosopher, Michel Foucault, has become a central figure in a postmodern movement that stresses the centrality of language in establishing a power/knowledge synthesis for rendering the individual calculable. Identified by Habermas (1987, p. 287) as "the theorist of power," the disciplinary paradigm established by Foucault to chronicle the history of closed institutions (asylums, prisons, barracks, schools) appears in many ways to parallel the factory system and other facets of modern life in which accountancy is implicated. In the factory and in other environments mediated by managerial action, it seems that accounting techniques serve as a vehicle for the normalizing gaze required to accommodate discipline at a microlevel.

One of Foucault's major contributions to the philosophy of history has been his analysis of the interconnections between power and knowledge (Dreyfus & Rabinow, 1982; Foucault, 1979), an "indissoluble unity" as Habermas (1987, p. 273) put it. The Foucauldian view of power differs from a more traditional definition of power as an agency of subjugation. Instead, power is construed as an "omnipresent web of relations," a network that operates from below as well as top-down (Thiele, 1986, p. 248). Power in the Foucauldian sense allows for the articulation of normalizing standards that provide individuals with the opportunity to increase their own well-being (Knights, 1990).

Much Foucauldian history has focused on the development of U.S. cost accounting. Hoskin and Macve (1986, 1988) detailed how cost accounting at the Springfield Armory in the 1830s and 1840s provided a technique of "hierarchical surveillance" that rendered labor "calculable" and "total human accountability" achievable. Miller and O'Leary (1987) traced the history of standard costing and budgeting through the first three decades of the 20th century to show how accounting and kindred disciplines (e.g. philosophy and sociology) constructed a "governable person" out of all individuals within the business enterprise. Similar studies have been conducted for the British Industrial Revolution (BIR). Walsh and Stewart (1993, p. 797) documented how Robert Owen utilized a reporting structure that became "the backbone of a regime of surveillance and hierarchy," permitting the monitoring of individual workers. Foucauldians in collaborative efforts have sought but failed to find in the BIR the genesis of modern management, labor controls that quietly order people about (Fleischman et al., 1995; Fleischman & Macve, 2002; see also Hoskin & Macve, 2000).

The bulk of commentary on Foucauldianism has come from Marxists who accuse Foucauldians of "symbolic reductionism," ignoring the materialist basis to reality occasioned by their pronounced emphasis on language and their failure to establish priorities in analyzing various discursive possibilities (Neimark, 1990, 1994). It is charged that Foucauldians undertheorize material, economic, and political realities, particularly issues of resistance and material conditions. "Without theorizing these features, researchers cannot articulate effective action to change regimes of power" (Cooper & Tinker, 1994, pp. 2–3). Armstrong (1994) found that the Foucauldian paradigm did not fit the pattern of worker resistance to disciplinary regimes and questioned Foucault's monolithic view of power, one common to all disciplinary regimes, serving universally to enhance human capacities.

Traditional historians have likewise participated in the Foucauldian critique. Tyson (1990, 1993) recast into economic-rationalist behavior the "transforming events," the historical discontinuity that Hoskin and Macve found at the Springfield Armory (Tyson, 1993, p. 7). Similarly, economic rationalists are critical of the Foucauldian emphasis on labor control to enhance efficiency as the sole preoccupation of management (Boyns & Edwards, 1996, 1997, 2000; Edwards et al., 1995; Tyson, 1993, 2000).

Marxism/Labor Process

Contemporary Marxist accounting historians, though not having lost contact with a Marxist view of class conflict, have moved away from an older economic reductionism into a broader investigation of the social, cultural, and political underpinnings that define industrial relations. This breadth of focus is evident in the work of historians Hobsbawm (1972), Meek (1976), Thompson (1964, 1967), and Hill (1986). Indeed, one of the obligations of Marxist historians is to update Marx as new stages of capitalism wax and wane. One seminal revision was the appearance of Braverman's *Labor and Monopoly Capital* (1974) that inaugurated a substantial volume of labor-process literature. Subsequent to Braverman, a spate of critique has appeared, usually not written by historians, underscoring a perceived narrowness in Braverman's perspective on labor process. The homogeneity and subjectivity of the work force are crucial issues (Gordon et al., 1982; Thompson, 1989). Braverman chose not to theorize workers' resistance to controlling labor processes through the development of a working class consciousness. These themes were taken up by others (Armstrong, 1986; Boreham et al., 1986; Clawson, 1980; K. Thompson, 1984; P. Thompson, 1984). Other labor-process theorists have urged a broadening of managerial motivations beyond the "conspiratorial, one-dimensional concept" (Knights & Willmott, 1986, p. 4) to a more linear, chronological evolution of labor process, featuring different control techniques (even consensual ones) at various stages of capitalism (Burawoy, 1985; Edwards, 1979).

Marxist accounting historians have actively fostered an agenda to communicate to academics the partisan nature of accounting records and the methodologies through which accounting practices can be deployed to suppress classes of people. Richardson (1987, p. 341) has written more generally of critical researchers' efforts to study accounting as a "legitimating institution," ranging from the existing social, political, and economic statuses quo (Cooper, 1980) to ideology (Tinker et al., 1982). For example, Bryer (1994, 1999) has investigated subjects as seemingly remote as feudalism and the FASB conceptual framework from a Marxist perspective, as well as most of what falls between. Hopper and Armstrong (1991) re-interpreted early American industrialization, formerly studied by economic rationalists Johnson and Chandler. Committed to an historical hypothesis that social and economic conflicts arising from labor-control practices give rise to new techniques, they demonstrated how cost accounting came of age to accomplish labor intensification.

In today's world the Marxist paradigm is under significant attack, not from the traditional, neoclassical enemy, but from Foucauldian scholars, kindred spirits in critical accounting. Foucault himself criticized Marxism for its positivism and conviction that its perspective dominated various conflicting interpretations of meaning. Marx's scientific approach, according to Foucault, allowed its adherents "to escape the figurality of language" and to advance definitive posturing where "no single order of validating method" should hold sway (Norris, 1991, pp. 86–87). Cooper (1997, pp. 21, 25) has complained how Marxism has become marginalized in postmodernism with Lyotard's (1984) invective against the "grand narrative" and postmodernism's emphasis upon pluralism and difference rather than enduring class interests. Arnold (1998, p. 666) has pointed out how much critical theory has to lose if the abandonment of historical materialism leads to an inability or a disinterest in critiquing capitalism.

NEW AND OLD ACCOUNTING HISTORY

When Miller et al. (1991) wrote an introduction to a collection of papers presented at the second Manchester Interdisciplinary Perspectives on Accounting Conference, the term "new accounting history" was introduced into debate. In an essay scarcely eight pages in length, the authors, all representatives of critical-research paradigms, summarized in a welcoming and democratic fashion certain of the central critical themes we have seen previously. However, on this occasion the message was less combative and was directed more specifically to accounting historians rather than mainstream traditionalists. A number of tenets central to the new accounting history espoused in Miller et al. include:

- a "pluralization" and "proliferation" of methodologies (p. 395), accompanied by a promise of the inappropriateness "to specify criteria that would exclude certain types of research on the basis of the methodological protocols" (p. 400). Also, it was declared inappropriate to specify those methodologies that would constitute the new accounting history;

- a "heterogeneous range of issues" (p. 396) and a "heterogeneous range of theoretical approaches" (p. 400);
- a greater interdisciplinarity (p. 395) that can both borrow and provide insights to other disciplines (p. 398) and that can free accounting history from "trained historians" (p. 396);
- a questioning of "received notions" from the old accounting history, such as the progressive and evolutionary nature of history (p. 395) and the traditional mandate to record historical events as they really happened (p. 396);
- a "challenge" to the older tradition's view of the "objectivity question" that facts are "unitary rather than perspectival" and that history and values, as well as history and fiction, are rigidly dichotomized (p. 397);
- a new focus on "the language and rationales that give significance to accounting practices" (p. 395);
- a recognition of the limitations of primary sources (problems of interpretation, authenticity, and completeness) (p. 400).

This testament of faith in a "new accounting history" paralleled a similar development in the larger discipline of history itself. Gaffikin (1998, pp. 633–635) noted corresponding directions of the "new" history – an expansion of focus beyond the political history traditionally privileged; analysis of structures rather than narration of events; concern with the histories of the disadvantaged rather than the elite; a movement away from dependence upon official, written records; a greater awareness of movements rather than single events; a questioning of objectivity in favor of a variety of opposing viewpoints; and an appreciation for the historical input of non-professional historians.

Carnegie and Napier (1996, p. 8), attempting a balanced view, provided a caricature of the new accounting historian in contradistinction to the traditionalist previously discussed. Traits here include an historian who writes to a paradigm, is willing to deploy speculation in lieu of hard evidence, and fills most of his/her published pages with "obscure theorization," albeit brilliantly written in many instances. Although overstated, these points do distinguish the old school that is more inclined to believe that the evidence presented represents some sort of an historical reality and, thus, must be respected. While many "old" accounting historians do subscribe to the economic-rationalist paradigm and are willing to debate issues with critical researchers, others, content to bring new information to light either with or without accompanying evaluation, do not choose to become involved in direct paradigmatic statement. As Napier (1989) suggested, these efforts should be respected given the importance of such "discovery" phase work in providing grist for the "contextualising" mills, lest the same articles be continuously rewritten. (The array of articles invoking Josiah Wedgwood's Potteries, aspects of the French transition from the Ancién Regime, and certain other oft-celebrated cases surely reinforce this plea.)

There are a number of substantial philosophical differences that separate old and new historians. Whereas the old attempts to make the past understandable, new narratives try to make "the familiar, strange" (Funnell, 1998, p. 144; Merino, 1998, p. 606). Old-school historians privilege the written archive of the past (Chua, 1998, p. 619), while the new are wary of primary sources, in part because of the silenced voices, and suggest an expanded view of what can constitute archival evidence (Carnegie & Napier, 1996, p. 8; Chua, 1998, p. 618). The new accounting history provides new forms of historical discourse, different lenses for viewing the past (Gaffikin, 1998, p. 632).

Debates between old and new historians have focused on some of these issues. A mutual distrust over the role and interpretation of evidence has been featured in archival research into the Springfield Armory and the New England textiles industry by Hoskin/Macve and Tyson (Funnell, 1998; Hoskin & Macve, 1988, 1994, 1996, 2000; Tyson, 1990, 1993, 1998, 2000). Disagreements over the relationship between past and present have informed an exchange between Miller and Napier (1993) and Fleischman and Tyson (1997) (see also Funnell, 1996). As Carnegie and Napier (1996, p. 14) have observed, some researchers on both sides are more tolerant; some are less so.

Theoretical disputes notwithstanding, the gulf separating new and old accounting historians seems more likely to be bridged than the divide between traditional and critical researchers. Funnell (1996, p. 41, 1998, p. 153) made two points. First, neither side is itself homogeneous so that discourse tends not to be so doctrinaire. Second, both new and old historians, even the most radical postmodernist, use the narrative form as a primary tool. Chua (1998, p. 620) observed that the "core difference" between the two schools is not large and that both share "a collective fear of dogma, of being duped or gagged, and of the pernicious exercise of despotic authority," particularly by other academics. She shares the perception of Merino and Funnell that substantial differences do not exist (Chua, 1998, p. 617). Funnell (1998, p. 157) agreed with Fleischman et al. (1995) that traditional, economic-rationalist historians could claim "new" history status with a widening of perspectives and perhaps a more questioning view of historical objectivity and facticity. By contrast, a traditionalist could not aspire to be a critical researcher, not so much because a traditionalist cannot be critical of capitalism or the status quo, but because the proactive component to change the system would in most cases be lacking.

MODERNISM/POSTMODERNISM

Marxists and Foucauldians appear to be soul mates when the demarcation of accounting history is between traditional and critical researchers or between the old and new accounting history. However, the alliance breaks down when the designations "modern" and "postmodern" become the basis of dichotomy. Now it is the Neoclassical and Marxist traditions that appear more in tune with one another.

It has been claimed that modernity as an "outgrowth of and reaction to" the Enlightenment was defined in the first instance by Baudelaire. Montagna (1997, pp. 125–128) characterized modernism in bipolar terms, a movement that was part "transient" and part "eternal." It had a fragmented, fleeting, and radically changing aspect (much as postmodernism), but that was combined with a search for "immutable elements" which provided a certainty and an order to replace uncertainty and chaos coexisting with the disruption.

Modernity is progressive in that it envisions a series of new presents while the foregoing, immediate pasts have to be destroyed to make way (Martin, 1998, p. 82). However, as Cooper (1997, p. 22) has pointed out, these new presents are very specific in that they are Western, ethnocentric, individualistic, democratic, capitalistic, scientific, and inattentive to gender issues. Merino (1998, p. 605) observed that modernity's "quest for certainty" permitted the rejection of values, ethics, and preferences as "subjective and non-rational." Part of modernism's rationality is its belief that markets are the ultimate "arbiter of what should happen" (Fogarty, 1997, p. 46). Here lies the legitimating of Neoclassicism and the source of Marxism's revolutionary fervor.

Lyotard (1984) has been prominently mentioned as the "high priest" of post-modernism (Martin, 1998, p. 80; see also, Montagna, 1997, p. 130), although many of his theories are not materially different from those of Foucault and Derrida. Lyotard attacked modernity on the basis that there is no underlying reality and that every interpretation of text is as legitimate as any other (Montagna, 1997, p. 130; see Funnell, 1996, p. 47 for an attribution of the same notion to Derrida).

Doomed in postmodernism is the search for the underlying laws that provide confidence to modernists that linear progress through history is possible (Fogarty, 1997, p. 57; Montagna, 1997, p. 125). Gone is "the modernist trap" (Merino, 1998, p. 613) that smugly assumes a "certified path to truth." It was this claim of knowing what was rational that allows modernism to silence the voices of suppressed peoples (Arrington & Francis, 1989, p. 3). However, as Martin (1998, p. 81) has astutely observed, postmodernism's "wallowing" in chaos and fragmentation is itself a universal or metanarrative that the philosophy so actively militates against. Blind to that reality, postmodernism has mounted an offensive against both Neoclassicism and Marxism as grand narratives doomed to failure. Cooper (1997) and Martin (1998) have urged a Marxist response to this onslaught that has declared the concept of class to be obsolete and reductionist and has professed a disillusion about change effectuated by this mechanism or any other. Should Marxism lose its vigor, the critique of capitalism would be materially weakened.

A CALL FOR CONFLUENCE

As we write, accounting history stands as a vibrant discipline, characterized by international interest, a breadth of scope that is near unique in academic accountancy, and a passion among its adherents that has driven its successes. It may well be that this body of work is now positioned for wider recognition within the North American orthodoxy; certainly, such recognition would be in keeping with the broader church of accounting research seen in Europe and elsewhere. There are signs of a new openness in North America, with leaders of key journals and other institutions being selected in part because of a perceived willingness to engage broader traditions of thought. Though there have been false dawns in the past, there are encouraging signs that the efforts of the Academy of Accounting Historians and other bodies may be close to bearing fruit within the broader academy through a wider awareness of the influence of history in shaping our present. In this sense, now is a propitious time for review of this fascinating body of work.

We have noted and characterized existing streams of work within the broad currents of accounting history, and while respecting the differences between various bodies of work, we conclude with a call for confluence, by which we mean a greater commitment to mutual learning and exchange. While we recognize the value in the passion that scholars have brought to their historical investigations, we feel that the early stages of debate among accounting historians should now rightfully be closed. It is now of paramount importance for the discipline to demonstrate a learning from debate and a willingness for all sides to hear one another. In the best representations of the old and the new, the epithets used to underline certain weaknesses of each tradition have always been somewhat ill-suited. It is time to retire the fiery rhetoric of "antiquarianism" and "ahistoricism" in favor of a period of reflection. While recognizing that not all may choose this path, we suggest that now may be an appropriate moment to draw on the experiences of recent debates. It is possible to use these as a window of opportunity to foster the development of the accounting historian's craft, irrespective of the tradition from which an individual author may heretofore have drawn a sense of identification and community.

In the traditionalist stream some, but not all, may choose to explore the theoretical underpinnings of their work. Whether explicitly working through the ideas undergirding their worldview, or with a more basic admission that one's frame of reference, however broadly stated, inevitably influences narrative, historians stand to develop work with a clearer sense of their own perspectives. Whether authors may or may not choose to engage in such self-reflection may be an open question, our second observation is that historians should do more to establish the particular interest of the materials that they study. Given the limitations in our knowledge of the development of accounting practices and techniques, it is not enough, and may be quite wasteful, for authors to simply present historical materials without a sense of how they illuminate broader developments of accountancy in the field. Historians have to do more to demonstrate the enduring consequence and relevance of the materials that they study; it is in these demonstrations that they will surely defeat charges of "antiquarianism" or an unearthing of isolated curios.

New accounting historians also have much work to do. If theoretical structuring and statement have been strengths of this stream of research, then the body of historical evidence that has been deployed in this work has surely been a weakness. Often relying on secondary sources, sometimes venturing into limited if not selective accounts of extant historical record, new accounting history stands to be greatly strengthened by a greater incorporation of primary sources, original work with historical materials, and the kinds of archaeological digging envisaged by some of its earliest adherents (Hopwood, 1987). Of course, as with traditional work, the best exemplars of this discipline have transcended the more widespread limitations of the genre as a whole. Yet, the ring of truth in traditional historians' charges that new historians have approached historical records with insufficient rigor and reverence cannot be ignored. For those committed to theory, there is a corresponding burden of proof that can only be drawn from the archive and other empirical sources.

Our sense is that as both traditional and new accounting history develop, the traits now seen in the best representations of each stream will influence the larger bodies of work of which they are a part. Amid these cross currents, we hope that each approach will develop new agendas and broader horizons through a process of mutual learning. In this way, the discipline will have had a worthwhile debate leading to a refinement of its work. In this paper, we have sought to illustrate general groupings of accounting historians and their work, and so have consciously focused on differences as a way of mapping the field. Yet, when viewed as a whole, accounting historians have, as we have noted, far more in common than recent debates might suggest. In rediscovering these commonalities, we sense that accounting history may now be poised for an exciting period of development and discovery.

REFERENCES

Annisette, M. (1999). Importing accounting: The case of Trinidad and Tobago. *Accounting, Business and Financial History*, *9*(1), 103–134.

Armstrong, P. (1986). Management control strategies and inter-personal competition: The cases of accountancy and personnel management. In: D. Knights & H. Willmott (Eds), *Managing the Labour Process* (pp. 19–43). Aldershot: Gower.

Armstrong, P. (1991). Contradiction and social dynamics in the capitalist agency relationship. *Accounting, Organizations and Society*, *16*(1), 1–25.

Armstrong, P. (1994). The influence of Michel Foucault on accounting research. *Critical Perspectives on Accounting*, *5*(1), 25–55.

Arnold, P. J. (1998). The limits of postmodernism in accounting history: The Decatur experience. *Accounting, Organizations and Society*, *23*(7), 665–684.

Arnold, P., & Hammond, T. (1994). The role of accounting in ideological conflict: Lessons for the South African divestment movement. *Accounting, Organizations and Society*, *19*(2), 111–126.

Arrington, C. E. (1997). Tightening one's belt: Some questions about accounting, modernity, and the postmodern. *Critical Perspectives on Accounting*, *8*(1/2), 3–13.

Arrington, C. E., & Francis, J. R. (1989). Letting the chat out of the bag: Deconstruction, privilege and accounting research. *Accounting, Organizations and Society*, *14*(1/2), 1–28.

Arrington, C. E., & Puxty, A. G. (1991). Accounting interests and rationality: A communicative relation. *Critical Perspectives on Accounting*, *2*(1), 31–58.

Arthur, A. (1999). Exploring an accounting paradigm: The cash account. *Critical Perspectives on Accounting*, *10*(1), 13–35.

Baker, C. R., & Bettner, M. S. (1997). Interpretive and critical research in accounting: A commentary on its absence from mainstream accounting research. *Critical Perspectives on Accounting*, *8*(4), 293–310.

Bebbington, J., Gray, R., & Owen, D. (1999). Seeing the wood for the trees. *Accounting, Auditing and Accountability Journal*, *12*(1), 47–51.

Boland, R. J. (1989). Beyond the objectivist and the subjectivist: Learning to read accounting as text. *Accounting, Organizations and Society*, *14*(5/6), 591–604.

Boreham, P., Clegg, S., & Dow, G. (1986). The institutional management of class politics: Beyond the labor process and corporatist debates. In: D. Knights & H. Willmott (Eds), *Managing the Labor Process* (pp. 186–210). Aldershot: Gower.

Boyns, T., & Edwards, J. R. (1996). The development of accounting in mid-nineteenth century Britain: A non-disciplinary view. *Accounting, Auditing and Accountability Journal*, *9*(3), 40–60.

Boyns, T., & Edwards, J. R. (1997). Cost and management accounting in early-Victorian Britain: A Chandleresque analysis? *Management Accounting Research*, *8*(1), 19–46.

Boyns, T., & Edwards, J. R. (2000). Pluralistic approaches to knowing more: A comment on Hoskin and Macve. *Accounting Historians Journal*, *27*(1), 151–158.

Boyns, T., Edwards, J. R., & Nikitin, M. (1997). *The birth of industrial accounting in France and Britain*. New York: Garland Publishing, Inc.

Braverman, H. (1974). *Labor and monopoly capital*. New York: Monthly Review Press.

Broadbent, J., & Guthrie, J. (1992). Changes in the public sector: A review of recent 'alternative' accounting research. *Accounting, Auditing and Accountability Journal*, *5*(2), 3–31.

Bryer, R. A. (1994). Accounting for the social relations of feudalism. *Accounting and Business Research*, *24*(95), 209–228.

Bryer, R. A. (1999). A Marxist critique of the FASB's conceptual framework. *Critical Perspectives on Accounting*, *10*(5), 551–589.

Burawoy, M. (1985). *The politics of production*. London: Verso.

Burchell, S., Clubb, C., & Hopwood, A. G. (1985). Accounting in its social context: Towards a history of value added in the United Kingdom. *Accounting, Organizations and Society*, *10*(4), 381–413.

Burchell, S., Clubb, C., Hopwood, A. G., Hughes, J., & Nahapiet, J. (1980). The roles of accounting in organisations and society. *Accounting, Organizations and Society*, *5*(1), 5–27.

Carnegie, G. D., & Napier, C. J. (1996). Critical and interpretive histories: Insights into accounting's present and future through its past. *Accounting, Auditing and Accountability Journal*, *9*(3), 7–39.

Catchpowle, L., & Cooper, C. (1999). No escaping the financial: The economic referent in South Africa. *Critical Perspectives in Accounting*, *10*(6), 711–746.

Chandler, A. D. (1977). *The visible hand: The managerial revolution in American business*. Cambridge: Harvard University Press.

Chua, W. F. (1986). Radical developments in accounting thought. *Accounting Review*, *61*(4), 601–632.

Chua, W. F. (1998). Historical allegories: Let us have dversity. *Critical Perspectives on Accounting*, *9*(6), 617–628.

Clawson, D. (1980). *Bureaucracy and the labor process*. New York: Monthly Review Press.

Cooper, D. J. (1980). Discussion of 'towards a political economy of accounting'. *Accounting, Organizations and Society*, *5*(1), 161–166.

Cooper, C. (1997). Against postmodernism: Class oriented questions for critical accounting. *Critical Perspectives on Accounting*, *8*(1/2), 15–41.

Cooper, D. J., & Tinker, A. M. (1994). Accounting and praxis: Marx after Foucault. *Critical Perspectives on Accounting*, *5*(1), 1–3.

Covaleski, M. A., & Dirsmith, M. W. (1988). The use of budgetary symbols in the political arena: An historically informed field study. *Accounting, Organizations and Society*, *13*(1), 1–24.

Cushing, B. E. (1989). A Kuhnian interpretation of the historical evolution of accounting. *Accounting Historians Journal*, *16*(2), 1–41.

Dreyfus, H. L., & Rabinow, R. (1982). *Michel Foucault: Beyond structuralism and hermeneutics*. Chicago: University of Chicago Press.

Edwards, R. (1979). *Contested terrain*. London: Heinemann.

Edwards, J. R. (1989). Industrial cost accounting developments in Britain to 1830: A review article. *Accounting and Business Research*, *19*(76), 305–317.

Edwards, J. R., & Boyns, T. (1992). Industrial organization and accounting innovation: Charcoal making in England 1690–1783. *Management Accounting Research*, *3*(2), 151–169.

Edwards, J. R., Boyns, T., & Anderson, M. (1995). British cost accounting development: Continuity and change. *Accounting Historians Journal*, *22*(2), 1–41.

Edwards, J. R., Hammersley, G., & Newell, E. (1990). Cost accounting at Keswick, England, c. 1598–1615: The German connection. *Accounting Historians Journal*, *17*(1), 61–80.

Elad, C. M. (1998). Corporate disclosure regulation and practice in the developing countries of Central Africa. *Advances in Public Interest Accounting*, *7*, 51–106.

Ezzamel, M. A., Hoskin, K. W., & Macve, R. H. (1990). Managing it all by numbers: A review of Johnson and Kaplan's *Relevance Lost*. *Accounting and Business Research*, *20*(78), 153–166.

Fleischman, R. K. (2000). Completing the triangle: Taylorism and the paradigms. *Accounting, Auditing and Accountability Journal*, *13*(5), 597–623.

Fleischman, R. K., Hoskin, K. W., & Macve, R. H. (1995). The Boulton & Watt case: The crux of alternative approaches to accounting history? *Accounting and Business Research, 25*(99), 162–176.

Fleischman, R. K., Kalbers, L. P., & Parker, L. D. (1996). Expanding the dialogue: Industrial revolution historiography. *Critical Perspectives on Accounting, 7*(3), 315–337.

Fleischman, R. K., & Macve, R. H. (2002). Coals from Newcastle: Alternative histories of cost and management accounting in northeast coal mining during the British industrial revolution. *Accounting and Business Research, 32*(3), 134–152.

Fleischman, R. K., & Parker, L. D. (1990). Managerial accounting early in the British industrial revolution: The Carron Company, a case study. *Accounting and Business Research, 20*(79), 211–221.

Fleischman, R. K., & Parker, L. D. (1991). British entrepreneurs and pre-industrial revolution evidence of cost management. *Accounting Review, 66*(2), 361–375.

Fleischman, R. K., & Parker, L. D. (1997). *What is past is prologue: Cost accounting in the British industrial revolution, 1760–1850*. New York: Garland Publishing, Inc.

Fleischman, R. K., & Tyson, T. N. (1997). Archival researchers: An endangered species? *Accounting Historians Journal, 24*(2), 91–109.

Fleischman, R. K., & Tyson, T. N. (2000). The interface of race and accounting: The case of Hawaiian sugar plantations, 1835–1920. *Accounting History, 5*(1), 7–32.

Fogarty, T. J. (1997). The education of accountants in the U.S.: Reason and its limits at the turn of the century. *Critical Perspectives on Accounting, 8*(1/2), 45–68.

Foucault, M. (1977). Nietzsche, genealogy, history. In: D. F. Bouchard (Ed.), *Language, Counter-Memory, Practice*. Oxford: Basil Blackwell.

Foucault, M. (1979). *Discipline and punish*. New York: Vintage Books.

Funnell, W. (1996). Preserving history in accounting: Seeking common ground between 'new' and 'old' accounting history. *Accounting, Auditing and Accountability Journal, 9*(4), 38–64.

Funnell, W. (1998). The narrative and its place in the new accounting history: The rise of the counternarrative. *Accounting, Auditing and Accountability Journal, 11*(2), 142–162.

Gaffikin, M. (1998). History is dead, long live history. *Critical Perspectives on Accounting, 9*(6), 631–639.

Gaffney, M. A., McEwen, R. A., & Welsh, M. J. (1995). Expectations of professional success in accounting: An examination of race and gender differences. *Advances in Public Interest Accounting, 6*, 177–202.

Gallhofer, S., & Haslam, J. (1997). Beyond accounting: The possibility of accounting and 'critical' accounting research. *Critical Perspectives on Accounting, 8*(1/2), 71–95.

Gordon, D. M., Edwards, R., & Reich, M. (1982). *Segmented work, divided workers*. Cambridge: Cambridge University Press.

Habermas, J. (1987). *The philosophical discourse of modernity*. Cambridge: MIT Press.

Habermas, J. (1990). *Moral consciousness and communicative action*. Cambridge: MIT Press.

Hacking, I. (1981). How should we do the history of statistics. *Ideology and Consciousness, 8*(Spring), 15–26.

Hammond, T., & Sikka, P. (1996). Radicalizing accounting history: The potential of oral history. *Accounting, Auditing and Accountability Journal, 9*(3), 79–97.

Hammond, T., & Streeter, D. W. (1994). Overcoming barriers: Early African-American certified public accountants. *Accounting, Organizations and Society, 19*(3), 271–288.

Hill, C. (1986). *The collected essays of Christopher Hill* (Vol. 3). Amherst: University of Massachusetts Press.

Hines, R. D. (1988). Financial accounting: In communicating reality, we construct reality. *Accounting, Organizations and Society, 13*(3), 251–261.

Hobsbawm, E. J. (1972). Karl Marx's contribution to historiography. In: R. Blackburn (Ed.), *Ideology in Social Science*. New York: Pantheon Books.

Hoogvelt, A. M. M., & Tinker, A. M. (1978). The role of colonial and post-colonial states in imperialism – A case study of the Sierra Leone Development Company. *Journal of Modern African Studies, 16*(1), 67–79.

Hopper, T. M., & Armstrong, P. (1991). Cost accounting, controlling labor and the rise of conglomerates. *Accounting, Organizations and Society, 16*(5/6), 405–438.

Hopwood, A. G. (1978). Editorial: Accounting research and the world of action. *Accounting, Organizations and Society, 3*(2), 93–95.

Hopwood, A. G. (1987). The archaeology of accounting systems. *Accounting, Organizations and Society, 12*(3), 207–234.

Hopwood, A. G. (Ed.) (1988). *Accounting from the outside*. New York: Garland Publishing, Inc.

Hoskin, K. W., & Macve, R. H. (1986). Accounting and the examination: A genealogy of disciplinary power. *Accounting, Organizations and Society, 11*(2), 105–136.

Hoskin, K. W., & Macve, R. H. (1988). The genesis of accountability: The West Point connections. *Accounting, Organizations and Society, 13*(1), 37–73.

Hoskin, K. W., & Macve, R. H. (1994). Re-appraising the genesis of managerialism: A re-examination of the role of accounting at the Springfield Armory, 1815–1845. *Accounting, Auditing and Accountability Journal, 7*(2), 4–29.

Hoskin, K. W., & Macve, R. H. (1996). The Lawrence Manufacturing Co.: A note on early cost accounting in U.S. textile mills. *Accounting, Business and Financial History, 6*(3), 337–361.

Hoskin, K. W., & Macve, R. H. (2000). Knowing more or knowing less? Alternative histories of cost and management accounting in the U.S. and the U.K. *Accounting Historians Journal, 27*(1), 91–149.

Johnson, H. T., & Kaplan, R. S. (1987). *Relevance lost: The rise and fall of management accounting*. Boston: Harvard Business School Press.

Kirkham, L., & Loft, A. (1993). Gender and the construction of the professional accountant. *Accounting, Organizations and Society, 18*(6), 507–558.

Knights, D. (1990). Subjectivity, power, and the labor process. In: D. Knights & H. Willmott (Eds), *Labor Process Theory* (pp. 297–335). London: Macmillan.

Knights, D., & Willmott, H. (1986). Introduction. In: D. Knights & H. Willmott (Eds), *Managing the Labor Process* (pp. 1–18). Aldershot: Gower.

Kuhn, T. S. (1970). *The structure of scientific revolutions*. Chicago: University of Chicago Press.

Laughlin, R. C. (1987). Accounting systems in organisational contexts: A case for critical theory. *Accounting, Organizations and Society, 12*(5), 479–502.

Laughlin, R. C. (1999). Critical accounting: Nature, progress and prognosis. *Accounting, Auditing and Accountability Journal, 12*(1), 73–78.

Lodh, S. C., & Gaffikin, M. J. R. (1997). Critical studies in accounting research, rationality and Habermas: A methodological reflection. *Critical Perspectives on Accounting, 8*(5), 433–474.

Loft, A. (1986). Towards a critical understanding of accounting: The case of cost accounting in the U.K., 1914–1925. *Accounting, Organizations and Society, 11*(2), 137–169.

Lyotard, J. (1984). *The postmodern condition: A report on knowledge*. Manchester: Manchester University Press.

Martin, R. (1998). Fragmentation and fetishism: The postmodern in Marx. *Critical Perspectives on Accounting, 9*(1), 77–93.

McCloskey, D. N. (1983). The rhetoric of economics. *Journal of Economic Literature, 21*(2), 481–517.

Meek, R. L. (1976). *Studies in the labor theory of value* (2nd ed.). New York: Monthly Review Press.

Merino, B. D. (1998). Critical theory and accounting history: Challenges and opportunities. *Critical Perspectives on Accounting, 9*(6), 603–616.

Merino, B. D., & Mayper, A. G. (1993). Accounting history and empirical research. *Accounting Historians Journal, 20*(2), 237–267.

Miller, P., Hopper, T. M., & Laughlin, R. C. (1991). The new accounting history: An introduction. *Accounting, Organizations and Society, 16*(5/6), 395–403.

Miller, P., & Napier, C. J. (1993). Genealogies of calculation. *Accounting, Organizations and Society, 18*(7/8), 631–648.

Miller, P., & O'Leary, T. (1987). Accounting and the construction of the governable person. *Accounting, Organizations and Society, 12*(3), 235–265.

Miller, P., & O'Leary, T. (1993). Accounting expertise and the politics of the product: Economic citizenship and modes of corporate governance. *Accounting, Organizations and Society, 18*(2/3), 187–206.

Mills, P. A. (1993). Accounting history as a social science: A cautionary note. *Accounting, Organizations and Society, 18*(7/8), 801–803.

Minson, J. (1980). Strategies for socialists? Foucault's conception of power. *Economy and Society, 9*(1), 1–43.

Montagna, P. (1997). Modernism vs. postmodernism in management accounting. *Critical Perspectives on Accounting, 8*(1/2), 125–145.

Moore, A. (1991). Accounting on trial: The critical legal studies movement and its lessons for radical accounting. *Accounting, Organizations and Society, 16*(8), 763–793.

Morgan, G., & Willmott, H. (1993). The 'new' accounting research: On making accounting more visible. *Accounting, Auditing and Accountability Journal, 6*(4), 3–36.

Napier, C. J. (1989). Research directions in accounting history. *British Accounting Review, 21*(3), 237–254.

Napier, C. J. (1998). Giving an account of accounting history: A reply to Keenan. *Critical Perspectives on Accounting, 9*(6), 685–700.

Neimark, M. K. (1990). The king is dead, long live the king! *Critical Perspectives on Accounting, 1*(1), 103–114.

Neimark, M. K. (1994). Regicide revisited: Marx, Foucault, and accounting. *Critical Perspectives on Accounting, 5*(1), 87–108.

Neimark, M. K., & Tinker, A. M. (1987). Identity and non-identity thinking: A dialectical critique of the transaction cost theory of the modern corporation. *Journal of Management, 13*(4), 661–673.

Neu, D. (1999). Discovering indigenous peoples: Accounting and the machinery of empire. *Accounting Historians Journal, 26*(1), 53–82.

Nietzsche, F. (1969). *On the genealogy of morals*. London: Vintage Books.

Norris, C. (1991). *Deconstruction theory and practice*. London: Routledge.

Preston, A. M., Cooper, D. J., & Coombs, R. W. (1992). Fabricating budgets: A study of the production of management and budgeting in the National Health Service. *Accounting, Organizations and Society, 17*(6), 561–593.

Radcliffe, V. S. (1998). Efficiency audit: An assembly of rationalities and programmes. *Accounting, Organizations and Society, 23*(4), 377–410.

Radcliffe, V. S., Cooper, D. J., & Robson, K. (1994). The management of professional enterprises and regulatory change: British accountancy and the Financial Services Act, 1986. *Accounting, Organizations and Society, 19*(7), 601–628.

Richardson, A. J. (1987). Accounting as a legitimating institution. *Accounting, Organizations and Society, 12*(4), 341–355.

Robson, K. (1991). On the arenas of accounting change: The process of translation. *Accounting, Organizations and Society, 16*(5/6), 547–570.

Robson, K. (1994). Inflation accounting and action at a distance: The Sandilands episode. *Accounting, Organizations and Society, 19*(1), 45–82.

Sarup, M. (1989). *An introductory guide to post-structuralism and postmodernism.* Athens: University of Georgia Press.

Shiozawa, Y. (1999). Economics and accounting. *Accounting, Auditing and Accountability Journal, 12*(1), 19–38.

Smith, C., Whipp, R., & Willmott, H. (1988). Case study research in accounting: Methodological breakthrough or ideological weapon? *Advances in Public Interest Accounting, 2*, 95–120.

Stewart, R. E. (1992). Pluralizing our past: Foucault in accounting history. *Accounting, Auditing and Accountability Journal, 5*(2), 57–73.

Thiele, L. P. (1986). Foucault's triple murder and the modern development of power. *Canadian Journal of Political Science, 19*(2), 243–260.

Thompson, E. P. (1964). *The making of the English working class.* New York: Pantheon Books.

Thompson, E. P. (1967). Time, work-discipline, and industrial capitalism. *Past and Present, 38*, 56–97.

Thompson, K. (Ed.) (1984). *Work, employment and unemployment.* Philadelphia: Open University Press.

Thompson, P. (1984). The labor process and deskilling. In: K. Thompson (Ed.), *Work, Employment and Unemployment* (pp. 67–86). Philadelphia: Open University Press.

Thompson, P. (1989). *The nature of work* (2nd ed.). London: Macmillan.

Tinker, A. M. (1988). Panglossian accounting theories: The science of apologising in style. *Accounting, Organizations and Society, 13*(2), 165–190.

Tinker, A. M., Lehman, C., & Neimark, M. K. (1991). Falling down the hole in the middle of the road: Political quietism in corporate social reporting. *Accounting, Auditing and Accountability Journal, 4*(2), 28–54.

Tinker, A. M., Merino, B. D., & Neimark, M. K. (1982). The normative origins of positive theories: Ideology and accounting thought. *Accounting, Organizations and Society, 7*(2), 167–200.

Tinker, A. M., & Neimark, M. K. (1988). The struggle over meaning in accounting and corporate research: A comparative evaluation of conservative and critical historiography. *Accounting, Auditing and Accountability Journal, 1*(1), 55–74.

Tyson, T. N. (1990). Accounting for labor in the early nineteenth century: The U.S. arms making experience. *Accounting Historians Journal, 17*(1), 47–59.

Tyson, T. N. (1993). Keeping the record straight: Foucauldian revisionism and 19th century U.S. cost accounting history. *Accounting, Auditing and Accountability Journal, 6*(2), 4–16.

Tyson, T. N. (1995). An archivist responds to the new accounting history: The case of the U.S. men's clothing industry. *Accounting, Business and Financial History, 5*(1), 17–37.

Tyson, T. N. (1998). Mercantilism, management accounting or managerialism? Cost accounting in early nineteenth century U.S. textile mills. *Accounting, Business and Financial History, 8*(2), 211–229.

Tyson, T. N. (2000). Accounting history and the emperor's new clothes: A response to 'knowing more or knowing less'? *Accounting Historians Journal, 27*(1), 159–171.

Walsh, E. J., & Stewart, R. E. (1993). Accounting and the construction of institutions: The case of a factory. *Accounting, Organizations and Society, 18*(7/8), 783–800.

Whitley, R. D. (1986). The transformation of business finance into financial economics: The roles of academic expansion and changes in U.S. capital markets. *Accounting, Organizations and Society, 11*(2), 171–192.

Whitley, R. D. (1988). The possibility and utility of positive accounting theory. *Accounting, Organizations and Society, 13*(6), 631–645.

Williams, R. B. (1997). *Accounting for steam and cotton*. New York: Garland Publishing, Inc.

Williamson, O. E. (1985). *The economic institutions of capitalism*. New York: The Free Press.

ARCHIVAL RESEARCH METHODOLOGY

Richard K. Fleischman and Thomas N. Tyson

INTRODUCTION

An archive is a dump without the seagulls (Shoe).

Traditionally, students of history are taught that research in the discipline mandates recourse to primary source materials. It is only thus that the figures of history are allowed to speak for themselves, absent the interpretive spin of the historian. For accounting history per se, Napier (1989) has identified the "discovery" and "contextualising" functions within the discipline. The "discovery" phase is the bailiwick of archival researchers for it is their responsibility to unearth the data to allow for subsequent theorizing ("contextualising"), grist for the paradigmatic mill, so to speak. However, a peaceful coexistence within the model suggested by this division of labor has been jeopardized of late for a variety of reasons, some of which are well founded while others appear rather shortsighted.

Critical historians, typically of a Marxist or Foucauldian persuasion, have questioned the facticity and neutrality of information derived from past accounting records. We have discussed in other venues the impossibility of historical objectivity (Fleischman et al., 1996a, b). The very questions for which researchers seek answers in the archives, as well as the selection process by which certain documents are presented in academic research while others are not, are inexorably linked to preconceived opinions and prejudices. The best we can do as historians is to inform readers of our paradigmatic groundings so that they can form

Doing Accounting History: Contributions to the Development of Accounting Thought
Studies in the Development of Accounting Thought, Volume 6, 31–47
ISSN: 1479-3504/PII: S1479350402060027

judgments as to whether the past or the historian is speaking to them at key junctures.

Tinker and his collaborators have written extensively about the partisan nature of accounting information, past and present (Tinker, 1991; Tinker & Neimark, 1988; Tinker et al., 1982, 1991). It is their contention that primary source material is of limited value because the accounting functions that traditional economic rationalists take for granted (such as striving for efficiency and cost reduction) have "conflictual underpinnings" (Tinker & Neimark, 1988; Tinker et al., 1991). Accounting ranges from a method "to bolster particular interest groups" (Tinker et al., 1982, p. 167) to an "ideological weapon" in the class struggle over wealth distribution (Tinker et al., 1991, p. 37). Critical history has also diminished the purported primacy of archival materials because of their failure to represent the suppressed voices of the past – the poor, the illiterate, women, the economically powerless for whom accounting records were not an available avenue of expression.

Less compelling, in our estimation, has been that facet of the "new accounting history" that suggests that the mere reporting of data without accompanying interpretive analysis is unacceptable scholarship (Miller et al., 1991; Miller & Napier, 1993). We have a distinct preference for history that marriages archival research to theory about the processes of change. However, as believers in the new accounting history's welcoming of a "pluralization of methodologies" and a "heterogeneous range of theoretical approaches" (Miller et al., 1991, pp. 395, 400), we respect those who wish to present research findings without becoming embroiled in the paradigmatic posturing that has come to characterize accounting historiography in the past two decades (Fleischman & Tyson, 1997). What is most enigmatic is how certain critical historians can accuse those archival researchers who choose to remove themselves from theorizing of "accounting antiquarianism" (Hopper & Armstrong, 1991, p. 405; Napier, 1989, p. 241; Stewart, 1992) when some of the most influential work of critical scholarship is not informed by reference to primary source material (e.g. Hopper & Armstrong, 1991; Miller & O'Leary, 1987).

It must not be assumed from the critique of traditional history methodology that practitioners of the new accounting history are loath themselves to get down and dirty in the archives (see, especially, Hoskin & Macve, 1988, 1994, 1996, 2000; Walsh & Stewart, 1993). Likewise, there can be no question that some exceptionally fine accounting history has been written by scholars who have not chosen to do archival research. However, these practitioners require a philosophical bent and a glib writing style with which most of us are not gifted. Consequently, the most that the majority of us can hope to accomplish is to deploy archival investigation to bring new knowledge to the light of day. This essay is designed to provide insights into archival research methodology and warnings about avoidable pitfalls.

PREPARATIONS FOR ARCHIVAL RESEARCH

Archival research is not only a long, laborious process, but in many instances it is an extraordinarily expensive proposition. Consequently, much preparation and budgetary planning must be done before embarking upon research projects. But for the happy circumstance when the archive you wish to examine is located near home, the expense of a research trip of sufficient duration to accomplish your ends can be astronomic. Sabbatical leaves and summer research support are the most convenient sources for both the required funding and sufficient released time from teaching duties. Since these benefits tend to be highly competitive, a well-documented proposal is often a first requirement. Even then, the amount of funding does not begin to cover the incremental expense of travel to and subsistence at remote locations. A distinct advantage exists for scholars fortunate enough to be at institutions where independent, discretionary funds are available for faculty research and development. At some universities where such endowments do not exist, a more proactive attempt on the part of accounting departments to raise money externally for such purposes could produce fruitful results. Application for foundation grants from some of the Big Five public accounting firms is another possibility. However, support via this avenue would be problematic at best since the firms are ultimately concerned with modern-day relevance in the projects they fund. The Academy of Accounting Historians in the past has underwritten the cost of research projects although available funds are quite constrained. External grants from private and public agencies, such as the Social Sciences Research Council, are possible, but they are highly competitive and the dollar amounts awarded are low. A further possibility, though a difficult one to be sure, is to arrange a faculty exchange for the geographic region in which you intend to do archival research. One final alternative would be to take on board a coauthor who lives in the vicinity of the archive in question with the understanding that the coauthor would undertake the archival exploration, leaving for you the writing and the analysis of the findings. Short of these possibilities, you must be prepared to finance your undertaking personally in the hope that the project will reap long-term dividends as you fulfill your research responsibilities (casting your bread upon the waters).

Since time and money are always of the essence for any archival research project, you must be prepared to take full advantage of your time away from home base. Frequently, a research project will require visiting business records in a variety of venues. It is important to know in advance the specific contents and locations of the archival collections you anticipate examining. A good starting point for planning an itinerary is to consult the work of economic historians who have previously examined records that you expect to be germane to your investigation. While their expertise in accounting may be limited or non-existent, their work may provide leads as to the location and contents of specific archival holdings. An excellent example is Sidney Pollard's *The Genesis of Modern Management* (1965), which is based upon a wide exploration of business records in the U.K. Direct contact with these scholars, if they are living, can provide even more information than might be gleaned from their published work. Additionally, there is a wealth of locator guides for archives, generally written by professional archivists. Consult the sections below on U.K. and U.S. business records for information on finding archives in those two countries. When the location of records becomes known, the researcher should contact the librarian or archivist in charge of the collection to see if an index to the resources might be available. Knowing where to go and advance selection of the materials to be examined can save much valuable time.

PITFALLS IN DOING ARCHIVAL RESEARCH

Once the researcher has located the archives to be investigated and borne the pecuniary expense and time commitment required, the difficulties of archival research do not magically melt away. A particularly vexing frustration is the low survival rate of old business records. It is most inconvenient that the makers of accounting documents did not take into account the interests and needs of future generations of historians whose task it is to figure out what they were doing. The best accounting history is that which can trace *ex ante* analyses and estimations into *post factum* business decisions and actions. However, when a mere 10% of the business records survive (our estimate for the British Industrial Revolution, for example), these linkages are virtually impossible to trace. In the absence of these relationships, it is most tenuous to gauge how accounting data came to inform operations and business decisions within past enterprises. The accounting historian must be prepared psychologically to find either the accounting basis for an action or the outcome of an estimation to be sadly absent from the archive. We must persevere and do our best where these gaps exist, even if it is to hypothesize intelligently what might have been.

It is also the case that business archives are maddeningly decentralized in most instances. For instance, if one were to study the British coal industry, one would have to travel to Northumberland/Durham, the South of Wales, Scotland, Lancashire, and the Black Country in order to survey the bulk of surviving records. There are occasional exceptions. For example, the English railroad records were collected at the Kew Public Record Office when the industry was nationalized. The National Archives in Washington, DC contains an immense volume of accounting records for industries and time periods that featured large-scale governmental intrusion into the economy. But, generally, it is the case that if the researcher is studying the whole of an industry or a region rather than a more narrowly defined record set, such as an individual company, he/she should be prepared to do some traveling.

Depending upon the age of the archive, surviving documents can be most difficult to use. Of course, many records are frail and will crumble if not handled with care. Older documents are entirely handwritten so that usability is sometimes a function of the recorder's hand or the researcher's eye. A magnifying glass, most portable in business-card size, is an essential tool. Even then, many records that predated printed forms or typewriting can be most difficult to read. Other problems include unfamiliarity with more arcane (though not necessarily inferior) accounting methods and terms or measurements commonly used in particular trades or industries. Preparation should be undertaken in the accounting methods used in foreign countries even if the archive under examination is so old that it does not conform to contemporary accounting practice. The methodologies and techniques that have evolved in various societies did not develop in a vacuum. They are descended from older usages and are culturally based in most instances. Unfortunately, consistency and comparability were not honored secondary qualities of record keeping until the 20th century. For the researcher studying a single enterprise or a particular industry, the development of a glossary reflecting the industry's nomenclature would be helpful preparation. For example, the abbreviation "chau" that appears in many English coal-mining records would be perplexing to a researcher unaware that "chauldron" was a common unit of measurement. Background study of standard economic histories would make this information readily available. For major industries, such as cotton or woolen textiles and coal, published glossaries are indispensable aids.

There are a number of exogenous pitfalls that can either ease or toughen the researcher's task in dealing with specific archival repositories. The attitudes of local archivists, for example, play an important role. Some are extraordinarily helpful, reflective of pride in the records under their care and a desire to see information therein contained widely disseminated. Very often these archivists are greatly pleased when a professional historian utilizes their records because they spend so much of their time servicing genealogists whose sole purpose is reconstructing their family trees. Other archivists translate their professional stewardship function into mere preservation. Consequently, they are happiest when their records are untouched by human hands. The facility of repository usage reflects these various attitudes. At the National Archives in Washington, for example, a researcher can have at hand an entire cart of documents at one time. The historian is able to go days without the need to replenish the supply. By contrast, at the Lancashire Public Record Office at Preston, the historian can order only three documents at a time. Each financial record book is carefully scrutinized, page-by-page, before release by an archivist, who maintains a log of each random piece of soiled blotting paper that happens to have survived the vagaries of disposal. Thus, one might have to wait 15 minutes both at pickup and at return for the bits and scraps to be logged out and in. Since it might take the researcher but 30 seconds to realize that the volume in question is not relevant or helpful to the undertaking, the time wasted in the process can be excessive. Moreover, it is embarrassing to use a document for so short a time after the archivist has expended so much energy.

The dwindling of governmental funds necessary to support archival staffs at many record repositories is a source of frustration for researchers as well. Many public record offices, particularly in the U.K., are now closed one day in midweek. This mandatory downtime can be extraordinarily inconvenient for a time-constrained research trip, but should be incorporated into planning one's schedule. Another public record office reality that must be anticipated is the booking requirement. Space is quite constrained in the research rooms of many depositories, and with the decline in public monies there is no chance for short-term remedy. Consequently, places in reading rooms can be booked weeks in advance. Space shortages can be especially galling when genealogical dilettantes freeze out legitimate scholars for seats.

Frequently, accounting historians will not want to expend valuable time in the archives replicating calculations in an effort to figure out what the accountants of bygone ages were about. Rather, researchers would prefer to have reproductions of the documents and to do these studies after hours. However, in the U.K. particularly, copies are extremely expensive and require substantial lead-time. One could expect to pay £2 for a single reproduction at the National Library of Wales, Aberystwyth, for example, if a photograph is required. This technique is frequently necessary with accounting journals since placing the volumes flat on reproduction machines would destroy the book's spine.

Thus, it will be observed that archival research is not "an evening in Paris." It is extremely laborious work and expensive in both temporal and pecuniary terms. Unfortunately, the products of these efforts do not always command the respect they deserve.

In the two sections that follow, we will consider issues related to locating archives in the U.K. and the U.S. It should be noted that, in recent years, a substantial volume of quality archival research has been done in other countries, particularly Australia, France, Italy, and Spain. Our experience does not extend to these venues; consequently, we have opted to stick to those environments for which we have first-hand knowledge.

LOCATING ARCHIVES IN THE U.K.

Although the major business archives in the U.K. are housed in a greater number of libraries and public record offices, the shorter distances and the superior locator services offered make their utilization easier than in the U.S. Each of the U.K. component countries has one or more centralized repositories of business records. In the case of England, the British Museum contains documents related to business history though its greater value lies in its immense collection of obscure tomes that no longer survive anywhere else. The Public Record Office, located at Kew, a London suburb, has substantial holdings related to business sectors that were nationalized in the 20th century, such as transport. Scottish business records are housed at the Scottish Record Office (particularly West Register House) and the National Library of Scotland, both in Edinburgh, and the Glasgow University Archives. Centralized holdings can also be found at the National Library of Wales, Aberystwyth, and the Public Record Office of Northern Ireland, Belfast. Notwithstanding these locations, however, there is nothing in the U.K. to compare to the collection of business documents housed at the National Archives in Washington. Each county in the U.K. has its public record office where local businesses have tended to deposit records over the years. University (e.g. Manchester, Leeds, Keele) and municipal public libraries (Manchester, Birmingham, Newcastle) tend to have more archival materials than similar installations in the U.S. Despite this dispersion, however, the British have taken greater pains to aid researcher access to these materials. The Royal Commission on Historical Manuscripts (HMC) maintains the National Register of Archives (NRA). The Business Index of the NRA [as per information sheet No. 5]:

> ... contains references to the records of business and commercial enterprises of all sorts. A search can be conducted for a particular firm by its name. Alternatively, business records from a particular sector of the economy can be selected by means of codes based on the Standard Industrial Classification. Searches can be refined further to take account of the geographical location of a business or the historical period in which it was active.

The NRA database may be accessed from the HMC's home page. The address is http://www.hmc.gov.uk/. Members of the public who have only e-mail capability may request information via nra@hmc.gov.uk. Inquiries in person or by post may be made to the HMC, Quality House, Quality Court, Chancery Lane, London WC2A 1HP.

Researchers in industrial accounting can be immeasurably aided by two published volumes of the Royal Commission – *Records of British Business and Industry 1760–1914: Textiles and Leather* (1990) and *Records of British Business and Industry 1760–1914: Metal Processing and Engineering* (1994). These books contain for specific firms the location, date, type, and catalog reference of all surviving business records in the U.K. A short illustration from the section on metal processing:

[570] **JOSEPH WRIGHT & CO. LTD.**, chain mfrs., Tipton, Staffs
Correspond and related papers (61 bundles and items) 1882–1915, misc.

drainage, specifications, etc. (20 items) 1855–1893, nd.
Sandwell Local Studies Centre (BS/W). NRA 34048.
Invoices (1 box, 2 vols. 1960–1961)
Dudley Archives and Local History Service (Acc 8264). NRA 25008.

It is with sadness that we report that the HMC is not planning to publish any further editions of the series because of funding cutbacks.

Finally, there is a wealth of published archival surveys completed for the following industrial sectors: banking, book trade, brewing, chemicals, computer manufacturing, insurance, railways, ship building, shipping, and woolen textiles. Full titles are available from the NRA's information sheet No. 5. Important general references include: Richmond and Turton (1992), *The Business Archive Council's Directory of Corporate Archives*; Armstrong and Jones (1987), *Business Documents, Their Origin, Sources, and Uses in Historical Research*; and Habgood (1994), *Chartered Accountants in England and Wales: A Guide to Historical Records*. This latter source details the extant records of public accounting firms plus the types and dates of clients' records in their possession. Of course, the availability to researchers of client records is problematic, a function of the individual client's policy, the age of the records, and whether or not the client remains a going concern.

LOCATING ARCHIVES IN THE U.S.

Although many accounting historians limit their investigations to formal accounting books and records, we approach our topics more broadly and include both labor and business/management perspectives. In our view, labor relations can have a significant impact on accounting policy since bonus schemes, standard costs, and performance review systems are implemented typically through compromise and negotiation, especially when strong unions are involved. To examine these and other managerial accounting topics without regard to labor's perspective can yield an incomplete interpretation of past events. Accordingly, we recommend that accounting historians not limit their investigations to business history archives. That said, historians can use hardcopy, database, and Internet resources to facilitate the search for historical materials.

One source that we have used to initiate several projects is *Labor History Archives in the United States*, by Leab and Mason (1992). In this volume, each institution's principal archivist describes his or her collection and identifies unique or particularly impressive holdings. Once we find a collection that appears fertile, we usually contact the archivist by telephone and describe our project's scope and purpose. In addition to providing objective feedback at an early stage, archivists furnish suggestions about accommodations, parking arrangements, travel directions, and even weather conditions, the latter being far from inconsequential for planning a visit to a remote location during the winter break.

We have had especially good fortune at Cornell University's Martin P. Catherwood Library in regard to our work on 20th century cost accounting history. In addition to its many arbitration proceedings and union records for the textile industry, the library houses the Academy of Management Archives that includes documents and personal correspondence from Frederick Taylor, Sanford Thompson, and other key figures in the scientific management movement. The head archivist, Richard Strassberg, knows his collections well and can identify other institutions that house materials relevant to the project. He can also place a person in contact with other scholars who are conducting research on similar or related topic areas.

Several other printed resource aids are worth noting. One of the most comprehensive is entitled *A Guide to Archives and Manuscripts in the United States* (Hamer, 1961). This volume contains information on 1,300 depositories and, at the very least, includes a general statement of the size and fields of special interest for each depository's holdings. A quick perusal reveals that some collections are described in extensive detail, second only to a particular collection's comprehensive finding aid. Notwithstanding, the volume's disadvantages are common to those of other old, hardcopy references – contact persons may be deceased; phone numbers and hours may have changed; and a collection may have been severely culled in the years since publication. The latter issue is of growing concern since accounting records are often the first to be discarded when archivists condense an institution's holdings. Despite these serious drawbacks, historians may find Hamer's and similar hardcopy guides helpful, at least in regard to forming an overall impression of the material included in a particular archive.

Accounting historians interested in conducting company studies may also find the *International Directory of Company Histories* (Derdak, 1988–1997) useful. In the words of the editor (Derdak, 1988, p. ix), "the *International Directory of Company Histories* provides accurate and detailed information on the historical development of 1,250 of the world's largest and most influential companies." The early volumes grouped companies by industry, while the more recent ones list new entries alphabetically. Each entry includes an interesting, but highly condensed, historical overview of the company. It also contains a list of references, although most refer to current issues involving the company and do not appear to be authored by historians. One other reference, *Subject Collections* (Ash & Miller, 1993, p. 360) contains condensed, self-reported listings for labor and business history. The citation for the Hagley Museum is representative:

> Our very strong collection documents American business history with a special emphasis on
> the development of the Mid-Atlantic region. Book and manuscript collections are especially

strong in the chemical, iron and steel, leather, railway, coal and petroleum industries from 1830 to 1950.

Using a database to locate archives is another very feasible approach, and the Research Libraries Information Network (RLIN) is clearly the most comprehensive. RLIN's Bibliographic Files include eight files organized by bibliographic material type for searching and interlibrary loan among its options. The Archive and Manuscripts Control file contains hundreds of thousands of records available in different archival collections. These records include the descriptions of literary and historical documents and other public documents, arranged by item, personal name, organization, and subject. RLIN is open to individual searching over the Internet or through an institutional searching agreement. Even if one's home institution is not a subscriber, its librarians may have established a sharing arrangement with a larger, local institution to conduct an occasional search. General information about RLIN is available on the Internet (http://lyra.rlg.org/rlin).

Scholars interested in both studying and writing history should avail themselves of Fordham University's excellent website at www.fordham.edu/halsall/mod/modshook.htm. The site provides a wealth of material for individuals especially interested in pre-19th century topic areas. For example, the site includes links to topics that include the Reformation, colonial America, and the Scientific Revolution. Once these topics are selected, the site visitor can then link to original documents that have been transcribed to the web. It is a simply fascinating site that can generate many unusual ideas for research.

Any discussion about locating archives in the U.S., or anywhere in the world for that matter, must include the Internet. Several websites are especially impressive and should be visited by accounting historians at various stages of the project. One of the best is the Labor and Business History site (www.iisg.nl/~w3vl.index.html). The site also provides links to a number of corporate archives and business history conferences. Linking to "Institutions" brings up a list of countries, that for the U.S. contains 61 libraries, museums, research institutions in labor and business history, meta-indexes of other repositories, university departments, historical societies, and business schools. The locations are listed alphabetically and, once accessed, can be saved to a researcher's favorites list. The site also contains a Web Search page for direct topic searching.

Another good site is Links for Business Historians (www.history.ohio-state.edu/buslinks.htm). Once on-line, the researcher can access individual companies, history discussion lists, and a variety of related topic areas such as management history. The site also provides links to a number of major corporate archives and business history conferences. Clearly, the number of Internet sites will continue to expand and the amount of historical data available for online searching will increase exponentially. Notwithstanding the greater ease in locating archives, scholars will still need to confront a variety of issues once they begin the gritty work of examining primary materials.

We wish to conclude this section by reporting on an important eleventh-hour development that will prove immensely beneficial to archival research opportunities in the U.S. The AICPA has just deposited its library of 26,000 volumes at the University of Mississippi. Access to this resource had been most difficult because the library was not cataloged. Researchers can anticipate that this important collection will be significantly more user friendly in the fullness of time.

METHODOLOGICAL ISSUES

There are a variety of methodological approaches for the presentation of archival research findings. Despite the jibes of the contextualizers, some historians are content to avoid paradigmatic posturing and to attempt to allow the facts to speak for themselves to every degree possible. However, as Miller et al. (1991, p. 397) have observed, the more modern tendency is to allow interpretations to be tested by the facts rather than to be derived from them. Traditional historians are not the objective purveyors of information they might perceive themselves to be. Both historical and philosophical literature suggests that the historian cannot escape his/her own subjectivity. Hegel saw the historian as "a part of the process he is studying, has his own place in that process, and can see it only from the point of view which at this present moment he occupies within it" (quoted in Gadamer, 1986, p. 468). We concur with Muller (1952, pp. 29–32) that "a historical fact never speaks for itself" and that every historian has some philosophy of history, "however vague or unconscious." Even the seemingly neutral task of selecting the appropriate documents in an archive to report, the "judgment of importance" in Ricoeur's (1965, pp. 26, 31) estimation, is a subjective action. Consequently, the historian does best who makes his/her philosophy "clear, conscious, and coherent" (Muller, 1952, pp. 29–32).

In today's world of the "new accounting history," writing to or within a paradigm has become a welcomed feature of much critical scholarship. The end result has been an interpretive richness that adds immeasurably to our understanding of the past. However, dangers lurk. Merino and Mayper (1993, p. 245 fn.; see also Merino et al., 1987) observed that "belief transference," the attribution of current concepts to past historical figures, "increases exponentially when researchers use a theoretical framework to explain a particular historical phenomenon." Bloch (1953, p. 20) warned that, "it is dangerous and foolhardy to pretend that we can fully eliminate the inescapable reality of our biases." Hill (1986, p. 14) chastised historians who believe that they are providing an objective account for they are "ignoring the distorting lens through which they observed past history." Given this environment, exposure to primary source materials is one way in which readers of historical narratives can begin to grapple with the issue of whether they are listening to the historian's voice or to the persona of the times. By gauging the historian's interpretation of archival materials, in combination with knowledge of the historian's frame of reference, the reader can evaluate how well the historian has done in offering a persuasive account within the context of his/her personal paradigmatic view.

There can be no doubt that archival evidence may be misinterpreted, manipulated, culled out, or selectively included to bolster a particular perspective. In the absence of primary sources, readers may place undue reliance on the historian's personal bias and interpretation. Thus, although there are critical questions regarding the objective reality of evidence, the complete substitution of data with theory, language, interpretation, and contextualism is even more problematic.

Another related methodological issue that has surfaced recently in accounting historiography concerns the intrusion of the present upon the evaluation of the past. The work of archival researchers Edwards (1989), Edwards et al. (1990), Edwards and Boyns (1992), and Fleischman and Parker (1990, 1991) has been criticized by Miller and Napier (1993) for using present-day methodology and vocabulary as a yardstick against which to measure the sophistication of past accounting practices. Specifically they charged, "within the traditional evolutionary model, the now is always present, if only *in utero*, in the then" (Miller & Napier, 1993, p. 639). This provocative observation requires a thoughtful response by those who undertake archival research. A first question, related to the objectivity issue, is whether the historian can so envelop him/herself in the past that the present can indeed be extirpated from historical narrative. We would agree with Bloch (1953, pp. 27, 36) who defined historical time as "a concrete and living reality with an irreversible onward rush." He warned of a "modernist climate" wherein the past is construed as unconnected to the present. A second question focuses on the desirability of dichotomizing past and present, even if it were possible to do so. Here Previts and Bricker (1994) and Carnegie (1997) have written that historical research in accounting can provide a greater understanding of contemporary practice and institutions (see also Previts et al., 1990). Muller (1952, p. 33) defined the relationship even more strongly, "the past has no meaningful existence but as it exists for us, as it is given meaning by us." Our response to Miller and Napier (Fleischman & Tyson, 1997) would center on the need for historians to involve their contemporary audience. Relating the historical narrative to the idiom of the present renders the account more meaningful and comprehensible to the reader, although the risks of distortion should be managed as carefully as possible. We do agree that the present should not be construed as best practice or that history evolves in a necessarily progressive fashion (the Whig interpretation of history).

Archival researchers are, thus, forced into many highly personalized decisions as they face the daunting prospects of bringing their research findings to light of day. They must draw conclusions about facticity in history, about whether truths are "unitary or perceptival" (Miller et al., 1991, p. 397). They must gauge their varying degrees of comfort at evaluating their source documents, whether it is an attempt to fill in the gaps existing in the data or to write unabashedly within a paradigm. They must come to decisions about how, and if, they will utilize the past to inform the present. However, there are two responsibilities/obligations that fall upon the shoulders of all archival researchers, in our opinion. First, they must attend to the needs of future investigators by informing their audience of the archive(s) examined – its location, the types of documents contained, reference numbers if cataloged, peculiarities or difficulties of access. Second, they have the obligation to inform the reader of their theoretical grounding, even if it is only to aid the reader to determine why certain documents were selected for reporting while others were left in silence. We aspire to Hill's (1986, p. 17) definition of a good historian as one who "questions his own assumptions and prejudices," though the task is difficult and the way unclear.

PUBLICATION OUTLETS

One of the significant attractions of archival research in accounting history is the number and variety of publication outlets available. Three journals particularly have specific missions to publish accounting history research. These are the *Accounting Historians Journal*, the journal of the Academy of Accounting Historians (U.S.); *Accounting History*, the journal of the Accounting History Special Interest Group of the Accounting Association of Australia and New Zealand; and *Accounting, Business and Financial History* (U.K.). Additionally, three international journals, perhaps geared in the first instance to critical history scholarship, are receptive as well to traditional archival research. These are the *Accounting, Auditing and Accountability Journal* (Australia); *Accounting, Organizations and Society* (U.K.); and *Critical Perspectives on Accounting* (U.S.). A significant percentage of the articles that appear in these journals are historically based. A number of periodicals that are substantially more presentist in their orientation but that do publish history articles periodically include *Abacus* (Australia), *Accounting and Business Research* (U.K.), *Contemporary Accounting Research* (Canada), *Management Accounting Research* (U.K.), and *Research in Accounting Regulation* (U.S.).

Archival researchers should not ignore the significant number of history (as distinct from accounting history) journals that periodically feature pieces in accounting. The most prominent of these are *Business and Economic History* (U.K.), *Business History* (U.K.), *Business History Review* (U.S.), and the *Economic History Review* (U.K.). This listing does not even begin to exhaust the outlet possibilities for articles within the history discipline.

Occasionally, extended archival research will produce findings in the form of a book-length manuscript. Here the Garland accounting history series, edited by Dick Brief, provided a well-respected outlet. In 1997–1998 alone, Garland published 13 new volumes of accounting history. While the Garland series has now run its course, other publishing houses, such as Elsevier Science, the publisher of this volume in the Studies in the Development of Accounting Thought series, continue to market accounting history, albeit on a more ad-hoc basis.

Finally and much more sporadically, volumes of original essays have been published to honor distinguished accounting historians or to commemorate important events. Examples include *The Costing Heritage*, a *festschrift* published by the Academy of Accounting Historians to honor S. Paul Garner (Graves, 1991), and *Accounting History from the Renaissance to the Present*, funded by the Institute of Chartered Accountants of Scotland to commemorate the quincentennial of Pacioli's *Summa* (Lee et al., 1996).

THE WAY FORWARD

Because accounting history as a research discipline is in its infancy, there remains an absolute wealth of archival material to be examined and evaluated. It falls upon us to reveal for the present knowledge derived from the past. It is through us that the voices of the past speak, albeit limited to those with sufficient status to be recorded in business archives and limited as well by the vagaries and the subjectivity of the historian's selection process.

English has heretofore been the *lingua franca* for reporting the findings of archival research, although many documents in other tongues have been examined. However, language barriers have limited our exposure to non-English primary sources. One way forward is collaboration between scholars with combinations of language skills that will allow for a wider examination and analysis of surviving records from different cultures.

Another way forward is to build upon the explanatory richness that is a feature of the new accounting history. However, we must be cautious not to allow paradigmatic posturing to harden into battle lines of demarcation. Only then, would we be deprived of the synergies and additive value forthcoming from discourse and collaborative efforts with advocates of rival intellectual traditions.

We have attempted in this essay to identify the most important methodological, controversial, and practical issues associated with archival research. While certain critical historians disdain the use of primary source materials, we find them essential for formulating, developing, and validating our own theory, or responding to the ideas proposed by other scholars. We are able to embark enthusiastically on new endeavors in this research path, in part because the journey can be as fulfilling as the final product. The excitement of finding buried treasures in the form of a key document or letter is unparalleled in most other forms of accounting scholarship. In addition, publication and international conference opportunities now abound, and the topic areas amenable to historical research appear limitless. Notwithstanding, we believe that the novice archival researcher will benefit from careful preparation and an awareness of certain pitfalls that we have sought to provide.

As we have mentioned, the rapid expansion of the Internet bodes well for scholars facing limited budgets. Where scholars formerly had to examine hundreds of nearly illegible documents to find one historical nugget, the Internet archival researcher of the present and future can greatly reduce this time-consuming, preliminary work. As pressures to publish accelerate, a dollar and a day's work saved in exploratory research may translate into additional publications. Nevertheless, archival researchers, both novice and experienced, must confront methodological concerns that include distinguishing fact from opinion, interpreting limited amounts of evidence, or writing to one's paradigm. These issues will remain contentious and central to future historical debates and, like other aspects of research, will benefit from examinations of primary materials.

REFERENCES

Armstrong, J., & Jones, S. (1987). *Business documents, their origin, sources, and uses in historical research*. London: Mansell.

Ash, L., & Miller, W. G. (Eds) (1993). *Subject collections* (7th ed.). New Providence, NJ: R. R. Bowker.

Bloch, M. (1953). *The historian's craft*. New York: Vintage.

Carnegie, G. D. (1997). *Pastoral accounting in colonial Australia*. New York: Garland Publishing, Inc.

Derdak, T. (Ed.) (1988–1997). *International directory of company histories*. Chicago: St. James Press.

Edwards, J. R. (1989). Industrial cost accounting developments in Britain to 1830: A review article. *Accounting and Business Research, 19*(76), 305–317.

Edwards, J. R., & Boyns, T. (1992). Industrial organization and accounting innovation: Charcoal ironmaking in England 1690–1783. *Management Accounting Research, 3*(2), 151–169.

Edwards, J. R., Hammersley, G., & Newell, E. (1990). Cost accounting at Keswick, England c. 1598–1615: The German connection. *Accounting Historians Journal, 17*(1), 61–80.

Fleischman, R. K., Kalbers, L. P., & Parker, L. D. (1996a). Expanding the dialogue: Industrial revolution costing historiography. *Critical Perspectives on Accounting*, *7*(3), 315–337.

Fleischman, R. K., Mills, P. A., & Tyson, T. N. (1996b). A theoretical primer for evaluating and conducting historical research in accounting. *Accounting History*, *1*(1), 55–75.

Fleischman, R. K., & Parker, L. D. (1990). Managerial accounting early in the British industrial revolution: The Carron Company, a case study. *Accounting and Business Research*, *20*(79), 211–221.

Fleischman, R. K., & Parker, L. D. (1991). British entrepreneurs and pre-industrial revolution evidence of cost management. *Accounting Review*, *66*(2), 361–375.

Fleischman, R. K., & Tyson, T. N. (1997). Archival researchers: An endangered species? *Accounting Historians Journal*, *24*(2), 91–109.

Gadamer, H. G. (1986). *Truth and method*. New York: Crossroad.

Graves, O. F. (Ed.) (1991). *The costing heritage: Studies in honor of S. Paul Garner*. Harrisonburg, VA: Academy of Accounting Historians.

Habgood, W. (1994). *Chartered accountants in England and Wales: A guide to historical records*. Manchester: Manchester University Press.

Hamer, P. M. (Ed.) (1961). *A guide to archives and manuscripts in the United States*. New Haven, CT: Yale University Press.

Hill, C. (1986). *The collected essays of Christopher Hill* (Vol. 3). Amherst, MA: University of Massachusetts Press.

Hopper, T. M., & Armstrong, P. (1991). Cost accounting, controlling labor and the rise of conglomerates. *Accounting, Organizations and Society*, *16*(5/6), 405–438.

Hoskin, K. W., & Macve, R. H. (1988). The genesis of accountability: The West Point connections. *Accounting, Organizations and Society*, *13*(1), 37–73.

Hoskin, K. W., & Macve, R. H. (1994). Re-appraising the genesis of managerialism: A re-examination of the role of accounting at the Springfield Armory, 1815–1845. *Accounting, Auditing and Accountability Journal*, *7*(2), 4–29.

Hoskin, K. W., & Macve, R. H. (1996). The Lawrence Manufacturing Co.: A note on early cost accounting in U.S. textile mills. *Accounting, Business and Financial History*, *6*(3), 337–361.

Hoskin, K. W., & Macve, R. H. (2000).Knowing more is knowing less? Alternative histories of cost and management accounting in the U.S. and U.K. *Accounting Historian Journal*, *27*(1), 91–149.

Leab, D. J., & Mason, P. O. (1992). *Labor history archives in the United States*. Detroit: Wayne State University Press.

Lee, T. A., Bishop, A., & Parker, R. H. (1996). *Accounting history from the renaissance to the present*. New York: Garland Publishing, Inc.

Merino, B. D., Koch, B. S., & MacRitchie, K. L. (1987). Historical analysis – a diagnostic tool for 'events' studies: The impact of the Securities Act of 1933. *Accounting Review*, *62*(4), 748–762.

Merino, B. D., & Mayper, A. G. (1993). Accounting history and empirical research. *Accounting Historians Journal*, *20*(2), 237–267.

Miller, P., Hopper, T. M., & Laughlin, R. C. (1991). The new accounting history: An introduction. *Accounting, Organizations and Society*, *16*(5/6), 395–403.

Miller, P., & Napier, C. J. (1993). Genealogies of calculation. *Accounting, Organizations and Society*, *18*(7/8), 631–648.

Miller, P., & O'Leary, T. (1987). Accounting and the construction of the governable person. *Accounting, Organizations and Society*, *12*(3), 235–265.

Muller, H. J. (1952). *The uses of the past*. New York: Oxford University Press.

Napier, C. J. (1989). Research directions in accounting history. *British Accounting Review, 21*(3), 237–254.

Pollard, S. (1965). *The genesis of modern management.* Cambridge: Harvard University Press.

Previts, G. J., & Bricker, R. (1994). Fact and theory in accounting history: Presentmindedness and capital market research. *Contemporary Accounting Research, 10*(2), 625–641.

Previts, G. J., Parker, L. D., & Coffman, E. N. (1990). Accounting history: Definition and relevance. *Abacus, 26*(1), 1–16.

Richmond, L. M., & Turton, A. (1992). *The business archive council's directory of corporate archives* (3rd ed.). London: London Business Archives Council.

Ricoeur, P. (1965). *History and truth.* Evanston, IL: Northwestern University Press.

Royal Commission on Historical Manuscripts (1990). *Records of British business and industry 1760–1914: Textiles and leather.* London: HM 50.

Royal Commission on Historical Manuscripts (1994). *Records of British business and industry 1760–1914: Metal processing and engineering.* London: HM 50.

Stewart, R. E. (1992). Pluralizing our past: Foucault in accounting history. *Accounting, Auditing and Accountability Journal, 5*(2), 57–73.

Tinker, A. M. (1991). The accountant as partisan. *Accounting, Organizations and Society, 16*(3), 297–310.

Tinker, A. M., Lehman, C., & Neimark, M. K. (1991). Falling down the hole in the middle of the road: Political quietism in corporate social reporting. *Accounting, Auditing and Accountability Journal, 4*(2), 28–54.

Tinker, A. M., Merino, B. D., & Neimark, M. K. (1982). The normative origins of positive theories: Ideology and accounting thought. *Accounting, Organizations and Society, 7*(2), 167–200.

Tinker, A. M., & Neimark, M. K. (1988). The struggle over meaning in accounting and corporate research: A comparative evaluation of conservative and critical historiography. *Accounting, Auditing and Accountability Journal, 1*(1), 55–74.

Walsh, E. J., & Stewart, R. E. (1993). Accounting and the construction of institutions: The case of a factory. *Accounting, Organizations and Society, 18*(7/8), 783–800.

ACCOUNTING HISTORIOGRAPHY USING ANCIENT SOURCES: PROBLEMS AND REWARDS

Gloria L. Vollmers

The work of the historian contains elements of science and art. Historical work is not, however, a science in a logical positivist sense. We do not find statistically significant experimental results or identify immutable laws that permit prediction. Philosophers of history have convincingly argued that neither scientific laws nor any other universal plans exist, at least in so far as they are identifiable (Berlin, 1950; Collingwood, 1993). It is a science in so far as the scholar adopts the attitude and some of the methods commonly ascribed to the scientist – a presumption of objectivity, a hunger for answers, a willingness to gather data painstakingly, and an attempt to explain and evaluate evidence in the most honest way possible. The historian organizes the data, the evidence, chronologically and places them within the prevailing culture and context to the degree that they are known and explanatory.

However, Collingwood (1993, p. 257) disparaged the practice of merely *describing* a chronological set of events as "scissors and paste history." Historians of this ilk continually look for data with which to fill in empty holes on a time line, as if an uninterrupted flow of events would explain history. Such a progression would be neither interesting nor particularly historical; hence, the element of artistry. Collingwood asks the historian to consider why events occurred and why they occurred in a particular way. What meaning lies behind this artifact? What might have been the thoughts of those who created or used it?

Doing Accounting History: Contributions to the Development of Accounting Thought
Studies in the Development of Accounting Thought, Volume 6, 49–62
Copyright © 2003 by Elsevier Science Ltd.
All rights of reproduction in any form reserved
ISSN: 1479-3504/PII: S1479350402060039

Historical work necessarily embraces description, but the best work is overlaid with creative narration. Command over oral and written expression is important, but the historian, moving beyond description, makes the logical inferences, the leaps of faith, necessary to tell a story that rings true. Certainly we hope the data align into a logical pattern, but at those points where the pattern is broken, or where the data are unclear or contradictory, the artist takes over, creatively filling in the narration. To say that inferences should not be made, to insist that the data speak for themselves, is to remove understanding from the discipline. The purpose of history is to find meaning in the evidence. What sort of people left this evidence? What did it mean to those who left the evidence behind? Why was it left in that way?

The historical imagination acts as a detective (Collingwood, 1993, p. 231). It looks for and creates the whys, the reasons, behind evidence and its sources. It enables the historian to marshal evidence and make inferences about it. It can also be used to access the validity of sources and to assess the degree to which they may be relied upon and incorporated into the story. The author of a written source may be biased; the historian tries to ascertain the degree and direction of that bias. A source written in an ancient language may not be fully translated or may be mistranslated because the intent of the message has not survived, leaving the translator to guess its meaning. If the evidence suggests a pattern, and it is one that sits well within the context of the people, period, and culture (to the degree we understand them), then random contradictory evidence may, in good conscience, be set aside. That is not to say it is thrown away, but if it does not fit within the overall pattern suggested by the majority of the evidence, then it may well be disregarded though it may later provide good evidence in answering some other historical question. Or, upon the discovery of new evidence, it may change an earlier interpretation.

A concern of any historian, but more particularly the historian working with ancient materials, is the degree to which he/she must depend on the work of others. Momigliano (1975, p. 370) observed that "between us and the facts lies the evidence." As individual scholars, we are rarely able to see the facts first hand. As interpreters of the ancient world, there is more distance between the scholar and the facts than is typical in more recent history. We rely on the reports of others, their photographs and descriptions, their writings and interpretations. These are the evidence; the historian sifts through it all to find facts. This is true universally, of course, since we would never move if everyone had to reinvent the wheel, but it seems particularly important here. It is not possible to acquire expertise in all the disciplines focused on the ancient world. Language is the most obvious barrier. Not only do few learn ancient languages, but also there are so many of them. One trilingual inscription had to be translated and published by three different scholars in different volumes of the same journal (Millar, 1983, p. 89). The scholar can only cross the language barrier by relying on the transcriptions and translations of others. Moreover, unless other experts have occasion to return to and correct early translations, it is impossible to check for errors. Contributions can be made. Schmandt-Bessarat (1988, 1992) has successfully established herself as a scholar of note in the field of ancient Assyrian clay tokens and envelopes (and hypothesizing links between accounting and writing) without knowing Assyrian or becoming an Assyriologist.

Language is only the most obvious problem. Archaeology is enormously important, but this discipline has its limitations. Remains may be misinterpreted, but even when there is a suspicion of misinterpretation, revisiting a site may be impossible or prohibitively costly. Artifacts may be cataloged incorrectly, misdated, or moved in haste, losing the record of their relative positions with other artifacts. Artifacts from different periods may be mixed together when buildings from one period are repeatedly constructed on top of another, leading to improper dating and unfortunate inferences. It is all too easy to carry theories to the site and to allow them to shape the understanding of the data found. Thus, the discovery of a single gold Egyptian ring and a piece of Italian pottery in a Babylonian city might lead to inappropriate generalizations about extensive trading practices the scholar expects.

It is not possible to coordinate site excavations with the studies of people not involved in archaeology. That is to say, the Biblical scholar studying a passage that refers to an ancient settlement cannot instruct archaeologists to go search for and excavate that venue. Or, should the funding for a site run out, it would not be possible for a scholar to re-examine some specific item there.

Another pressing problem for the historian of the ancient world is insufficient and/or missing evidence. That which survives necessarily takes on an importance that it might not deserve if everything had survived. Some material from the ancient world is of enormous importance to scholars but was of little consequence to its contemporaries. Pottery is the best example. It is the most voluminous of ancient artifacts because it was common, had little intrinsic value, and was virtually indestructible compared to goods composed of wood, cloth, or metal. We have it because it was easy to make, was easy to replace, and was tossed out and left behind without care. It has provided historians an amazing amount of information, particularly in the area of dating, but its ubiquity should not be confused with its importance *in situ*.

By contrast, there are vast areas of human life about which virtually no evidence has remained. Why, for example, did ancient peoples fail to write about the economy of their world? If our world were suddenly destroyed, an archaeologist excavating a millennium from now would, with almost 100% probability, no matter how few textual materials remained, find plenty of written materials referring to jobs, inflation, prices, trade, and interest rates. By contrast, references to any kind of economic topic are exceedingly rare in ancient texts. A great variety of contracts remain, but it is highly unusual for an historian or other writer from the ancient world to write about his economic life. What does this silence mean? One must conclude that an entirely different mindset existed, one that, I believe, cannot be understood by the modern historian.

The historian does bring present beliefs, understandings, and modern common sense into the past. It is impossible to suppress all of one's own assumptions and, hence, to approach evidence without preconceptions. As we continually reconstitute our own reality, we try to recast the past in that image. Known assumptions can be stated but may not be the problem. Others, however, lie so deeply beneath the surface that the historian is unaware of their existence. For example, if everyone knows the earth is flat, then it does not seem to be an assumption.

Momigliano (1975) said that the historian cannot avoid approaching evidence with some expectations or theories and that those pre-existing conditions guide the choice of evidence. However, the hypothesis that leads to a search for evidence does not preclude recognizing the unexpected and revising the initial hypothesis. The historian should be open to surprise and change.

Opportunities for accounting research in the ancient world abound despite all the problems associated with that research. The primary reason is that of all the documents that have survived, the vast majority is accounting artifacts. There are contracts for land, slaves, marriage, exchanges, and work. There are inventory lists of household items, as well as personnel, land, grain, and livestock holdings. There are documents recording the settlement of debts, the compensation of workers, and the collection of taxes. There are rich collections of private business documents from the Achaemenid period from the houses of Egibi and Murashu, as well as the temple archives of Eanna and Ebabbar (Clay, 1904; Dandamaev & Lukonin, 1989; Lutz, 1927). The sheer abundance of these documents has allowed scholars in disciplines other than accounting to learn the languages, to determine diet, to expand knowledge of religious practices, to date events with near certainty, to make inferences about business and social practices, as well as family structures, and to determine the type and extent of control of regimes. What tends not to be of interest to scholars from other disciplines is the accounting itself. What part did it play in the lives of individuals and regimes? It is here that accounting historians can find the space to work. What controls were exercised over people, property, and activities? How did regimes feed and monitor vast empires?

The question of what constitutes accounting should not be ignored. There are many who would say that the existence of these lists and other documents are not sufficient to justify accounting research. Littleton (1980) maintained that accounting is "modern accounting," born only with the advent of double-entry bookkeeping with its duality (books and entries), its equilibrium (balance), and its proprietary claims on gains and losses. Double-entry bookkeeping arises in the presence of capital, money, credit, and commerce. "If either property or capital were not present, there would be nothing for records to record. Without money, trade would be only barter; without credit, each transaction would be closed at the time; without commerce, the need for financial records would not extend beyond governmental taxes" (Littleton, 1980, p. 12). Strict agreement with Littleton would eliminate most interest in ancient accountings. Indeed, Stevelinck (1985) dismissed all research in ancient accountings because, in his opinion, the relatively small number of translated documents and the remoteness of the times in which they were created defy our understanding. However, there are others who have a much broader perspective on accounting. This accounting facilitates exchanges (whether money or barter) and can provide a mechanism for control, for evaluation, and for adjudicating between parties. This expansive view of accounting does not require, but does not exclude, double-entry bookkeeping and calculation of income. It is important though that these accountings have some importance in themselves. It is not surprising that a list of inventory would be more interesting to an anthropologist than an accountant. Standing alone, it would not be of great interest to the accounting historian. However, if there is evidence that the list was audited, then it brings to light the existence of an occupation that was important to those ancient peoples. We now see that controls were being exercised through the accounts. Or if the list is a compilation from other sources, we perhaps are seeing a greater organization of information than first appreciated. Ancient accounting then becomes interesting.

The second reason for scholarly opportunity is that few historians of any type have written about ancient accounting. The articles described in the following few paragraphs represent a substantial sampling of the entire population of literature written either by accountants or by others whose focus was accounting. The inescapable conclusion is that there is abundant room for accounting historians to find accountings of interest within vast periods of human history. There is, of course, some mention of accounting in standard texts on ancient peoples and civilizations, at least as a tangential topic. These references must not be ignored if one is to pursue this area.

Schmandt-Bessarat (1992) is not an accounting researcher, but did present papers at the fifth and sixth World Congresses of Accounting Historians. She has studied Assyrian clay tokens and the clay envelopes that enclosed them, a system used to account for commodities from 8000 to 3000 B.C. before there was writing. Mattessich (1987, 1994) used her work to theorize that the clay token-envelope system was an ancient version of debit and credit. Nissen et al. (1993) complied a formidable collection of tablets and constructed a convincing account of bookkeeping in the third millennium B.C. Mattessich (1998a) continued his debit/credit theory, integrating the works of both Schmandt-Bessarat and Nissen et al. just mentioned. A brief note by Keister (1974) drew attention to but did not analyze the accounting references in the Code of Hammurabi, dating from about 2200 B.C. For example "If a merchant give to an agent grain... with which to trade, the agent shall write down the value and return it to the merchant. The agent shall take a sealed receipt for the money which he gives to the merchant." The Code requires written records of transactions, as well as the assignment of values to various activities, people, and animals. Much more could be done from an accounting perspective with this Code and other ancient law codes that survive.

Hagerman (1980) brought forward examples of Biblical references to financial and managerial accounting and internal controls. Jose and Moore (1998) looked at income, property, poll, special assessment, and indirect taxes that appear in the Bible to track their development over the centuries during which the texts were written. Nurnberg (2000) theorized that accounting's choice of a 40-year amortization period for goodwill had a Biblical basis, citing its frequent references to the assertion that the life of a generation was 40 years. Much more could be done here.

Setting a standard for accounting research in this area, Ezzamel (1997, p. 596) examined, in a richly contextualized work, how Egyptian scribes in the New Kingdom (1552–1069 B.C.) accounted for the conversion of grain into bread. He discovered that Egyptians used input/output ratios and allowed for loss due both to evaporation and varying flour quality:

> Accounting developed a simple, yet extremely powerful, metric that made calculable and visible the activities of individuals who inhabited state organization. By engaging in the process of quantifying and reporting economic activities, it played a major role in defining, and thereby constituting, the domain of economic transactions that were deemed of concern.

Costouros (1977, 1978) wrote about accounting and auditing during Greece's Golden Age (500–300 B.C.). He reported, for example, that all those responsible for handling any public funds were subject to audit by state auditors. His access to actual written documents describing the requirements minimized the need to make uncomfortable inferences. Ste. Croix (1956) looked broadly at Greek and Roman accounting from the sixth to the first century B.C. Mattessich (1998b), delved into Indian accounting history. He believes that the Indian accounting tradition's (dating from 300 B.C. at the latest) notion of debt as a negative amount contributed to medieval Indian mathematicians accepting the reality of negative numbers much earlier that did mathematicians in the western world. Another welcome and unusual piece of research is Zaid's (2000, p. 73) argument that "links between Muslim traders and their Italian counterparts (prior to Pacioli) influenced the development of accounting books in the Italian Republics." A fascinating piece of research appeared decades ago. Fu (1971) reported on governmental accounting in China during the Chou Dynasty (1122–256 B.C.). The Chous, building on even earlier concepts of accounting, auditing, and accountability, added fund accounting, budgeting, and financial reporting, while expanding the audit process. They had several governmental funds that were specific as to their purposes and sources of revenue, including both contributions of money and produce. For example, there were funds for worship and sacrifice, for state funerals, for the maintenance of the royal household, and for the support of the older relatives of deceased governmental officials. Various periodic reports were required and all were audited. More work of this type, particularly expanding into civilizations not normally appearing in western accounting journals, would be welcome.

If one has a broader view of what is considered "ancient," it is possible to expand this examination. If "ancient" may be defined as encompassing periods about whose accounting we know little or as accounting in the absence of modern notions of bookkeeping or income calculation, then much more recent periods may be included.

Oldroyd (1997) challenged the view that the Anglo-Saxon period (450–1066) played no part in accounting history. Contrary to the experience of historians of the very ancient world, Oldroyd had few accounting documents but many other written documents with which to work. He primarily wished to identify areas to be explored at a later time but did conclude that systematic accounting was used by the church, the state, and estates. Godfrey and Hooper (1996, p. 38) made a case for the Domesday Book (~1086) as a "multi-dimensional document combining accountability and decision-making." There is little doubt that there are accountings waiting to be studied across time and across countries.

I have worked with an archive of cuneiform tablets that came from the ancient city of Persepolis (in modern Iraq), dating from about 500 B.C., during the regime of Darius I, an Achamenid king (Vollmers, 1996). This collection was translated, organized, and discussed by Hallock (1969). I relied upon his translations and accepted his interpretations of these texts as they were based on a lifetime of scholarship and many years of working with this archive. The tablets are accounting records primarily of distributions of food rations to workers, animals, and travelers. These tablets are highly formulaic and, with exceptions, record amounts distributed, the people responsible for the distribution, the people receiving them, their location, and the date. They also record seed set aside for planting and fodder, rations for religious services. There are records for food deposits, of food transported, and food inventories.

What assumptions did I knowingly bring to this work? First, the archive is an accounting of common events. Second, the records were created for a purpose;

that is, that they were to be used for planning or budgeting for the following year. Third, controls over these events existed with the type or amount of control varying as a function of the peculiarities of the event. Fourth, there existed an economy recognizable in its outlines if not in its particulars.

The first assumption is easily supportable. Without doubt, these are common accounting records. Not only does the size of this archive suggest this (over 2000 tablets), but also these types of records (clay cuneiform tablets) have been found all over the Mesopotamian area for thousands of years (Nissen et al., 1993; Postgate, 1992). Finley (1973, p. 28) asserted that the word "rationing" fairly well describes the bureaucratic, record-keeping economic world of the Near East over many millennia. In addition to the voluminous archaeological finds, there are also many Biblical references to the rationing practices of the Babylonian and Persian kings in Ezra, Ezekiel, Nehemiah, and Esther.

The second assumption, that these transactions were recorded for the benefit of managerial or administrative planning, cannot be proven although the existence of some specialized tablets are indicative of those practices. For example, if I, a thousand years from now, were to unearth a cache of voided checks, I would have something similar to the bulk of this archive of cuneiform tablets. Modern checks are dated, an amount is recorded, and the payee and the payer are listed. On the reverse, the payee's signature or stamp is applied and on some the purpose of the check is indicated. Individually we write large numbers of checks and many of us record these payments in checkbooks, but very few use the information recorded over the years for planning purposes. We want to be sure that we *have* cash available for the next purchase, but we do not typically categorize these expenditures into food, books, or clothing so that we can budget later. Classifications are indeed made by businesses for tax and income reporting. They may use them for budgeting purposes, but this is not a common practice of an individual. So, was the Achamenid regime recording these transactions to track or confirm current inventory levels, to minimize the occurrence of duplicate distributions, or were these records meant to meet more extensive needs of the regime, or to provide information for decision-making purposes? The answer is not obvious.

There are tablets on which scribes have compiled information gathered from other tablets recording ration distributions from a single location. The fact that the tablets were forwarded from surrounding locales to Persepolis, were there classified by location, and were recopied onto larger tablets suggests at least that someone was monitoring the reductions in inventory from individual supply depots.

There are other large tablets that record not the individual distributions or deposits but only the gross increases and decreases in inventory over one or many years. Many include a line saying, "this accounting took place in x year." The accounting cited often took place a considerable period of time after the last stated year of the inventory. It was as if the accountant were to write, "the inventory at the end of year 1995 included 500 barrels of figs. We figured this out in 1997."

Obviously the inventory had not just been counted. Perhaps the scribe was recording information gathered from a number of other tablets. If this is true, then why? What could have been the purpose of a compilation done years after the fact? Parallel modern situations can be illustrated. When the IRS audits prior-year tax returns, their work papers would be dated several years after that of the return. State funding agencies often audit the organizations they fund a few years after the fact. So, many modern audits take place long after the period at issue. Might that ancient tablet represent an audit directed towards a person whose fiduciary responsibilities regarding inventory were in question? A fraud audit? Might this have merely been a training exercise for a new scribe/bookkeeper? Since all of the tablets were found in a section of wall, used as fill, and not in a special storeroom, there is no evidence whatsoever of the relative importance of any of them. However, the historian/accountant is greatly tempted to ascribe to these tablets a purpose grounded in the same needs that created modern managerial or administrative control systems. Absent evidence to the contrary, such a conclusion appears warranted.

There is substantial evidence for the third assumption that control systems were well in place. The very existence of any of these tablets points to that. More important, however, is that most of them are inscribed with at least one seal denoting an authorization of or a witness to a transaction. The use of seals on documents to authorize or ensure contents is undisputed and was common throughout the ancient world for, quite literally, thousands of years (Postgate, 1992). Modern society still uses seals in the same way. For example, notaries impress their seals certifying their witness. Birth and marriage certificates are impressed with state seals. Similarly, and at its simplest, the ancient authority sanctioned a transaction by appending his or her seal. A step above this in complexity included the mutual appending of seals by two equal-status parties to the transaction. Thus, "I delivered the grain" and "I received the grain."

The archive reveals that tablets recording common transactions tend to have one or two seals while those marking less usual events have more. Such evidence points to the existence of a control system established to encourage the fluidity of repetitive work while protecting the regime's assets. Unfortunately, a rather high level of exceptions (about 25% within some categories of tablets) casts a shadow over this conclusion. There are tablets with no seals that belong to populations that "require" two. There are tablets with three seals that only "need" one. What does this mean? Does it throw into question the entire modern understanding of internal control? I think not. I believe that there were prescribed processes and

procedures that most officials and others followed, and that the anomalies that
appeared were either breakdowns in the system or varied for reasons that have not
survived.

What about the economy? Was it similar to that of the modern world? We might
first look at the ration allocations. We see two major types of food distributions,
grain (or flour) and wine. This combination is not sufficiently nutritious to support
a population according to people working in the agricultural extension of this
university. So what are the possibilities? Were grain distributions accompanied by
unmentioned measures of vegetables, fruit, meat, and salt? The possibility that
other tablets recorded the distribution of those necessities is unlikely since none
have been found, but we do know that these foodstuffs were grown all over the
area. Did workers have their own gardens and time to tend them? Were these
distributions in excess of workers' needs so that they could be used to barter for
other necessities? The amounts cited on the tablets do *not* suggest an excess; they
meet the normal daily requirement for an average adult. Might the workers have
been fed on the job and received the allotments as excess? Were the work periods
limited to a certain number of months after which groups would return home where
they would eat more nutritiously?

The answer to this question must remain a mystery although a possible
explanation may be discerned from the rations given out to soldiers more recently.
"A daily bread ration of between $1\frac{1}{2}$ to 2 lbs was established for the Army of
Flanders during the 1590s . . . and British soldiers during the 1690s received daily
a single 1 lb. loaf of rye bread." All armies expected men to supplement their
diets in local markets or by foraging (Corvisier, 1994, pp. 684–685).[1] Perhaps
this describes the situation of the Persian workers.

What about the work performed? Sadly, there is little information. The majority
of the tablets identify the area where laborers were located but nothing about their
skills. A few tablets do name the job (archer, auditor, treasurers, Persian boys
copying texts, and delivery man), but this is infrequent. Persepolis was under construction during this time, so a considerable amount of basic hard labor was needed;
e.g. clearing land, digging foundations, hauling stone. We do know that many
applied their skills to the artistic side of the city, including carving massive reliefs,
sculptures, and wood; applying gold leaf; and painting. The handful of tablets that
specify the work is sufficient to let us know that there was little or no differentiation
of payment for the type of work performed. The custom was to give a worker a
set amount for a day's work, regardless of the job. Laborers were compensated (or
better, fed) for their labor, not for their skill. We do not have much evidence for
changes in rates (rations) over time. Similarly, Finley (1973, p. 23) reported that
labor payments in the Greek and Roman worlds stayed the same over very long
periods. Usually one or more people received more in rations than others, but they

were probably supervisors. We also see differential allotments to men, women, boys, and girls.

Who were the workers? There were many of them. Were they all slaves? The evidence is not at all conclusive. Finley (1973) found that throughout the ancient Greek and Roman world, the concept of slavery was one of degree, and that freedom was a function more of wealth than of social status. Greek and Roman slaves had families and often managed the estates of their owners for their own use and enrichment. Often their offspring were politically and socially free. On the other hand, a "free" debtor manifested the characteristics of a slave. He was bound to the creditor until the debt was paid and, if unable to pay off his debt during his life, his children would remain bound. A slave could rely on the owners providing food and shelter whereas the poor freeman might be free to starve.

In the Achamenid period, slavery had a role, but scholars disagree about the extent of royal or noble slave holdings and the status of the slave. As in Finley's analysis, Achamenid slavery encompassed a spectrum of possibilities. Most slaves were foreign and worked on royal estates or work projects, such as Persepolis. But it is unlikely that they were the only workers and equally unlikely that their status remained unchanged over time. Semi-free people, working for their subsistence, contributed as well as landowners whose contracts required state work (Dandamaev & Lukonin, 1989, pp. 166–171).

A mix of free, semi-free, and slave labor underscores the finding that labor was "paid" by the day or month and that the payment equaled a measure of a daily food allowance. People cannot be paid less than a measure of grain per day since survival would be threatened. Among the slaves were the most skilled of workers, goldsmiths and sculptors, none of whom received more than anyone else. Logic suggests that if the most highly skilled workers were paid subsistence wages, then there was little incentive for the regime to distribute more to those who were not slaves. What emerges from this scenario is unfamiliar terrain, requiring a creative imagination. This was a bureaucratic regime, with an economy of stasis, not growth. It was a society moving with the seasons, agriculturally based, artistic, and healthy, but not dynamic in a modern sense and apparently lacking markets of any vitality. Currency existed but payment-in-kind was the common method of remunerating labor. There are no or few changes in wage prices because there was little to buy beyond subsistence. Indeed, if work had for millennia been traded for food, then it would have taken a substantial change in cultural behavior to reward beyond the subsistence level. There was no reason to pay more for skilled than unskilled laborer since a skilled laborer cannot consume more food than an unskilled worker and, in the absence of excess remuneration, the accumulation of other goods was difficult. There must be surplus and something to expend that excess upon in order for true markets to develop. Land, the heart of wealth, was acquired by conquest or inheritance so major changes in an individual's status were limited.

Working with ancient materials is fascinating because it offers a view, although doubtlessly distorted, of worlds that have disappeared and that operated in ways foreign to the modern observer. To a degree, developing even a partial understanding of past accountings brings us some flavor of familiarity. The organization of documents reminds us of our own checks and receipts. Counting inventories (protecting assets), applying seals (verification and authorization), and holding people responsible are also familiar. Rationing was like feeding an army. On the other hand, the scholar seeking certainty or even probabilities will not be comfortable here – there are just too many unknowns. Drawing conclusions based on limited evidence is a requirement. The accounting historian who has an inclination for histories beyond our paper-filled modern era will find richness and pleasure working in the distant past.

NOTES

1. By contrast, the daily ration for a Union soldier in the Civil War between August 3, 1861 and June 20, 1864 was "12 oz of pork or bacon, or, 1 lb and 4 oz of salt or fresh beef, 1 lb and 6 oz of soft bread or flour, or, 1 lb hard bread, or 1 lb and 4 oz of corn meal; and to every 100 rations, 15 lbs of beans or peas, and 10 lbs of rice or hominy; 10 lbs of green coffee or 8 lbs of roasted coffee, or, 1 lb and 8 oz of tea; 15 lbs of sugar; 4 quarts of vinegar . . . 3 lb, 12 oz of salt, 4 oz of pepper, 30 lbs of potatoes and 1 quart of molasses" (Wiley, 1952, p. 224). This ration allocation was unusually generous compared to those distributed in other wars and other countries. Soldiers also lived off the land to a considerable extent and took certain items, such as coffee and sugar, as well as full meals, from local communities (Shannon, 1965; Wiley, 1952).

REFERENCES

Berlin, I. (1950). *Concepts and categories*. New York: Viking Press (1978 reprint).

Clay, A. (1904). *Business documents of Murashu Sons of Nippur dated in the reign of Darius II (424–404 B.C.)*. Philadelphia: Department of Archaeology and Palaeontology of the University of Pennsylvania.

Collingwood, R. G. (1993). *The idea of history*. Oxford: Clarendon Press.

Corvisier, A. (Ed.) (1994). *A dictionary of military history*. Oxford: Blackwell.

Costouros, G. J. (1977). Development of an accounting system in ancient Athens in response to socio-economic changes. *Accounting Historians Journal*, 4(1), 37–54.

Costouros, G. J. (1978). Auditing in the Athenian state of the golden age (500–300 B.C.). *Accounting Historians Journal*, 5(1), 41–50.

Dandamaev, M., & Lukonin, V. (1989). *The culture and social institutions of ancient Iran*. Cambridge: Cambridge University Press.

Ezzamel, M. (1997). Accounting, control and accountability: Preliminary evidence from ancient Egypt. *Critical Perspectives on Accounting, 8*(6), 563–604.

Finley, M. I. (1973). *The ancient economy*. Berkeley and Los Angeles: University of California Press.

Fu, P. (1971). Governmental accounting in China during the Chou dynasty (1122–256 B.C.). *Journal of Accounting Research, 9*(1), 40–51.

Godfrey, A., & Hooper, K. (1996). Accountability and decision making in feudal England: Domesday book revisited. *Accounting History, 1*(1), 35–54.

Hagerman, R. (1980). Accounting in the Bible. *Accounting Historians Journal, 7*(2), 71–76.

Hallock, R. (1969). *Persepolis fortification tablets*. Chicago: University of Chicago Press.

Keister, O. (1974). Unexpected accounting. *Accounting Historians Journal, 1*(1), 16–18.

Jose, M., & Moore, C. (1998). The development of taxation in the Bible: Improvements in counting, measurement, and computation in the ancient middle east. *Accounting Historians Journal, 25*(2), 63–79.

Littleton, A. C. (1980). *Accounting evolution to 1900*. University, AL: University of Alabama Press (reprint of 1933 edition).

Lutz, H. F. (1927). *Neo-Babylonian administrative documents from Erech* (2 parts). Berkeley: University of California Press.

Mattessich, R. (1987). Prehistoric accounting and the problem of representation: On recent archaeological evidence of the middle-east from 8000 B.C. to 3000 B.C. *Accounting Historians Journal, 14*(2), 71–92.

Mattessich, R. (1994). Archaeology of accounting and Schmandt-Bessarats's contribution. *Accounting, Business and Financial History, 4*(1), 5–28.

Mattessich, R. (1998a). Recent insights into Mesopotamian accounting of the 3rd Millennium B.C. – Successor to token accounting. *Accounting Historians Journal, 25*(1), 1–27.

Mattessich, R. (1998b). From accounting to negative numbers: A signal contribution of medieval India to mathematics. *Accounting Historians Journal, 25*(2), 129–145.

Millar, F. (1983). Epigraphy. In: M. Crawford (Ed.), *Sources for Ancient History* (pp. 80–136). Cambridge: Cambridge University Press.

Momigliano, A. (1975). Historicism revisited. In: A. Momigliano (Ed.), *Essays in Ancient and Modern Historiography* (pp. 365–373). Middletown, CN: Wesleyan University Press.

Nissen, H., Damerow, P., & Englund, R. (1993). *Archaic bookkeeping: Early writing and techniques of economic administration in the ancient near east*. Chicago and London: University of Chicago Press.

Nurnberg, H. (2000). Biblical basis of forty-year goodwill amortization. *Accounting Historians Journal, 27*(2), 165–176.

Oldroyd, D. (1997). Accounting in Anglo-Saxon England: Context and evidence. *Accounting History, 2*(1), 7–34.

Postgate, J. N. (1992). *Early Mesopotamia*. London: Routledge.

Ste. Croix, G. (1956). Greek and Roman accounting. In: A. C. Littleton & B. Yamey (Eds), *Studies in the History of Accounting* (pp. 14–74). London: Sweet and Maxwell.

Schmandt-Bessarat, D. (1988). Tokens at Uruk. *Baghdader Mitteilungen, 19*, 1–12.

Schmandt-Bessarat, D. (1992). *Before writing* (2 vols.). Austin: University of Texas Press.

Shannon, F. A. (1965). *The organization and administration of the Union Army 1861–1865* (Vol. 1). Gloucester, MA: Peter Smith.

Stevelinck, E. (1985). Accounting in ancient times. *Accounting Historians Journal, 12*(1), 1–16.

Vollmers, G. (1996).The Persepolis fortification texts: Accounting and control in ancient Persia from
    509 to 494 B.C. *Accounting Enquiries, 6*(1), 1–43.
Wiley, B. (1952). *The life of Billy Yank*. Indianapolis: Bobbs-Merrill Co.
Zaid, O. (2000). Were Islamic records precursors to accounting books based on the Italian method?
    Accounting Historians Journal, 27(1), 73–90.

THE THEORY/PRACTICE SCHISM IN COST ACCOUNTING HISTORY: NEW INSIGHTS FROM ARCHIVAL RESEARCH

Richard K. Fleischman

INTRODUCTION

The word "schism" has become a prominent part of accounting parlance over the past two decades. In 1979, the American Accounting Association (AAA) actually constituted what was called the Schism Committee. Bricker and Previts (1990) wrote an article about "schism" that appeared in *Accounting Horizons* a decade ago, while a team of authors several years ago published an entire book on the subject, *The Schism in Accounting* (Bloom et al., 1994). However, the schism central in these efforts, the divide between the practice and the teaching of accounting, is not the focal point here, but will be discussed in way of introduction. The theory/practice schism that is the focus of this chapter involves the differing chronologies according to which new costing methodologies appear in the literature, on the one hand, and in industrial enterprises, on the other. It is a rebuttable assumption that practice comes to mirror innovative techniques articulated in textbooks and journals. It will be argued here that, in historical environments, it is only through the agency of archival research that the assumption can be rebutted and the schism's depth measured.

Doing Accounting History: Contributions to the Development of Accounting Thought
Studies in the Development of Accounting Thought, Volume 6, 63–79
ISSN: 1479-3504/PII: S1479350402060040

The current schism between academic accounting and practice that has generated so much attention has two distinct parameters – the relevance of the material that we teach in the classroom and the relevance to practitioners of the research that we do. The teaching relevance question has been brought into focus recently in the U.S. with the grant program administered by the Accounting Education Change Commission. It is also the case that very recently the leading accrediting organization in the U.S., the American Assembly of Collegiate Schools of Business, has rewritten its standard on relevant professional experience to foster a greater interaction between academics and professionals. It seems that steps are being taken in the U.S. to address the gulf separating the "ivory tower" and "the real world" as identified in the famous Bedford Report (1986) and the 1988 survey of the AAA's practitioner membership (Bricker & Previts, 1990, p. 2).

Concomitant forward steps, however, are not happening with respect to a perceived research schism. The accounting research that appears in mainstream U.S. journals such as the *Accounting Review*, the *Journal of Accounting Research*, and many others is not only irrelevant to practice but also unintelligible to practitioners as it is to most of us. The Carnegie and Ford Foundations are frequently blamed for defining the rules of the research game 40 years ago (e.g. Panozzo, 1997; Whitley, 1986, 1988), but it is not at all clear why the called-for application of statistics and a social sciences methodology to practical problems has given rise to this genre of published research. Likewise, the positivism and natural sciences paradigm of the Rochester School cannot really be blamed. Rather, it all seems to be a conspiracy on the part of faculty at prestigious universities to force their graduate students into duplicating that which got them to the top so as to perpetuate an elite standing, both individually and institutionally. We hear that U.S. academic research is tied to funding opportunities, but does big accounting really embrace this output? What motivates big accounting is the desire for recruits from prestigious schools, and firms have been willing to pay part of the research tab in order to improve their chances. But funders of research would be just as happy to have their dollars go into the accounting research the rest of the world does, that which is historical, multidisciplinary, qualitative, and "less in need of scientific legitimation" (Panozzo, 1997, pp. 466–467). It is doubtful that these research alternatives are any more germane to the art of accounting practice, but at least the output would be more intelligible and enjoyable to read.

The "schism" that this study purports to discuss is that which divides accounting theory and practice. In point of fact, in an historical sense, the theory/practice schism may just be an older version of the current academe/practice divide, and that it is only the relative youthfulness of accounting education that has modified the schism's parameters. Accounting writing/theory has evolved through three distinct historical epochs. Precedent to the turn of the 20th century, when there was no accounting education per se, virtually all that was written about accounting was instructional – "how-to" manuals, authored by practitioners. Commencing around 1900, an accounting professorate began to develop, but this cadre of professors was quite different from what constitutes academe today. Most educators had been or continued to be practitioners, with the result that the nature of accounting writing changed little from what it had been before the advent of university-level business and commerce programs. It was really not until the last quarter of the 20th century that academic accounting developed a research agenda apart from practice, and that the accounting theory relevant to U.S. practitioners came to be articulated by organizations such as the Financial Accounting Standards Board and the American Institute of Certified Public Accountants. It was only at this point of time that the theory/practice schism evolved into the academe/practice schism of today.

Since this study will focus on two seminal periods in the history of cost accounting, it is imperative to consider whether cost/managerial accounting is immune from schism possibilities. Panozzo (1997, p. 455) suggested that perhaps management accounting has been "liberated" from the "mainstream orthodoxy" because of the greater suitability of field-based research in that branch of the discipline. However, this view is problematic in light of Johnson and Kaplan's (1987b) indictment of academe as being partially responsible for the failure of costing methods to allow U.S. industry to identify which 20% of its product lines generate 80% of its revenue. Furthermore, the lag of nearly a decade just concluded between the operationalization of just-in-time manufacturing systems and activity-based costing with their appearance in standard managerial and cost accounting textbooks is indicative of the fact that the theory (academe)/practice schism is flourishing in this branch of the discipline as well.

This paper is organized as follows. In the succeeding two sections, the costing innovations of the British Industrial Revolution (BIR) and the development of standard costing in the U.S. are discussed in terms of the theoretical literature and the practical applications in each of the respective periods. The inescapable conclusion is that, in the absence of archival research, it is frequently misguided to make assumptions about the extent of methodologies in practice based solely upon evidence related to the accounting theory that prevailed contemporaneously.

THE BIR COSTING PROJECT

At a history session at the 1985 national meeting of the AAA, Tom Johnson spoke to the subject of "the organizational awakening in management accounting history," featuring his conviction that sophisticated costing commenced at the Lyman textile mills in the U.S. in the 1850s. Although Johnson's (1972) article on

Lyman and *Relevance Lost* (Johnson & Kaplan, 1987a) had little to say about BIR accounting (only a footnote in *Relevance Lost* (p. 44) about "intriguing results" at Wedgwood's Etruria pottery works, citing McKendrick, 1970), it was in this forum that I first heard of Pollard's (1965, p. 248) conclusion that BIR costing was not helpful for entrepreneurial decision making. Given my prior knowledge of BIR business records (Fleischman, 1985), this judgment seemed at odds with the remarkable sophistication of BIR entrepreneurs in diverse economic activities, such as capital accumulation, technological innovation, and the development of marketing/distribution structures. How could they have failed to appreciate the advantages cost accounting could bring to their enterprises?

My first task in confronting this issue was to seek understanding on how widespread was this indictment of BIR costing and the conditions that gave rise to this perception. In terms of accounting history per se, the judgment appeared universal in venerated texts that predated Pollard. Littleton (1933), Edwards (1937), Yamey (1949), Solomons (1952), and Garner (1954) were just several of the giants of our discipline who seemingly dismissed the genesis of sophisticated managerial accounting during the BIR in favor of the Age of Taylor and scientific management of which Solomons (1952, p. 8) declared the coming of a "costing renaissance." It is not difficult to appreciate why these fathers of our craft universally subscribed to that opinion. There was an almost total dearth of cost accounting literature during the BIR. Until Charles Babbage's rather late effort, *On The Economy of Machinery and Manufacturers* (1835), only three manuals of the age – Thompson's *The Accountant's Oracle* (1777), Hamilton's *An Introduction to Merchandise* (1777), and Cronhelm's *Double Entry by Single* (1818) – reflected any awareness of industrial accounting topics. Dozens of texts that went through multiple editions took no cognizance of costing. When Brown wrote his classic, *The History of Accounting and Accountants* (1905), he took no notice of industrial accounting methods in over 300 pages of narrative. Couple this shortfall with the lack of accounting education (Stacey, 1954), the absence of an accounting profession (Parker, 1986), and the non-existence of universally accepted accounting conventions (Yamey, 1960), it would have been difficult for the writers of generations ago to have reached any other conclusion in the absence of archival research.

However, Pollard, in writing *The Genesis of Modern Management*, had undertaken a wider sweep of BIR business records than any other historian up until his time. Yet, his negative conclusion is almost universally referenced as the process of rehabilitating BIR cost accounting has progressed, primarily during the past decade. But if the thrust of this article is that archival research is necessary to understand and evaluate theory/practice schisms, how can it be that Pollard, given his wide sweep of original sources, got it so wrong?

Pollard (1965, p. 233) identified four failings of financial accounting during the BIR – suspect profit calculations, "confusion between capital and revenue," non-recognition of depreciation, and the treatment of owners' investment as a cost. Ultimately his bill of particulars boiled down to three indictments:

(1) High profit margins during the BIR made entrepreneurs oblivious to cost factors. However, it is the judgment expressed in Fleischman and Parker (1997) that profit margins were distinctly narrow and competition extremely fierce, at least in the textiles and iron industries. It has now also been acknowledged that even in luxury trades such as pottery, margins could be narrow in times of depression. Wedgwood's famous calculation of vase prices (McKendrick, 1970) was occasioned by the economic distress of the 1770s.

(2) The number of surviving cost estimates from the BIR is impressive, but their accuracy is so questionable as to render them worthless and reflective of what Pollard called pejoratively a "cavalier attitude" about costing. This charge is extraordinarily difficult to answer because it raises issues as to whether "managing by the numbers" is appropriate irrespective of the time period under review. If the managerial accounting of the late 1980s could not resolve the dilemma that Johnson and Kaplan (1987b) posed of determining which products to manufacture, why should BIR costing be held to a high standard? It may just be that the mere act of generating an impressive array of data was sufficient to establish a panoptic accounting eye to effectuate a degree of labor and managerial control. An accounting system as exact as what Hoskin and Macve (1988, 1994) observed and documented at the Springfield Armory, but not at Boulton & Watt (Fleischman et al., 1995) or in the Northeast coal industry during the BIR (Fleischman & Macve, 2002), is not required to achieve some measure of labor and managerial discipline. Moreover, it might be argued that the very survival of many BIR firms over an extended time frame testifies to some measure of success, irrespective of the accuracy of the accounting numbers generated.

(3) Where Pollard is on firmer ground in his skepticism of BIR cost accounting is his questioning of whether or not accounting data were used to facilitate business decisions. Here the argument takes two directions. The first is whether or not integration was achieved between costing and financial record keeping. This issue has not yet been resolved as Jones (1985) and Edwards (1989) reported a successful integration at Cyfarthfa, while Fleischman and Parker (1990) found that at Carron the hopelessness of the financial accounting made any attempt at integration with the vastly more sophisticated costing efforts an abortive exercise.

Of more immediate consequence is the absence of vital linkages between *ex ante* accounting estimation and *post factum* business decision making in directions indicated by the accounting. My research has uncovered precious few of these linkages although several surfaced in the Stella Coal Company archive. However, I am more optimistic than Pollard who feels they simply did not exist and that their absence is indicative of a simplistic accounting methodology. My more optimistic vision is that business decisions were undertaken based upon accounting data but that with a survival rate of perhaps 10% for BIR business records overall, the chances for both ends of the chain to be extant are small.

Until recently, I would have answered Pollard's bottom-line judgment in the foregoing terms. However, a recent review of *The Genesis of Modern Management* has induced me to revise my opinion as to why Pollard got it wrong. Of the archives I have visited, Pollard was also privy to the Boulton & Watt, Cyfarthfa, Dowlais, Gott, Herculaneum, Mona, Newton Chambers, and Wedgwood business records. The first three are substantial and relatively sophisticated archives, but in the case of all three, Pollard looked mainly at correspondence rather than at accounting record books. Gott, Herculaneum, and Mona all had a measure of sophisticated accounting in my view, but they were all very small collections that have frustrated researchers into wishing for more. Newton Chambers, a substantial, Yorkshire iron firm, had the poorest accounting system of any major concern in the industry (Fleischman & Parker, 1992). Wedgwood, everybody's favorite BIR firm, was both a substantial and fairly sophisticated archive, but not cataloged at the time of Pollard's visitation. Pollard, through the vagaries of the collections he chose to visit, did not see the best of what was available. He did not see records from the Carron or the Coalbrookdale iron firms, Stella Coal, or the Marshall or the Strutt textile enterprises. Rather, he depended upon the histories of these firms written by Campbell (1961), Raistrick (1953), and Rimmer (1960). Notwithstanding, Pollard's approach to archival research ought not to be condemned. Given that his archival investigations constituted a groundbreaking project, it was eminently practical for him to visit only those repositories of business records that had not yet been examined and to depend upon the narratives of his fellow economic historians for those archives that had been more extensively mined. It must also be recalled that his focus was on the whole of modern management of which accounting is only a part. In a way it was an unlucky happenstance that the records his colleagues had examined contained the best accounting. Pollard, who had a keener sense of appreciation for accounting methodology than they, might have formed a different conclusion had he observed the best the age had to offer.

Given this introduction, the question remains, what information has been conveyed via the mechanism of archival research that differs from the venerated cost accounting histories whose authors were not privy to these records and to

Pollard, also venerated, whose access to the best sources was limited? Were the entrepreneurs of the BIR engaged in cost accounting activities not thought to have existed at any level of sophistication for decades, whether the genesis was felt to have been the New England textile mills as per Johnson (1972), the Springfield Armory (Hoskin & Macve, 1988, 1994), the U.S. railroads (Chandler, 1977), or the Age of Taylor and scientific management? Was there a schism between the practice of accounting in the BIR and a theoretical shortfall occasioned by the aforementioned absence of an accounting literature?

Archival research, undertaken for the most part in the past decade, has accomplished the rehabilitation of BIR costing in the estimation of many, albeit not all, accounting history scholars. Archival investigations have been conducted at various levels of focus – specific BIR business firms, specific industrial sectors, and the BIR at the macrolevel. Single enterprise studies include those by Stone (1973) of the Chorlton mills, Edwards and Baber (1979) of Dowlais iron, Fleischman and Parker (1990) of Carron iron, Walsh and Stewart (1993) of New Lanark textiles, Fleischman et al. (1995) and Williams (1997a, b, 1999) of Boulton & Watt, and Williams (1997a) of the Oldknow cotton firm. Industry-specific results have been reported for coal and iron, including Baber and Atkinson (1987), Edwards and Boyns (1992), Fleischman and Parker (1992), Edwards et al. (1995), Oldroyd (1996), McLean (1997), and Fleischman and Macve (2002). Global sweeps of BIR costing archives are evident in Jones (1985), Edwards (1989), Edwards and Newell (1991), Fleischman and Parker (1991, 1997), Fleischman and Tyson (1993), Boyns and Edwards (1996, 1997), and Boyns et al. (1997).

The paragraphs that follow chronicle a "best case" scenario of the BIR's cost/managerial accounting. Further explanations of these methodologies, including archival reproductions and references, may be found in Fleischman and Parker (1997).

The control of costs would be an anticipated first step in the process through which sophisticated costing systems are developed. J. & N. Philips, tape makers, tracked indirect material costs for all nine steps of its bleaching process (Fleischman & Parker, 1997, p. 91). John Marshall, the Leed's flax spinner, generated cost data in 40 expense categories for each productive process in the operation (Fleischman & Parker, 1997, p. 82). Included was overhead allocation as exemplified by an 1811 table of the Shrewsbury accounts where subsequent allocation percentages were changed periodically (Fleischman & Parker, 1997, pp. 36, 90). It is known that overhead allocation on the basis of predetermined formula was used at Carron as early as the 1760s and almost universally in the South Wales iron industry in the 1840s (Fleischman & Parker, 1997, pp. 151, 177). Stone (1973) made a similar claim for the Chorlton textile mills.

The generation of cost data most likely served a higher purpose when comparative costings were undertaken. Carron in the 1770s was producing ironstone yields and associated cost reports for its various mineral fields that were used in making abandonment decisions and served as a source for transfer prices (Fleischman & Parker, 1997, pp. 178–180). Similar concerns about raw materials cost was reflected at Mona Mine where the refining charges of varieties of copper ore were calculated taking into account differential raising and smelting costs (Fleischman & Parker, 1997, pp. 149–150). At textiles enterprises Ashworth and Strutt, waste costs were computed for various raw material mixtures (Fleischman & Parker, 1997, pp. 83–84).

Within firms the expenses incurred in shops of the same function were compared. Strutt tracked costs in its various carding and spinning rooms, while a similar costing exercise was done at Boulton & Watt with respect to its lathing and drilling operations (Fleischman & Parker, 1997, pp. 38–39). The productivity and raw material consumption of Carron's five blast furnaces were provided in monthly production reports, along with explanations for departures from the norm (Fleischman & Parker, 1997, pp. 183–185). The Darby ironworks in Shropshire, as well as the Marshall and Ashworth textile enterprises, generated comparative costing and/or production information for its individual mills (Fleischman & Parker, 1997, pp. 54–56, 95–96).

The Strutt cotton firm of Derbyshire had a most impressive inventory control system in place. Its raw materials inventory was maintained at both average and standard cost. Work-in-process was tracked with regard to location and state of completion. Products in finished goods were qualitatively rated on a one-to-five decimal scale (Fleischman & Parker, 1997, p. 45).

Standard costing achieved renown in the Age of Taylor as a prime indicator of improved costing methodology. Depending upon one's definition of this practice, it was evident to a greater or lesser degree among certain BIR firms. The Boulton & Watt engine books serve as a classic example as hundreds of components were costed therein at standard for completed steam engines. These engine standards were derived scientifically through trials and observations. However, they did lack more modern accuracy as they tended to be quite rounded and infrequently amended (Fleischman & Parker, 1997, pp. 211–214). J. & N. Philips deployed standards in the early 1770s in order to gauge the quantity of inputs necessary to achieve a certain level of output (Fleischman & Parker, 1997, p. 82). The Mona copper mine in Anglesey found it was encountering difficulty in applying industry-wide standards to its individual situation (quoted in Fleischman & Parker, 1997, p. 148):

We ought not to place such reliance upon the Cornish Standard in our Calculations to regulate Mining operations; and I recommend as a Rule to be generally observed with respect to the produce of Mona Mine that £90 per Ton of Metal in Cake should be taken as the Average Standard – limiting all your workings by that Standard, except such as are pursued with a reasonable prospect of Discovery, or for other ultimate objects necessary to the success of the Mines.

There is also a surviving 1822 document from Mona in which a coal input standard is established for six operations (two each from smelting, roasting, and refining). A time standard for labor also appears for the two smelting processes (Fleischman & Parker, 1997, pp. 156–158).

There exists virtually no evidence that variance analysis was undertaken comparing actual results to standards. However, one very busy document for mining and marketing coals at Halbeath Colliery in Scotland compares 1798 and 1799 expenses with detailed explanations for significant deviations (Fleischman & Parker, 1997, pp. 156–158).

Surviving business records from the BIR feature a galaxy of cost estimates to support business decisions with regard to technological innovations or upgrades, transport construction or alternatives, and capital improvements. Most remarkable is a differential analysis between estimated and actual expenses incurred in the sinking of the Emma Pit at Stella Coal in the 1840s. The document is some 34 pages long and includes the original estimate of cost, a restatement of estimated costs with corresponding actuals, a narrative explaining key differences, a statement of "delay days," and a final reconciliation of differences distinguishing those where actuals exceeded estimates and those that had not been estimated at all (Fleischman & Parker, 1997, pp. 119–121).

In addition to the above evidence, sporadic tidbits reflective of modern usages appeared. Sensitivity analyses were done at Carron in 1770 and at the Ashington Coal Company in 1843, gauging the effects of reduced production and increased sales respectively (Fleischman & Parker, 1997, pp. 139, 183). Henry Ashworth and Carron did business forecasting, albeit infrequently (Fleischman & Parker, 1997, pp. 42–44, 185). There is evidence that transfer pricing was done with some regularity at Carron and in the standardized South Wales iron production reports of the 1840s (Fleischman & Parker, 1997, pp. 52–54).

In my estimation, the sum total of the above archival evidence puts paid to Pollard's evaluation of BIR cost accounting and demonstrates the existence of a schism between theory and practice. It is also my contention that this revision is best defended with archival research. These investigations also disprove a theory advanced by many to explain the absence of published cost accounting theory at this point in history. It has been argued that competitive advantage mandated secrecy about costing techniques (Chatfield, 1977; Edwards, 1937; Garner, 1954; Urwick & Brech, 1964; Wells, 1978). However, Henry Ashworth frequently visited his competitors' operations and possessed an 1845 survey of 40 Bolton-area textiles mills that divulged vast quantities of information about operations (Fleischman & Parker, 1997, pp. 80–81). Boulton & Watt knew moulders' piece rates at its competition (Fleischman & Parker, 1997, p. 207). The Tyneside coal-owners' cartels likewise collected and disseminated data on their memberships, information that would have been highly confidential had secrecy been the order of the day (Fleischman & Macve, 2002).

Scholars are not in universal agreement, however, that the archival evidence outlined above constitutes a "costing renaissance" in the sense that it represents the genesis of cost accounting's use as a tool of modern management. Hoskin and Macve (1988, 1994), based on archival research at the Springfield Armory in the U.S., have dated the "genesis of modem management" from the disciplinary regime instituted there to control labor in the 1830s and 1840s. Both have undertaken joint venturing with me into selected BIR archives with the conclusion that accounting was used to control expenses and/or to measure the efficiency of machines, but that this attention was not parallelled by similar developments in the area of labor control (Fleischman et al., 1995; Fleischman & Macve, 2002). In my view and in the perception of most economic rationalists, relating the significance of accounting to a single purpose excluding all other potential benefits is reductionist. A recent debate in the *Accounting Historians Journal* provides valuable perspectives on this and other issues that may prove irreconcilable in Foucauldian and Neoclassical theory (Boyns & Edwards, 2000; Hoskin & Macve, 2000; Tyson, 2000).

U.S. STANDARD COSTING

The introduction of standard costing in the U.S. during the Age of Taylor and beyond is another fruitful area of investigation where archival research has shed light on the myths and realities associated with another theory/practice schism. Solomons (1952) bespoke a "costing renaissance" that featured an unprecedented theoretical outpouring, much of which, but not all, was authored by Americans or British émigrés to the U.S. Many of the foremost theorists were not accountants at all, but like the most famous of these scientific managers, Frederick Wilmslow Taylor, had been trained as engineers. Very little had been written on either side of the Atlantic between Babbage's book (1835) and the 1880s when the scientific management tradition started with works by Towne (1885–1886), Metcalfe (1885), Garcke and Fells (1887), and Norton (1889). The costing literature became more prolific and more perceptive in the early 20th century, featuring classics by Taylor (1903, 1911), Emerson (1908–1909), Whitmore (1908), and Church (1901), just to mention a few of the more prominent.

The same venerable authors, who saw no merit in BIR costing because of the absence of a literature, have likewise proclaimed the dawning of the new era of scientific management based upon these works. They extrapolated from this writing the existence in practice of a gamut of scientific management practices – standard costing, variance analysis, time-and-motion studies, budgeting, centralized purchasing, etc. This period's significance as a formative age has been further established by two influential Ph.D. dissertations subsequently published as books – those of Sowell (1973) and Epstein (1978). The first two decades of the 20th century became an important, albeit not central, focus for an emerging tripartite historiographic debate over the pattern of cost accounting development in the U.S. Johnson and Kaplan, from an economic-rationalist perspective, wrote in *Relevance Lost* (1987a, pp. 49–50):

> ... these 'scientific managers' focused their attention on predetermining 'standard' rates at which material and labor should be consumed in manufacturing tasks. The methods they devised to determine standards for material and labor inputs included engineering design of bills of material and time-and-motion study.

Miller and O'Leary (1987, p. 238), in a classic Foucauldian rendering, discussed accounting's contribution in providing the knowledge to permit the U.S. industrial worker to be transformed into a "governable person":

> Standard costing is, we suggest, intertwined with other attempts within the enterprise and outside it to embark on a vast project of standardisation and normalisation of the lives of individuals .... It is the positive conditions of a complex group of relations with which accounting exists that we should address.

Hopper and Armstrong (1991, p. 433), drawing upon Marxist ideology and the labor-process investigations of Braverman (1974), concluded:

> Standard cost systems were pioneered as an aspect of the fragmentation and deskilling of craft labour, which had hitherto resisted employers' attempts at intensification through piecework payment systems. Once the American industrial engineers had gained control over working methods, it became possible for them to make 'scientific' decisions on the pace of work, and to issue these in the form of standard costs.

It seems apparent that these quoted scholars had accepted the judgment of the authors of the traditional accounting history texts that there was a substantial costing advance occurring in practice during the years immediately precedent to World War I. However, in this regard they were merely seconding perceptions that had only been assumed on the basis of the theoretical outpouring. There is absolutely nothing remiss in this acceptance by Johnson/Kaplan, Miller/O'Leary, and Hopper/Armstrong. They had bigger fish to fry than to question the accumulated wisdom regarding one small subperiod of their larger surveys. If accounting historians were not to accept certain of the perceptions of their forebearers, the vast majority of many careers would be exhausted reinventing the wheel. The vitality of history as a discipline lies not only in re-interpreting what is thought to be known, what Napier (1989) called the "contextualising" phase, but also in discovering new information that revises what was formerly thought to be known. "New" accounting historians seem preoccupied by the former; archival researchers find greater comfort with the latter.

When Tyson and I decided to do work on the history of U.S. standard costing, it was clearly not done with revisionist thoughts as had inspired my BIR project. It was more a function of seeking closure on an issue we had debated between ourselves; namely, what are the parameters and implications of the term "standard costing" and at what point does the utilization of standards reflect a sophisticated costing methodology? We decided initially to investigate the relationship between big government and big business during the New Deal era by looking at the archives of the National Recovery Administration (NRA), established in 1933 to seek cures for the Great Depression but subsequently declared unconstitutional in 1935. We found much to our surprise that despite the fact that the National Association of Cost Accountants (NACA) initially had felt this event was going to usher in a golden age for cost accountancy, nothing tangible was achieved in the attempt to include uniform cost accounting in the various industrial codes of practice that were articulated and operationalized by the NRA. Even more surprising was the primitive state of industrial cost accounting in the U.S. as reflected in the voluminous data the NRA gathered as background for its operations. There was neither evidence of standard costing in the returns nor any manifestation of the costing sophistication suggested by the theory penned decades before (see Fleischman & Tyson, 1999, for a full discussion of these findings).

Our next foray was to see whether anything was different during an earlier episode of large-scale governmental intrusion into the economy – U.S. involvement in World War I. In particular, our plan was to examine the archive of the Price-Fixing Committee (PFC) of the War Industries Board. Not only did the war effort come immediately on the heels of scientific management's heyday, but Loft (1986, 1990) had found such substantial advances in U.K. cost accountants' professionalization and costing methodology that she had proclaimed the "coming into the light." But these results were not in evidence on this side of the Atlantic. Despite the professionalization reflected by the formation of the NACA in 1919, the same year as the Institute of Cost and Works Accountants in the U.K., once again the research findings were negative (Fleischman & Tyson, 2000). The record just did not show that scientific management had penetrated the industries that the PFC attempted to regulate through its price-fixing mechanism.

The next step was to gather more information on the practice side of cost accountancy during the time when industrial consultants such as Taylor, Emerson,

Gantt, Gilbreth, and others had their shingles out, proclaiming their availability to install scientific management systems. Here much of the legwork had been done by Epstein (1978) and Nelson (1974), the latter a prolific economic historian, both of whom had done archival research into the Taylor archive at the Stevens Institute in Hoboken, NJ. Additionally, there was a significant volume of primary source materials that were written and published contemporaneously in the 1910s. Taylor himself testified at length to a Congressional committee in the aftermath of a 1911 strike at the Watertown Arsenal, a governmental installation that had adopted some of his time-study methods. Also, R. F. Hoxie, a University of Chicago economist, undertook a survey of scientific management in 1915 under the auspices of the U.S. Commission on Industrial Relations in which the leading consultants were asked to name those business enterprises that had availed themselves of their services. C. B. Thompson, a Harvard professor and defender of Taylor, published a survey in 1917 in which he presented evidence of scientific management applications in American industry.

Utilizing these materials, I have attempted to determine whether scientific management was as widespread in practice as the literary bounty would suggest (Fleischman, 2000). Epstein (1978), Hoxie (1920), and Nelson (1974) all presented lists of specific businesses wherein evidence of scientific management adoptions had apparently taken place, either because the Taylor archives had so indicated or because the prime movers had nominated them to Hoxie. Given the interest this period has generated, doubtlessly because of the notoriety engendered by the prevalence of theory, one might have expected hundreds, maybe even thousands, of entrants on a merged list. The resulting number was a paltry 80. Practice was clearly running far in arrears of theory.

A secondary focus of Fleischman (2000) was to draw upon each of the three prevailing paradigms, from whose advocates representative but not archival-informed quotes were provided above, to furnish a part of the explanation for the Taylorism phenomenon in the U.S. The argument goes that Taylorism itself, with its effort to discipline labor for the mutual advantage of all participants in the organization, was essentially Foucauldian, with the significant drawback that power was top-down imposed rather than reflective of a "nexus" of power relationships typified in Foucauldian thought. Labor's negative reaction and resistance to Taylorism is understood in Marxist terms; time study, task en-gineering, and standard costing were all perceived as speeding and sweating devices. Finally, the extraordinarily limited number of actual adoptions of scientific management, now brought to light through archival research, suggests hesitancy on the part of entrepreneurs explained essentially in cost/benefit terms. Thus, the explanatory triangle is completed within the context of economic rationality.

CONCLUSION

Archival research does represent a substantial commitment to the historian's craft. It is a time-consuming and extraordinarily expensive process. Notwithstanding these significant drawbacks, archival research can contribute significantly to sorting out historical myth and reality. Through this mechanism the proposition can now be suggested with some confidence, and supported with evidence, that the entrepreneurs of the BIR deployed in practical application a cost accounting methodology of some sophistication despite the absence of a literature, while business enterprises in the pre-World War I U.S. failed to incorporate into practice the innovations suggested by the robust scientific management theory of the times.

REFERENCES

Babbage, C. (1835). *On the economy of machinery and manufactures*. New York: Augustus Kelley Publishers (1963 reprint).

Baber, C., & Atkinson, M. (1987). *The growth and decline of the South Wales iron industry 1760–1880*. Cardiff: University of Wales Press.

Bloom, R., Heymann, H. G., Fuglister, J., & Collins, M. (1994). *The schism in accounting*. Westport, CT: Quorum Books.

Boyns, T., & Edwards, J. R. (1996). The development of accounting in mid-nineteenth century Britain: A non-disciplinary view. *Accounting, Auditing and Accountability Journal, 9*(3), 4–60.

Boyns, T., & Edwards, J. R. (1997). Cost and management accounting in early Victorian Britain: A Chandleresque analysis. *Management Accounting Research, 8*(1), 19–46.

Boyns, T., & Edwards, J. R. (2000). Pluralistic approaches to knowing more: A comment on Hoskin and Macve. *Accounting Historians Journal, 27*(1), 151–158.

Boyns, T., Edwards, J. R., & Nikitin, M. (1997). *The birth of industrial accounting in France and Britain*. New York: Garland Publishing, Inc.

Braverman, H. (1974). *Labor and monopoly capital*. New York: Monthly Review Press.

Bricker, R. J., & Previts, G. J. (1990). The sociology of accountancy: A study of academic and practice community schism. *Accounting Horizons, 4*(1), 1–14.

Brown, R. (1905). *A history of accounting and accountants*. Edinburgh: C. & E. C. Jack.

Campbell, R. H. (1961). *Carron Company*. Edinburgh: Oliver & Boyd.

Chandler, A. D. (1977). *The visible hand: The management revolution in American business*. Cambridge: Harvard University Press.

Chatfield, M. (1977). *A history of accounting thought*. Huntington, NY: Robert E. Krieger Publishing Co.

Church, A. H. (1901). The proper distribution of establishment charges. *The Engineering Magazine, 21*, 508–517, 725–734, 904–912; *22*, 31–40, 231–240, 367–376.

Cronhelm, F. W. (1818). *Double entry by single: A new method of book-keeping*. New York: Arno Press (1978 reprint).

Edwards, R. S. (1937). Some notes on the early literature and development of cost accounting in Great Britain. *The Accountant, 97*, 193–195, 225–231, 253–255, 283–287.

Edwards, J. R. (1989). Industrial cost accounting developments in Britain to 1830: A review article. *Accounting and Business Research, 19*(76), 305–317.

Edwards, J. R., & Baber, C. (1979). Dowlais Iron Company: Accounting policies and procedures for profit management and reporting purposes. *Accounting and Business Research, 9*(34), 139–151.

Edwards, J. R., & Boyns, T. (1992). Industrial organization and accounting innovation: Charcoal ironmaking in England 1690–1783. *Management Accounting Research, 3*(2), 151–169.

Edwards, J. R., Boyns, T., & Anderson, M. (1995). British cost accounting development: Continuity and change. *Accounting Historians Journal, 22*(2), 1–41.

Edwards, J. R., & Newell, E. (1991). The development of industrial cost and management accounting before 1850: A survey of the evidence. *Business History, 33*(1), 35–57.

Emerson, H. (1908–1909). Efficiency as a basis for operation and wages. *The Engineering Magazine, 35* and *36*.

Epstein, M. J. (1978). *The effect of scientific management on the development of the standard cost system.* New York: Arno Press.

Fleischman, R. K. (1985). *Conditions of life among the cotton workers of southeastern Lancashire, 1780–1850.* New York: Garland Publishing, Inc.

Fleischman, R. K. (2000). Completing the triangle: Taylorism and the paradigms. *Accounting, Auditing and Accountability Journal, 13*(5), 597–623.

Fleischman, R. K., Hoskin, K. W., & Macve, R. H. (1995). The Boulton & Watt case: The crux of alternative approaches to accounting history? *Accounting and Business Research, 25*(99), 162–176.

Fleischman, R. K., & Macve, R. H. (2002). Coals from Newcastle: Alternative histories of cost and management accounting in northeast coal mining during the British industrial revolution. *Accounting and Business Research, 32*(3), 134–152.

Fleischman, R. K., & Parker, L. D. (1990). Managerial accounting early in the British industrial revolution: The Carron Company, a case study. *Accounting and Business Research, 20*(79), 211–221.

Fleischman, R. K., & Parker, L. D. (1991). British entrepreneurs and pre-industrial revolution evidence of cost management. *Accounting Review, 66*(2), 361–375.

Fleischman, R. K., & Parker, L. D. (1992). The cost-accounting environment in the British industrial revolution iron industry. *Accounting, Business and Financial History, 2*(2), 141–160.

Fleischman, R. K., & Parker, L. D. (1997). *What is past is prologue: Cost accounting in the British industrial revolution, 1760–1850.* New York: Garland Publishing, Inc.

Fleischman, R. K., & Tyson, T. N. (1993). Cost accounting during the industrial revolution: The present state of historical knowledge. *Economic History Review, 46*(3), 503–517.

Fleischman, R. K., & Tyson, T. N. (1999). Opportunity lost? Chances for cost accountants' professionalization under the National Industrial Recovery Act of 1933. *Accounting, Business and Financial History, 9*(1), 51–75.

Fleischman, R. K., & Tyson, T. N. (2000). Parallels between U.S. and U.K. cost accountancy in the World War I era. *Accounting, Business and Financial History, 10*(2), 195–216.

Garcke, E., & Fells, J. M. (1887). *Factory accounts, their principle and practice.* London: Crosby, Lockwood & Son.

Garner, S. P. (1954). *Evolution of cost accounting to 1925.* University, AL: University of Alabama Press.

Hamilton, R. (1777). *An introduction to merchandise.* Edinburgh: privately printed.

Hopper, T. M., & Armstrong, P. (1991). Cost accounting, controlling labor and the rise of conglomerates. *Accounting, Organizations and Society, 16*(5/6), 405–438.

Hoskin, K. W., & Macve, R. H. (1988). The genesis of accountability: The West Point connections. *Accounting, Organizations and Society, 13*(1), 37–73.

Hoskin, K. W., & Macve, R. H. (1994). Re-appraising the genesis of managerialism: A re-examination of the role of accounting at the Springfield Armory, 1815–1845. *Accounting, Auditing and Accountability Journal, 7*(2), 4–29.

Hoskin, K. W., & Macve, R. H. (2000). Knowing more as knowing less? Alternative histories of cost and management accounting in the U.S. and the U.K. *Accounting Historians Journal, 27*(1), 91–149.

Hoxie, R. F. (1920). *Scientific management and labor.* New York: D. Appleton & Co.

Johnson, H. T. (1972). Early cost accounting for internal management control: Lyman Mills in the 1850s. *Business History Review, 46*(4), 466–474.

Johnson, H. T., & Kaplan, R. S. (1987a). *Relevance lost: The rise and fall of management accounting.* Boston: Harvard Business School Press.

Johnson, H. T., & Kaplan, R. S. (1987b). The rise and fall of management accounting. *Management Accounting, 68*(7), 22–30.

Jones, H. (1985). *Accounting, costing, and cost estimation: Welsh industry 1700–1930.* Cardiff: University of Wales Press.

Littleton, A. C. (1933). *Accounting evolution to 1900.* New York: American Institute Publishing Co., Inc.

Loft, A. (1986). Towards a critical understanding of accounting: The case of cost accounting in the U.K., 1914–1925. *Accounting, Organizations and Society, 11*(2), 137–169.

Loft, A. (1990). *Coming into the light.* London: Chartered Institute of Management Accountants.

McKendrick, N. (1970). Josiah Wedgwood and cost accounting in the industrial revolution. *Economic History Review, 23*(1), 45–67.

McLean, T. (1997). Agent's reputation, accounting and costing in organizational control structures. *Accounting Historians Journal, 24*(1), 1–23.

Metcalfe, H. (1885). *The cost of manufacturers.* New York: John Wiley & Sons.

Miller, P., & O'Leary, T. (1987). Accounting and the construction of the governable person. *Accounting, Organizations and Society, 12*(3), 235–265.

Napier, C. J. (1989). Research directions in accounting history. *British Accounting Review, 21*(3), 237–254.

Nelson, D. (1974). Scientific management, systematic management, and labor, 1880–1915. *Business History Review, 48*(4), 479–500.

Norton, G. P. (1889). *Textile manufacturers' bookkeeping for the counting house, mill and warehouse.* London: Simpkin, Marshall, Hamilton, & Kent.

Oldroyd, D. (1996). The costing records of George Bowes and the Grand Allies in the north-east coal trade in the eighteenth century: Their type and significance. *Accounting, Business and Financial History, 6*(1), 1–22.

Panozzo, F. (1997). The making of the good academic accountant. *Accounting, Organizations and Society, 22*(5), 447–480.

Parker, R. H. (1986). *The development of the accountancy profession in Britain to the early twentieth century.* London: Academy of Accounting Historians.

Pollard, S. (1965). *The genesis of modern management.* Cambridge: Harvard University Press.

Raistrick, A. (1953). *Dynasty of iron founders.* Newton Abbot: David & Charles (1970 reprint).

Rimmer, W. G. (1960). *Marshalls of Leeds flax-spinners 1788–1886.* Cambridge: Cambridge University Press.

Solomons, D. (1952). *Studies in costing.* London: Sweet & Maxwell, Ltd.

Sowell, E. M. (1973). *The evolution of the theories and techniques of standard costs*. Tuscaloosa, AL: University of Alabama Press.

Stacey, N. E. H. (1954). *English accountancy 1800–1954*. London: Gee & Co., Ltd.

Stone, W. E. (1973). An early English cotton mill cost accounting system: Charlton (sic) Mills, 1810–1889. *Accounting and Business Research, 4*(17), 71–78.

Taylor, F. W. (1903). *Shop management*. New York: Harper and Brothers (1911 reprint).

Taylor, F. W. (1911). *The principles of scientific management*. New York: Harper and Brothers (1913 reprint).

Thompson, W. (1777). *The accountant's oracle*. York: N. Nickson.

Thompson, C. B. (1917). *The theory and practice of scientific management*. Boston: Houghton Mifflin Co.

Towne, H. R. (1885–1886). The engineer as an economist. *Transactions of the American Society of Mechanical Engineers, 7*(2), 28–32.

Tyson, T. N. (2000). Accounting history and the emperor's new clothes: A response to 'knowing more or knowing less? . . .'. *Accounting Historians Journal, 27*(1), 159–171.

Urwick, L., & Brech, E. F. L. (1964). *The making of scientific management*. London: Sir Isaac Pitman & Sons, Ltd.

Walsh, E. J., & Stewart, R. E. (1993). Accounting and the construction of institutions: The case of a factory. *Accounting, Organizations and Society, 18*(7/8), 783–800.

Wells, M. C. (1978). *Accounting for common costs*. Urbana, IL: Center for International Education and Research in Accounting.

Whitley, R. D. (1986). The transformation of business finance into financial economics: The roles of academic expansion and changes in U.S. capital markets. *Accounting, Organizations and Society, 11*(2), 171–192.

Whitley, R. D. (1988). The possibility and utility of accounting theory. *Accounting, Organizations and Society, 13*(6), 112–123.

Whitmore, J. (1908). Shoe factory cost accounts. *Journal of Accountancy, 4*(1), 12–25.

Williams, R. B. (1997a). *Accounting for steam and cotton*. New York: Garland Publishing, Inc.

Williams, R. B. (1997b). Inscribing the workers: An experiment in factory discipline or the inculcation of manners? A case in context. *Accounting History, 2*(1), 35–60.

Williams, R. B. (1999). Management accounting practice and price calculation at Boulton & Watt's Soho foundry: A late 18th century example. *Accounting Historians Journal, 26*(2), 65–87.

Yamey, B. S. (1949). Scientific bookkeeping and the rise of capitalism. *Economic History Review, 1*(2/3), 99–117.

Yamey, B. S. (1960). The development of company accounting conventions. *Three Banks Review, 47*, 22–37.

HISTORIES OUTSIDE THE MAINSTREAM: ORAL HISTORY AND NON-TRADITIONAL APPROACHES

Theresa D. Hammond

INTRODUCTION

Accounting research is increasingly heading off in directions unexpected a decade or two ago. While the majority of academic institutions and accounting journals fail to appreciate the contributions of non-traditional research streams, conferences and journals that promote alternative perspectives on accounting are flourishing. A glance at the titles of the papers presented at the Third Asian Pacific Interdisciplinary Research in Accounting Conference in Australia in July 2001 is one indication of this welcome change.

There are many alternatives to the positivist methodologies that dominate the accounting literature. In my research on African-American CPAs, I have found that qualitative methods are essential to understanding. Oral history, archival work, and immersion of self into one's research area are critical to avoiding dilettantism and furthering the understanding of marginalized groups.

THE IMPORTANCE OF EXAMINING UNDERREPRESENTED GROUPS

In the late 20th century, white people comprised 74% of new graduates with bachelor's degrees in accounting, closely approximating white representation in

Doing Accounting History: Contributions to the Development of Accounting Thought
Studies in the Development of Accounting Thought, Volume 6, 81–96
Copyright © 2003 by Elsevier Science Ltd.
All rights of reproduction in any form reserved
ISSN: 1479-3504/PII: S1479350402060052

the U.S. population. But fully 88% of those hired by CPA firms were white. Given these statistics, it is arguable that white people are the most overrepresented group in public accounting. Other statistics point to African Americans as the most underrepresented group. While African Americans constitute 12% of the U.S. population and over 8% of accounting graduates, they compose less than 3% of hires by white-owned CPA firms. The disparity gets even larger in the higher levels of the firms. Of approximately 80,000 partners in non-minority-owned firms surveyed by the AICPA in 1996, only 60 were African American (AICPA, 1998).

Statistics on women in the firms are quite different. For the past decade, women have composed over half of accounting graduates and over half of accounting firm hires. Research on women in accounting, therefore, focuses not on the absence of entry-level opportunity for women in the profession, but rather on the relative absence of women in management positions. Women experience higher rates of turnover than men, which lead to smaller percentages of women in the higher ranks of the firms. In the mid-1990s, for example, only 19% of new partners in CPA firms were women (Doucet & hooks, 1999; hooks & Cheramy, 1994).

These current statistics about the dearth of African Americans at all levels of the profession and the underrepresentation of women managers and partners are a cause for concern among practitioners, educators, and students. Practitioners are interested in attracting and retaining talented individuals who will meet the needs of their clients. Recently, several firms have cited client demands for diverse consulting teams as an impetus to diversify their staffs (hooks, 1996). Educators and students are concerned about underrepresentation because they hope that applicants and employees will be treated fairly and rewarded based on merit.

Understanding and addressing the conditions facing prospective women and African-American CPAs requires an understanding of the history of the composition of the profession. There is a tension between the current discussions of inclusiveness in the profession and the exclusive nature of professions. Those who study the development of the professions in the U.S. point out that one of the primary means of enhancing the prestige of an occupation is to increase the exclusivity of its membership. Thus, those who formed the American Medical and Bar Associations in the 19th century prided themselves on their discrimination against immigrant groups and attempted to confine participation in their professions to native-born Americans of British extraction. This tactic worked; the status of both professions rose dramatically, and, by the turn of the century, law and medicine were the most prestigious professions in the country, a status that endures today (Collins, 1979).

As the professions developed, leading doctors and attorneys discussed the potential effectiveness of various barriers to access. Apprenticeship, the traditional means of entry to a profession, ensured current practitioners complete control over new entrants. Educational and testing barriers were sometimes viewed as more democratic means of entry since they convey an aura of meritocracy. Unequal distribution of educational opportunity, however, meant professions that excluded those lacking elite educational records effectively excluded those from undesirable backgrounds (Collins, 1979).

In the U.S., accounting was a late entrant in the quest for professional status, but its tactics were similar to those of the earlier, better-established professions. The growth of the accounting profession coincided with the consolidation of financial capital at the end of the 19th century. Despite its late start, accounting's origins in Scotland and England enhanced its credibility and spurred its ascent in a society struggling to absorb immigrants from southern and central Europe. Debates ensued between an exclusive approach based on the British system of requiring purchase of an apprenticeship and, on the other hand, requiring examinations and education. The former approach was designed to ensure that prospective accountants would come from families with the financial means to pay for the apprenticeship, as well as forego the apprentice's income during the apprenticeship period. Ultimately, each state earned the autonomy to develop its own system. By the late 1920s, most states had adopted an approach combining education, examination, and apprenticeship, what we now call the experience requirement (Miranti, 1990).

Although exclusivity is a primary characteristic of professions, including accounting, it is not the only characteristic that must be cultivated. Because professions seek state-sanctioned autonomy, they must also develop legitimacy. With regard to professional workforce composition, the requirements for legitimacy have changed dramatically over time. Early in the 20th century, excluding immigrants from Italy or Germany did not attract negative attention. Likewise, during the first half of the century, many large firms excluded Jewish accountants, and some would not hire Catholics. As recently as the late 1960s, firms routinely denied professional opportunities to women and African Americans. Far from decreasing their legitimacy, the firms believed their exclusivity *enhanced* their professional status. On the rare occasion that this discrimination was acknowledged, the firms typically claimed that exclusion was a way of meeting their clients' demands that women and African Americans not review their financial records (e.g. *Journal of Accountancy*, 1923; Mitchell, 1969).

Accounting's exclusion of women and African Americans was not unique: Employment discrimination was so widespread that the U.S. Congress passed the Civil Rights Act of 1964 explicitly to put an end to it. Research in accounting on this underexplored topic can draw on the parallels between its experience and the experience of other professions in the area of workforce composition, as well as seek to understand the characteristics of accounting that have led to its unique demographics – public accounting has more women than most professions, but fewer African Americans.

Thoughtful histories of exclusion in the professions go beyond an examination of the mechanisms of exclusion to analyze the impact of that exclusion both on those who were excluded and on the profession itself. Kanter's (1977) landmark study of a multi-national corporation showed that the behavior of both majority-group and minority-group members changed when the previous professional homogeneity was disrupted. Women and African Americans were pressured to conform to the white-male-defined culture. Moreover, white men frequently exaggerated that culture to test the limits of outsiders' willingness to adapt and fit in. Harding (1986) has argued that the dearth of women in science does not simply curtail the professional opportunities of women who would have chosen the field, it also curtails the choice of subjects worth studying. One example is the increasing research into uniquely female medical conditions, such as breast cancer, that has developed only with increasing numbers of women becoming doctors.

No history of accounting could ever be "complete," but the absence of research that includes the experience and the impact of women and African Americans on accounting represents a crucial omission. For example, other than a mention of the first woman to become a partner or the first woman to become a CPA in a given state, most histories of major accounting firms or state CPA societies completely overlook marginalized groups. This historical approach that considers only the experiences of the dominant group has been challenged by historians for decades (e.g. Burrows & Wallace, 1998). It is time that accounting historians took a more holistic approach to understanding our profession's past. The remainder of this article considers ways to incorporate these "invisible histories" into the academic literature.

RENDERING THE INVISIBLE VISIBLE

The very fact that the histories of African Americans and women in accounting are invisible poses challenges to researchers interested in a broader perspective. Most indices in accounting history books do not include categories such as "women," "African Americans," or "employment discrimination." Other common historical sources frequently suffer from the same limitation. For example, in my ongoing research on African-American CPAs, I found that, between 1933 and 1969, not a single article discussing African-American CPAs appeared in the *Journal of Accountancy*. Because of an absence of documentation in the mainstream sources, investigating these non-traditional histories requires examining non-traditional sources.

Traditional approaches to historiography were challenged during the civil rights movement of the 1960s, which led to questioning not only the political and economic foundations of U.S. society, but also to challenges in the academy. Demands for Afro-American and Women's studies programs proliferated, and the recognition that traditional course requirements were biased in favor of the most dominant groups became widespread. Historians called for a "bottom up" history that included the experiences of common people to correct the previous distorted focus on powerful politicians, heroes, and business leaders (Hammond & Sikka, 1996).

Oral History

Understanding these more common lives required examining new documentary sources, including the use of "oral history" (talking to people about their experiences). Prior to the 1960s, these oral histories had been used primarily to gather the reminiscences of powerful leaders. In 1948, the Oral History Association was established, and Columbia University began an oral history project that includes interviews with U.S. Presidents and Cabinet Members (Frisch, 1990; Thompson, 1988). In the 1960s, the increasing availability of audiotape technology combined with the new emphasis on common people's history led to a new use for oral history – documenting the experiences of the less powerful members of society.

This approach was not without precedent. President Franklin Delano Roosevelt's New Deal included the Federal Writers' Project, that dispatched hundreds of writers, including novelists Zora Neale Hurston and Richard Wright, around the U.S. to document the experiences of ordinary Americans such as factory workers, sharecroppers, former slaves, and coal miners. The Writers' Project was designed to combat unemployment during the Depression, and the more than ten thousand interviews that were gathered remained largely untouched until the 1960s' surge of interest in grassroots history.

Along with the growing interest in oral history came several books, articles, and journals addressing oral history techniques (e.g. Vansina, 1973). Much of this literature addresses concerns that oral history is too soft and subject to bias; it focuses on making oral history more "scientific" by avoiding the pitfalls of subjectivity in research dependent on individuals' accounts of the past. As the field of oral history developed, however, the emphasis in these journals shifted. Instead of efforts to remove all bias from oral history research, leading historians recognized that *all* histories are selective and biased, although traditional researchers rarely acknowledge this reality (Chomsky, 1989; Said, 1994). Contemporary literature on the use of oral history grapples with questions of validity and authority without contending that a purely scientific and unbiased approach is possible (Gluck & Patai, 1991).

This acknowledgment of the lack of objectivity is, in fact, key to the contribution of oral history. Understanding the experiences of women and African Americans in accounting must be based on interviewees' own interpretations of their experiences. That there were only 100 African-American CPAs in the U.S. in 1965 is an important fact that underscores the intense discrimination that existed. But to learn how that discrimination was experienced by and overcome by the few African Americans who did become CPAs before 1965 is essential to understanding what it meant to be an African-American CPA at the time.

Accounting researchers who are interested in the history of women and African Americans in the profession are fortunate that our profession is young: Many of the pioneers in these groups are still alive and willing to talk about their experiences. Nevertheless, gathering oral histories poses several challenges to the researcher. Editing and transcribing interviews is necessary for their dissemination, but important clues as to meaning, including tone of voice, pauses, and gestures, are all lost in the process of transcription (Rosengarten, 1984). These distortions underline the importance of trust between the researcher and the informant; oral history inevitably leads to coauthored work. I always return transcriptions to my informants in order to give them an opportunity to correct or edit their interviews. I have found this technique particularly useful when it comes to places, names, and dates. But there are risks inherent in this approach. Although it has never happened to me, an informant may reconsider his or her responses and decline to participate after seeing the transcription.

Openness on the part of the informant is critical to the success of an interview. Authorities on oral history have recognized that timing is important in predicting the openness of interviewees. Oral historians have suggested that retirement can be an ideal time to conduct an interview, both because informants are in a period of "life review" that can lead to willingness to share stories, and because informants are no longer concerned with the consequences of honesty on their professional lives (Thompson, 1988). I have found that retired African-American CPAs are much more forthcoming in describing the barriers they faced than are those who are still practicing professionals, although this willingness may be partially due to the fact that conditions improved for the younger group (Hammond, 1997, 2002; Hammond & Streeter, 1994).

Openness can also be affected by the relationship between the researcher and the informant. Surveys have found that informants respond to the same questions differently depending upon who is asking the questions (Thompson, 1988). Film director Spike Lee argued that only an African American could elicit open responses from Malcolm X's associates; therefore, only an African American could direct a movie about his life (Hruska, 1993). Other researchers point out that since subjectivity is so inherent in historical research, there is no correct "match" between researcher and informant. Because of these inevitable barriers, experts recommend that researchers gain a thorough familiarity with the subject matter before conducting interviews (Thompson, 1988).

As a young (I was 26 when I began conducting interviews), white woman whose typical informant is a retired, African-American man, I have been concerned with the potential barriers to communication. Before I visited Chicago's pioneering African-American CPAs in 1992, I sent them a paper I had written that was largely based on the experience of African-American CPAs in New York. This had the desired effect of demonstrating my familiarity with the field. But it also backfired in part, because several informants said, "Yes, my experience was just like in your paper," rather than telling me their own fresh stories without reference to the experiences of others.

The relationship between informant and researcher also affects the amount of analysis that should be included in the final publication. Overanalysis sometimes means that informants are only quoted when their comments fit the researcher's preconceived theories of history, thus obliterating the contribution of the oral histories (Thompson, 1988). Underanalysis, on the other hand, can leave readers without the context to interpret the experiences about which they are reading. Oral historians recommend a "shared authority" (Frisch, 1990), in which the researcher includes extensive material gleaned from informants but also brings his or her own expertise to bear. The proper balance is difficult to achieve, and authors are criticized when they are perceived as going too far in either direction. For example, Behar's (1993) oral history of a poor Mexican marketing woman includes parallel stories from Behar's own life as a female professional in a male-dominated institution. This juxtaposition has elicited criticism that her affluent life in U.S. academia cannot fairly be compared to the experiences of her destitute informant (Perera, 1993). Mellon (1998), who collected and edited slave narratives that were gathered during the Federal Writers' Project, was criticized for the opposite reason – his work lacked details (e.g. the age of the interviewee) that were essential to readers' ability to derive meaning from their stories (Bradley, 1929).

The value of oral history goes well beyond introducing the stories of those previously ignored in accounting research into academic literature. By interviewing individuals and documenting their unique experiences, oral history emphasizes the diversity *within* groups, a recognition that both leads to opportunities to discover commonalities across groups and makes it more difficult to categorize and stereotype non-dominant groups (Hammond & Preston, 1992). hooks and Cheramy (1994), for example, found that many male, accounting-firm partners assumed that female hires would leave their firms as soon as they had children. This stereotype affected these partners' willingness to devote training and mentoring energy to new female hires, and, perhaps, became a self-fulfilling prophecy. Interviews with then Big-Six leaders revealed more complexity in this issue, including an increased understanding of the (slowly) changing division of child-care responsibilities and an increased demand by men to spend more time with their families (hooks, 1996). They also revealed that the women who left the firms continued to work, albeit within organizations that displayed more flexibility. Interviews with women who left firms, as well as those who pursued partnership, would undoubtedly illuminate their individual experiences in a way that would make it more difficult for employers to assume that all women will forfeit a public accounting career for a family. Interviews with women who tried to pursue careers in accounting firms in the 1950s, 1960s, and 1970s without success would also contribute to an understanding of the attitudes that shaped the current culture of public accounting, and would also demonstrate that, even decades ago, women did not fit the stereotypes that persist today.

While axes of power such as race and gender have clear effects on the experiences of subordinate groups, oral history also reveals the fact that women and African Americans are not simply powerless victims. The stories of how people overcame the barriers to access in the profession and then helped others to succeed provide an important lesson in empowerment and personal agency. The fact that many white men helped African Americans become CPAs, either as professors who provided guidance or as the rare professional mentor who helped African Americans meet the experience requirement, underscores the difference that individual behavior can make in ending discrimination.

Oral history also allows researchers to examine the impact of several individual characteristics simultaneously. In 1982, a landmark feminist book appeared, entitled *All the Women are White, All the Blacks are Men, but Some of Us are Brave: Black Women's Studies* (Hull et al., 1992). This title reflects a tendency to ignore overlapping categories. The feminist literature of the 1970s was roundly criticized in the 1980s and 1990s for focusing exclusively on the concerns of white, middle-class women. Likewise, the movement to enhance opportunities for African Americans has been criticized for excluding the concerns of African-American women. These criticisms led to an expansion of the literature to address specifically the experiences of people who are marginalized on the basis of more than one characteristic – in the case of African-American women, by both race and gender (see, for example, Hine, 1989; Robinson-Backmon & Weisenfeld, 2001). Oral history allows informants to describe their experiences of exclusion or inclusion from their individual perspectives, not part of an ostensibly all-inclusive category.

Other Sources

While I consider oral history to be the most promising methodology for exploring the history of women and African Americans in accounting, there are other sources of information that should be explored. Since it is impossible to "fact check" individuals' experiences, many historians find oral history an insufficiently robust frame upon which to hang a history of the profession. However, there are ways to verify the reasonableness of responses and to provide context for individual experience.

First, various interviews that reveal similar stories bolster confidence that my informants' memories are not playing tricks on them. For example, early in my series of interviews, Dr. Lincoln Harrison told me that he was required to sit in the back of the room at an American Accounting Association (AAA) meeting held in Memphis in 1948 (Harrison, 1992). Similar stories followed. Two informants told me of not being welcome at an American Institute of Certified Public Accountants (AICPA) meeting held in Houston in the 1950s (Austin, 1992; Pittman, 1992). The similar stories not only verified that accounting's main professional organizations held segregated annual meetings, they also underscored the importance of such rejection in these professionals' early experiences in the field. Similarly, I learned from several southern African-American CPAs that their applications for membership in the state societies in Georgia, Texas, and Louisiana were denied until the end of the 1960s. While none of them had kept their rejection letters, the consistency in their stories makes them more than plausible.

In these cases there were other means of verifying the validity of these stories. I checked issues of the *Journal of Accountancy* for the 1950s and found that the AICPA held its annual meeting in Houston in 1952 at the Shamrock Hotel. Research on de-segregation in the South indicated that this famous hotel did not allow black guests until the 1960s. Similarly, contacting the AAA yielded a program for its annual meeting at the "air-conditioned" Hotel Peabody in Memphis, Tennessee in September 1948. These checks also helped determine exact dates; many informants remember general time periods in which events occurred, although they are unlikely to recall the exact year since they experienced similar discrimination in other circumstances.

Another recurring story concerned the difficulty faced in trying to meet the experience requirement. Most African Americans who became CPAs in the 1940s or 1950s worked for other African-American CPAs, sometimes moving across the country to do so. The unwillingness of white CPAs to hire African Americans was verified not only in the disheartening consistency of my informants' stories, but also by late-1960s accounting publications urging CPAs to end their discrimination (*Journal of Accountancy*, 1969).

The AICPA library, having now moved to the University of Mississippi, is a key resource for most accounting histories. For a while, I was mystified as to how the *first* African Americans became CPAs since there were no predecessors to provide the experience requirement. The AICPA library keeps records of past and present CPA requirements by state, and I discovered that these pioneers had earned their CPAs *before* the experience requirements were instituted.

Several informants, who talked about their educational experiences at leading universities such as Columbia and Illinois, took pride in having studied under leaders of the profession such as A. C. Littleton and Robert Montgomery. One informant, who attended graduate school at Columbia in the early 1920s, also described being inspired to become a CPA by her undergraduate accounting professor at Howard University, O. C. Thornton (Rutherford, 1992). The Howard University libraries include old yearbooks, in which I was able to verify Rutherford's graduation at the top of her class, and old catalogues, in which I noted that Thornton taught *all* the accounting courses offered at the school. His course descriptions emphasized preparation for the CPA examination, even though at the time there were no African-American CPAs in the country. Other libraries at historically black colleges were also very helpful. Old course descriptions indicate the changing course offerings in business and accounting that corresponded with changing opportunities for African-American students who wanted to enter the accounting profession. Also, since many of the earliest African-American CPAs were also professors at black colleges, these libraries are good sources of information on these individuals. For example, the Atlanta University Library had a clipping file on Jesse Blayton, the first African-American CPA in Georgia, who was also a professor.

The *Accountants' Index* is invaluable for finding related literature that provides context and support for oral histories. Volumes have been published throughout this century, and I found many obscure publications listed that I would not otherwise have discovered, including a 1939 report on "Negro" Accountants that was published by the "Colored Division" of the Georgia branch of the National Youth Administration (Blayton, 1939).

The *Accountants' Index* can also be effectively used as a primary source for histories of accounting. Lehman's landmark "Herstory" in accounting (1992) relied primarily on articles she found through the *Index*. Fortunately for researchers on gender issues, there are many more entries in these indexes for "women" than for other groups. She found dozens of articles, starting as early as 1909, wherein members of the profession openly discussed the opportunities, or lack thereof, for women in public accounting. She unearthed articles that indicated that women were not welcome in most accounting firms because clients would not accept them as auditors and because travel requirements made the employment of "heterogeneous personnel" untenable (e.g. *Accountant*, 1915; *Journal of Accountancy*, 1923). During World War II, Lehman found articles discussing the use of women accountants to meet the *man*power shortage created by the draft and editorials decrying old-fashioned thinking that women could not be good accountants (e.g. *Journal of Accountancy*, 1942). Suddenly the profession seemed to have concluded that women's participation in the profession was desirable after all. After the war, attitudes changed again, with women giving up their positions for returning soldiers (*Journal of Accountancy*, 1951).

Post-war changes in the U.S. corresponded with changes for women in the profession, and articles in the accounting literature, indexed in the *Accountants' Index*, reflected these changes. Articles in *The Woman CPA*, which began publication in 1942, and in mainstream accounting journals reflected the increasing participation of women despite several backlashes against their inclusion. The variety of articles available on women in accounting throughout this century provides a good perspective on the various conditions they faced. Lehman effectively utilized these articles to illustrate the changes experienced by female CPAs during the 20th century.

Articles concerning African-American CPAs are rare, but fortunately there are some sources specifically on African-American accountants upon which I could draw. The AICPA began a Minority Initiatives Committee in 1968, and in 1976 it began annual publication of the *Report on Minority Accounting Graduates, Enrollment and Public Accounting Professionals* (formerly known as the *Minority Recruitment and Equal Opportunity Committee Reports*). Although the data provided varied somewhat over the years and publication was suspended from 1989 to 1994, the *Report* includes information on Asian/Pacific Islander, Black, Hispanic, and Native American/Alaskan Native accounting majors, graduates, and hires. The pre-1989 reports include more extensive data on women in the profession than do later reports. From these reports, researchers can determine some of the trends in employment and graduation rates of various underrepresented groups in accounting. In addition, the National Association of Black Accountants (NABA), founded in 1969, has many publications, including its 1990 compilation of the first 100 African-American CPAs (NABA, 1990).

There remains a dearth of literature explicitly addressing these non-dominant groups among CPAs; therefore, researchers must often take an oblique approach to their study. After learning what I could from the AICPA Minority Initiatives Committee and the NABA literature, I explored both research on accounting history and on African-American history. The former includes general histories of accounting (e.g. Carey, 1970; Edwards, 1978; Miranti, 1990; Previts & Merino, 1998), histories of state societies (e.g. Tinsley, 1983), and histories of individual, typically large firms (e.g. DeMond, 1917; Spacek, 1989). Most of these books virtually ignore the composition of the profession, although some provide the date on which the first woman became a professional member of a firm or became a CPA in the state being studied. Nevertheless, these books are valuable because they provide details on accounting's efforts to become recognized as a profession and, thus, add to the understanding of motivations for exclusion. Also, some of the books include directly relevant material. Miranti (1990), for example, explicitly addressed the bias against immigrants that helped shape the profession. Tinsley's (1983) book on the Texas Society of CPAs narrated the history of the only state society that acknowledged its discrimination against African Americans who desired to become members. Tinsley reported that in the early 1950s Dr. Milton Wilson received his Texas CPA through a reciprocity agreement with Indiana, but that the Texas State Society of CPAs would not admit him as a member until 1969 (Tinsley, 1983, p. 172; Wilson, 1991). Sometimes the relevant information in these books clearly was not intended as such, as when Leonard Spacek, the former Chairman of Arthur Andersen & Co., discussed his firm's political clout in Chicago, including how he helped stop Martin Luther King, Jr.'s marches on the city (Spacek, 1989, p. 205).

Inadvertent sources of information on conditions for marginalized groups can also come from AICPA publications and meeting minutes. When I looked in AICPA (then the American Institute of Accountants) Council Meeting minutes for the early 1940s to find discussions on admitting the first African-American member, I found several racist "jokes" instead. These "jokes" clearly indicated that the leading CPAs of the 1940s did not expect African Americans to fill professional roles. Reviewing Council minutes from the 1960s in search of the origins of the AICPA's Minority Initiatives Committee revealed debates over the "ability" of African Americans to become CPAs, again providing me with insight into then-current attitudes.

In order to understand a group whose history has been largely ignored, however, a researcher cannot limit him or herself to materials available within the profession. An investigation into the history of the group under analysis is also necessary. In my research on African-American CPAs, I reviewed African-American periodicals, including black newspapers, magazines, and journals from black organizations such as the National Association for the Advancement of Colored People and the Urban League. Although African-American CPAs were ignored within the profession until the late 1960s, they were often leaders in the black community, and their accomplishments were cited by local African-American newspapers as well as national publications such as *Jet* magazine. Some African-American newspapers are indexed in the *Black Newspapers Index*; other indexes can be found at African-American library collections such as the Schomburg Center for Research in Black Culture, part of the New York Public Library.

Research is often inseparable from personal involvement. My research grew along with my participation in organizations designed to enhance diversity in the profession. In the past decade I have been a member of the AICPA Minority Initiatives Committee, the American Accounting Association's Minority Faculty Development Committee, the African-American Accounting Doctoral Student Association, and the National Association of Black Accountants. While not my reason for joining these organizations, the memberships have given me a much better understanding of contemporary issues in diversity and the profession, as well as having provided me valuable contacts.

Other Groups

Women constitute over half of Americans, so it is no surprise that literature concerning women in accounting is relatively plentiful and that there has been significant research in this area. Other groups are not as easy to study, but should have their place in the literature. The associations for Filipino, Asian-American, and Hispanic CPAs, although they are smaller than NABA, provide good starting points for research on these groups. The histories of large CPA firms often include names and pictures of partners, which reveal that there were Latino partners in these firms well before there were African-American partners, although all these partners were from Puerto Rico or South America. The relationship between immigration and acceptance into the profession is particularly relevant when considering the history of Latino and Asian-American accountants. This research should draw on Miranti's work (1988, 1990) analyzing the experiences of earlier immigrant groups.

While it is important to investigate the histories of diverse groups of accountants, it is also crucial to cease ignoring these groups in more general histories of the profession. One good example of an accounting history that did not omit marginalized groups is Sheldahl's (1982) history of *Beta Alpha Psi*, accounting's honor society, which recognized the history of Jewish exclusion in the profession. Sheldahl (1982, pp. 171–177) reported that in the late 1920s, leaders of the fledgling organization were uncomfortable with the "Hebrew" dominance of Boston University's chapter of *Beta Alpha Psi* and suspended the chapter on what seems to have been a trumped-up technicality. This history of an important accounting organization would not be as valuable without an examination of this event.

RESISTANCE

While there is much good news, in the form of *Critical Perspectives on Accounting, Advances in Public Interest Accounting, Accounting, Auditing and Accountability Journal*, as well as the increase in historical journals and conferences in accounting, resistance remains to publishing non-traditional work. Getting hired and promoted, particularly in the U.S. but increasingly elsewhere, can be difficult if your focus is in an area perceived as critical to the accounting industry. Some researchers advocate developing a mainstream line of research and pursuing non-traditional work almost as a sideline. I have talked to many doctoral students who plan to do exactly that. However, this choice may prove impossible for them because developing expertise is so time-consuming that it is difficult to accomplish in one research area, let alone two or more.

CONCLUSION

Public accounting comprises some of the largest and most powerful professional organizations in the U.S. Histories of the field have long ignored the role of exclusion in developing the profession as well as the role of women, African Americans, and other marginalized groups in shaping the industry. Through the use of non-traditional historical sources, such as oral history, accounting historians can begin to rectify this lapse and provide richer, more comprehensive understandings of our profession's past.

These richer understandings are not achieved easily. Research that treats all women or all African Americans as interchangeable will not lead to useful insights. Oral history provides the opportunity to achieve these insights, but it poses challenges of its own. Traditional measures of objectivity cannot be achieved, but there are ways of increasing the reliability of data, such as immersing yourself in the research context and understanding the contemporaneous social and political facets of the historical period studied.

The editors of the non-traditional journals and conferences have opened a space in accounting for those of us who value this research. In turn, by pursuing the work ourselves, we can continue to expand the borders and create opportunity for others.

REFERENCES

The Accountant (1915). The admission of women into the profession (January 23, 127–129).
American Institute of Certified Public Accountants (1998). *Report on Minority Accounting Graduates, Enrollment and Public Accounting Professionals – 1997*. New York: AICPA.
Austin, R. (1992). Interview (first African-American CPA in Michigan, 1941; Secretary of State of Michigan).
Behar, R. (1993). *Translated woman: Crossing the border with Esperanza's story*. Boston: Beacon.
Blayton, J. B. (1939). *Bulletin No. 11*. Atlanta: National Youth Council, Colored Division.

Bradley, D. (1929). A powerful lot of tribulations. Review of: J. Mellon, *The Slaves Remember*, *New York Times* (January 8, Sect. 5, p. 1).

Burrows, E. G., & Wallace, M. (1998). *Gotham: A history of New York City to 1898*. New York: Oxford University Press.

Carey, J. L. (1970). *The rise of the accounting profession to responsibility and authority, 1937–1969*. New York: AICPA.

Chomsky, N. (1989). *Necessary illusions: Thought control in democratic societies*. London: Pluto Press.

Collins, R. (1979). *The credential society: An historical sociology of education and stratification*. New York: Academic Press.

DeMond, C. W. (1917). *Price, Waterhouse & Co. in America: A history of a public accounting firm*. New York: Price Waterhouse & Co.

Doucet, M., & hooks, K. (1999). Toward an equal future. *Journal of Accountancy, 187*(6), 71–76.

Edwards, J. D. (1978). *History of public accounting in the United States*. University, AL: University of Alabama Press.

Frisch, M. (1990). *A shared authority: Essays on the craft and meaning of oral and public history*. Albany, NY: State University of New York Press.

Gluck, S. G., & Patai, D. (Eds) (1991). *Women's words: The feminist practice of oral history*. London: Routledge.

Hammond, T. (1997). From complete exclusion to minimal inclusion: African Americans and the public accounting industry, 1965–1988. *Accounting, Organizations and Society, 22*(1), 29–54.

Hammond, T. (2002). *A white-collar profession: African-American CPAs since 1921*. Chapel Hill: University of North Carolina Press.

Hammond, T., & Preston, A. (1992). Culture, gender, and corporate control: Japan as 'other.'. *Accounting, Organizations and Society, 17*(8), 795–808.

Hammond, T., & Sikka, P. (1996). Radicalizing accounting history: The potential of oral history. *Accounting, Auditing & Accountability Journal, 9*(3), 79–97.

Hammond, T., & Streeter, D. (1994). Overcoming barriers: Early African-American certified public accountants. *Accounting, Organizations and Society, 19*(3), 271–288.

Harding, S. (1986). *The science question in feminism*. Ithaca, NY: Cornell University Press.

Harrison, L. (1992). Interview (first African-American CPA in Louisiana, 1946).

Hine, D. C. (1989). *Black women in white: Racial conflict and cooperation in the nursing profession, 1890–1950*. Indianapolis: Indiana University Press.

hooks, K. L. (1996). Diversity, family issues and the big 6. *Journal of Accountancy, 182*(1), 51–56.

hooks, K. L., & Cheramy, S. J. (1994). Facts and myths about women CPAs. *Journal of Accountancy, 178*(4), 79–86.

Hruska, B. (1993). When directors cross over. *The New York Times* (April 4), 20.

Hull, G. T., Scott, P. B., & Smith, B. (Eds) (1992). *All the women are white, all the blacks are men, but some of us are brave: Black women's studies*. Boston: Feminist Press.

Journal of Accountancy (1923). Women in accountancy: What militates against them (Vol. 36, No. 6, pp. 443–444).

Journal of Accountancy (1942). Women in accounting (Vol. 73, No. 4, pp. 295–296).

Journal of Accountancy (1951). Women in public accounting (Vol. 91, No. 5, 675).

Journal of Accountancy (1969). Editors' notebook: On black CPAs (Vol. 128, No. 4, 39).

Kanter, R. M. (1977). *Men and women of the corporation*. New York: Basic Books.

Lehman, C. (1992). 'Herstory' in accounting: The first eighty years. *Accounting, Organizations and Society, 17*(3/4), 261–286.

Mellon, J. (Ed.) (1998). *Bullwhip days: The slaves remember: An oral history.* New York: Avon.

Miranti, P. J. (1988). Professionalism and nativism: The competition in securing public accountancy legislation in New York during the 1890s. *Social Science Quarterly, 69*(2), 361–380.

Miranti, P. J. (1990). *Accountancy comes of age: The development of an American profession, 1886–1940.* Chapel Hill: University of North Carolina Press.

Mitchell, B. (1969). The black minority in the CPA profession. *Journal of Accountancy, 128*(4), 41–48.

National Association of Black Accountants (1990). *The history of black accountancy: The first 100 black CPAs.* Washington, DC: NABA.

Perera, V. (1993). Borderline case. *The Nation* (September 20), 290–293.

Pittman, H. T. (1992). Interview (Illinois CPA, 1949).

Previts, G. J., & Merino, B. D. (1998). *A history of accountancy in the United States: The cultural significance of accounting.* Columbus: Ohio State University Press.

Robinson-Backmon, I., & Weisenfeld, L. (2001). An investigation of perceived discrimination and career advancement curtailment: The African-American female accountant's perspective. *Advances in Accountability: Regulation, Research, Gender and Justice, 8*, 261–274.

Rosengarten, T. (1984). *All God's dangers: The life of Nate Shaw.* New York: Knopf.

Rutherford, T. (1992). Interview (first African-American CPA in West Virginia).

Said, E. W. (1994). *Culture and imperialism.* London: Fontana.

Sheldahl, T. K. (1982). *Beta Alpha Psi, from alpha to omega: Pursuing a vision of professional education for accountants, 1919–1945.* New York: Garland Publishing.

Spacek, L. (1989). *The growth of Arthur Andersen & Co. 1928–1973: An oral history.* New York: Garland Publishing.

Thompson, P. (1988). *The voice of the past: Oral history.* Oxford: Oxford University Press.

Tinsley, J. (1983). *Texas Society of Certified Public Accountants: A history, 1915–1981.* College Station: Texas A&M University Press.

Vansina, J. (1973). *Oral tradition: A study in historical methodology.* Chicago: Aldine.

Wilson, M. (1991). Interview (first African-American CPA in Indiana, 1951).

BIOGRAPHICAL RESEARCH IN ACCOUNTING

Dale L. Flesher and Tonya K. Flesher

There is properly no history, only biography (R. W. Emerson).

As indicated in the above quote from Emerson, history is really the story of those individuals who helped make history; history and biography are actually one and the same. Thomas Carlyle (1832) made a similar statement: "Biography is the only true history." The history of any field, including accounting, is dependent upon the contributions of the practitioners and theoreticians in the field. As a profession, such as accountancy, reaches a level of maturity, that maturity is supported by recognizing the contributions of the pioneers who laid the foundation on which the profession is based. Parker (1977, p. 6) expressed the importance of studying and assessing the influence of individuals on the development of accounting thought and practices with the following comment:

> Accounting historians should concentrate on accountants as well as accounting; partly because accounting thought and practice are clearly not independent of *who* thought and *who* practiced; partly because accounting history is part of social history and not just the history of a technique.

Indeed, a history of accounting cannot be separated from the biographies of those individuals who made that history. Kerrigan (1985, p. 1) explained:

> There are a small group of individuals whose labors have contributed significantly and selflessly to the status, prestige, and public esteem of accountants and accounting in their time. Like others before, during, and since their time, this group deserves to be included as developers of accounting thought as expounded and professionally practiced, to the position it has achieved today, as one of society's great moral forces, that will grow even greater with time.

Doing Accounting History: Contributions to the Development of Accounting Thought
Studies in the Development of Accounting Thought, Volume 6, 97–120
Copyright © 2003 by Elsevier Science Ltd.
All rights of reproduction in any form reserved
ISSN: 1479-3504/PII: S1479350402060064

Norman E. Webster, an accounting historian of the 1940s and 1950s, is quoted as saying essentially the same thing another way: "Every lasting institution is the lengthened shadow of a person." To Webster, accounting history is "the story of the lives of persons in the form of associations and societies" (Flowers, 1974, p. 21). Solomons also recognized this need to focus on people as well as ideas when he wrote "The Historical Development of Cost Accounting." Commenting on this work at the 1993 Accounting Biography Conference at the University of Mississippi, Solomons (1994, p. 136) stated:

> The history of costing, when it comes to be written, ought, I think, to be more than a bald account of ideas. Some information about the men who formed the ideas ought surely to be available to a later generation.

Romeo and Kyj (2000, p. 137), when discussing the contributions of Anson O. Kittredge, noted that institutions and journals are often given credit for changes in accounting, but that the people behind those organizations are forgotten. "The work becomes greater than the individual who created it." The authors concluded:

> Leafing through early accounting journals from the last two decades of the 19th century, accounting historians and enthusiasts are able to piece together the history of accountancy in the U.S. Yet, precious little attention is paid to the editors of these journals who, at times, almost single-handedly willed their very existence.

It was not just editors who single-handedly willed the existence of change in accounting; virtually every change had a champion who moved the cause forward. Biography is simply a research technique that focuses on the "movers and shakers" of a profession. This paper examines many published biographies to develop a model for accounting biographical research.

EXAMPLES OF ACCOUNTING BIOGRAPHIES

A number of excellent accounting biographies have been written in the past quarter century, the most in-depth of which were several dissertations (see Appendix 1 for titles and authors). The gathering of basic biographical material is rarely the primary purpose of dissertation research (perhaps because of the assumed need for quantitative analysis); however, such data must be gathered to place the contributions of an individual into the proper perspective and to learn the probable influences on the subject's life. Often, it is something outside the domain of accounting that influences the work of notable accountants.

In addition to dissertation research, there have been a few books (i.e. Howlett, 1969; Previts & Taylor, 1978; Zeff, 2000) and dozens of biographical articles published on accountants in recent years. Most accounting journals, including both research-oriented and practitioner journals, have published biographies. Thus, there are many quality biographies of accountants that can be studied to gain insights into the biographical research process. In addition, new technology is making the biographical research process even easier. It should also be noted that accounting biographies are not limited to "good" people. Biographical research can also be used to understand the motives of those who have taken advantage of the accounting process for purposes of ill-gotten gains. For instance, Flesher and Flesher (1986) detailed Ivar Kreuger's fraud activities. Similarly, an understanding of Philip Musica helps explain the McKesson and Robbins fraud of the 1930s (Keats, 1964).

Researching accounting biographies involves the discovery of facts about an individual's life. However, a collection of facts does not make a biography. From facts, a biographer may shape a story about how a person lived, but a good biography should also have a theme and a plot. The events of the subject's life are the outline, or framework, for the plot. The theme of a biography gives the reader a clue as to what the subject's life was all about and reflects the dominant thread that pervaded that life. Sometimes that theme is reflected in a single anecdote that can serve as an opening paragraph; alternatively, the theme can be reflective of an entire life rather than a single instance. The final result is a shaping of an accumulation of facts and anecdotes into a meaningful work of art. Indeed, a biographer is a metaphoric portrait painter (Pachter, 1979, p. 3). Alternatively, Virginia Woolf (quoted in Young-Bruehl, 1990) purportedly stated that biographers must somehow combine "gravity" and "rainbow," the weight of the facts with the colors of literary imagination.

The gist of the preceding paragraphs was captured over two centuries ago by Samuel Johnson, who, in 1750, criticized biographers who began with pedigrees and ended with funerals. According to Johnson, a person's character is revealed by conversations, not by pedigrees (Clifford, 1970, p. 42). Johnson also advised biographers not to shirk from the truth. However, Johnson's own biographer, James Boswell, did not follow this advice. Boswell stated: "I think it proper to say that I have suppressed everything which I thought could really hurt anyone now living" (Pottle & Bennett, 1963, p. 402).

A recent accounting biography that presented a balanced approach to the subject's character was Richardson's (2000) work on Canadian pioneer, George Edwards. Richardson included Edwards' attempts to keep women out of the accountancy profession because he felt they undermined the profession. Richardson also discussed his subject's attempt but failure to stop the creation of alternative accounting organizations in Canada. Inclusion of these "politically incorrect" topics provides readers with a better understanding of Edwards' character.

Most accounting biographies that have heretofore been published have been of major characters in the history of accounting, but this is not to say that lesser-known figures are not suitable for their own biographies. The entire concept of microhistory focuses close attention on seemingly minor or intensely local events from the past to discover what possibilities and constraints shaped human behavior at specific historical moments. Scandals and trials provide an example of this sort of analysis, as do biographies of individuals who probably would not be well known at a national level. The idea is to explain ideas, attitudes, or cultural patterns by an intensive examination of a particular person. Abraham (2000, p. 1) illustrated this methodology in her presentation at the Eighth World Congress of Accounting Historians in Madrid: "Just as William Blake (c. 1802) saw 'a world in a grain of sand,' so microhistory operates like a microscope by concentrating attention on one slide which is brought into a sharp revealing focus." Abraham further noted:

> Microhistories . . . have shown that a detailed study of individual lives, using a variety of quantitative and qualitative sources, can lead to a deeper understanding of contemporary social and cultural climate. Thus, microhistory demonstrates that individuals must be taken seriously as historical agents.

Indeed, biography does fall into the category of microhistory, and as such can be used to evaluate the movement of cultural, social, and other changes. One recent example of an accounting microhistory would be the biography of Warren W. Nissley, authored by Slocum and Roberts (1996). An Australian example would be the biography of Edward Wild by Carnegie and Varker (1995).

Two conflicting problems facing biographers are a lack or an abundance of material. Typically, biographical researchers will either be starved for meaningful documents and impressions or will be inundated by thousands of such chronicles. More will be said about inundation later. Initially, the concern is with the shortage of research materials.

Locating and gathering material may be the most difficult aspect of conducting biographical research studies in accounting. One must necessarily dig for information in any fertile ground. Examples of fertile ground include previously published works, including those by or about the subject; library or company archives; interviews with the subject if he or she is still living; interviews with individuals who knew the subject; visits to the subject's hometown and/or cemetery; and government files that can be accessed via the federal Freedom of Information Act.

RESEARCHING PUBLISHED RESOURCES

Researching published resources is the easiest way to conduct biographical research, particularly in this age of the Internet and on-line library resources.

Also, it is best to learn first what others have said about an individual before proceeding to a search for original materials. After conducting electronic searches at the local library for materials both published by and about the subject, the next step is to search via WORLDCAT, which allows a search of virtually every major library in the U.S. For example, when Previts et al. (1997) were looking for material on Charles Waldo Haskins and Elijah Watt Sells, they first searched for every book ever *authored* by either subject. After exhausting those resources, the next step was to list each gentleman as the *subject* of a search. The result was the discovery of a book entitled *A Land Lover and His Land* (McCulloch-Williams, 1909), a volume that had been published in an edition of only 200 copies. Only one library in the country had a copy, but it was possible to obtain this copy through interlibrary loan. That book, the publication costs of which were underwritten by Sells, was not about Sells the CPA, but Sells the gentleman farmer. That volume, which the authors had never found cited in any other place, depicted a different Sells than is available from accounting sources. Flesher et al. (1996a) used WORLDCAT to uncover a previously unknown book authored by Joseph Hardcastle, the first man to pass the CPA exam. The only existing copy was in the library at Stanford University, far from Hardcastle's New York hometown. Unfortunately, once obtained, it was found that the book was nothing more than a series of journal articles that had been clipped out and bound together in a hard binding. Although the bound volume provided no new research materials, it did result in the question, who had clipped and bound the articles? Were Hardcastle's materials being used for a class at Stanford University? The question remains unanswered.

Although the *Accountants' Index* has long been a research resource for all kinds of accounting articles, there are now many electronic tools that can be used to find journal articles. For instance, NEXIS/LEXIS and ABI-INFORM allow keyword searches in a variety of published articles.

Another source of published information is the subject's obituary. When Flesher et al. (1996b) were researching their history of early CPA educators, they were able to find obituaries for many of their subjects in the *New York Times*. The *New York Times Index* dates back to 1851, which makes researching obituaries quite easy. Obituaries in areas other than New York City may be more difficult to find, but if the date of death is known, microfilm copies of other newspapers can be utilized for a particular obituary. Flesher and Flesher (1985) knew the date James O. McKinsey died and were able to find the obituary in the Chicago papers. Alternatively, some accountants have had their obituaries published in accounting journals. Previts distributed an index of accounting biographies, many of which were obituaries, at the 1993 Academy of Accounting Historians Biography Conference at the University of Mississippi. That index, probably compiled by New Yorker Norman Webster in the 1950s, lists hundreds of biographies of accountants that appeared in accounting journals from the 1880s to the 1950s. Some of these so-called biographies are only a few lines about the author of an article, but, nevertheless, the information may be useful.

Another source of accounting biographies that should not be overlooked is the Accounting Hall of Fame at Ohio State University. Each year, the Accounting Hall of Fame inducts one or more outstanding accountants into its ranks. More than 60 individuals have been so honored since the Hall was established in 1950. Brief profiles of these inductees have been published in book form in past years (Burns & Coffman, 1976, 1991), and each new inductee is now profiled in the *Accounting Historians Journal* (e.g. Jensen, 1999). In addition, the Accounting Hall of Fame has in recent years begun publishing the collected written works of some of the members of the Hall of Fame under the editorship of Jensen and Coffman. These volumes open with a biography of the person whose publications and speeches are being reprinted (for example, see Coffman & Jensen, 1996, 2000).

Other sources of published information that should not be overlooked include *The Wall Street Journal Index, Business Periodical Index, Reader's Guide to Periodic Literature, Dissertation Abstracts, Biography Index, Dictionary of American Biography*, and the various *Who's Who* publications. There is also a 1939 reference book entitled *Biography by Americans, 1658–1936: A Subject Bibliography* (O'Neill, 1939) that supposedly lists most of the book-length biographies written in the U.S. up until that time.

LIBRARY OR COMPANY ARCHIVES

Many biographies are enhanced by documents made available to the researcher in archival holdings either in some library or company storage facility. For example, Flesher and Flesher (1989) were able to examine the personal papers of Accounting Hall of Famer T. Coleman Andrews that are available at the University of Oregon library. The Fleshers, after having researched the contributions of Andrews for four years, happened to find an archival collection catalog at the Library of Congress. That catalog listed the contents of the T. Coleman Andrews papers. Although surprised that the collection existed, the Fleshers were even more surprised to learn that the collection was housed in Oregon since there was no apparent connection between Andrews, a native Virginian, and Oregon. The answer was that the University of Oregon housed documents relating to the John Birch Society, and that Andrews' papers had been acquired because he was a founder of that organization in 1958. Although much of the archival material related to Andrews' fringe activities, there was a sufficient quantity relating to accounting and Andrews' position as Commissioner of the Internal Revenue to make a research trip to Oregon worthwhile. The Fleshers had concentrated their search for information on Andrews to the Virginia and Washington DC areas; it was only happenstance that the Oregon archives were discovered.

Employee personnel files are one archival source that should not be forgotten. For instance, when studying A. C. Littleton, Buckner (1975) used the personnel and biographical files held by the Alumni, the President's, the Bureau of Research, and the Department of Accountancy Offices at the University of Illinois. Similarly, when Flesher (1997, p. 5) was researching the career of Clive Dunham, an early professor at the University of Mississippi, he found the Personnel Office had a 1937 letter in which a job offer was made to Dunham. Dunham's birth date was also still on file, 36 years after his retirement.

Some archival records may not even be viewed as resources by many biographers, but accounting biographers should recognize that old ledgers in a storeroom may be important biographical sources. For instance, do the levels of receivables or payables say anything about a subject's level of success at a particular point in time? Most biographers would likely be uncomfortable trying to use accounting documents as sources, but not accounting biographers.

Unfortunately, these archival resources are often simply not available. Personal papers have been lost or destroyed, often by well-meaning relatives who dispose of the "trash" in the subject's file cabinets shortly after death. Occasionally, archival materials are intentionally destroyed by the subject of a biography. If there is anything potentially embarrassing in a person's past, documentation for those events may be missing when the biographer shows up. Many literary figures, such as Charles Dickens, James Joyce, and even Sigmund Freud, took the trouble to burn their own papers. Others, such as Somerset Maugham and George Orwell, left instructions for their executors to destroy anything that might be of interest to future biographers. However, given the number of biographies that have been written on the aforementioned personages, those efforts seemingly accomplished little.

A new, high-tech research tool to help in archival searching is a CD-ROM database that catalogs the holdings of hundreds of archives around the U.S. The database costs several thousand dollars and is thus available in only a few large libraries. Many other archival holdings are available free on the Internet. Many of these have been designed for genealogical researchers. Excellent resources are www.ancestry.com and www.genealogy.com. For those subjects who immigrated to the U.S., their arrivals can be documented on the manifests made available at www.ellisislandrecords.org. Flesher et al. (1996b) used the latter site to learn that 19th century CPA Arthur Lowes Dickinson arrived in New York on November 26, 1894, aboard the ship *Britannic*. According to the manifest, Dickinson was then 25 years of age and had emigrated from Liverpool.

INTERVIEWS

Interviews are frequently the best source of material if the subject is of recent vintage. For example, Previts and Flesher (1996) conducted interviews with former Securities and Exchange Commission Chief Accountant Andrew Barr to obtain data on Barr's contributions to the SEC and financial accounting principles. Besides using the interviews for their current research, Previts and Flesher provided a database for other researchers by videotaping their interviews. The resulting tapes are available from the Academy of Accounting Historians' Videotape Center (Barr, 1992).

Interviews with elderly subjects, however, do not always turn out as planned. A well-prepared interviewer often knows more about an early aspect of the subject's life than the subject himself remembers. For example, Previts and Flesher found that Barr, although strong mentally, could not remember various events in his life, events that had been previously recorded in Barr's writings. Similarly, Buckner (1984, p. 20) could not conduct an interview with Littleton because Mrs. Littleton felt that such an interview would not be productive. Alternatively, Cooper (1981, p. 4) found that his interview with former Chief Accountant Carman Blough went extremely well despite Blough's advanced age: "Throughout the interview he amazed me with his ability to recall dates, places, and events that affected his career."

Interviews with friends and acquaintances of the subject (regardless of whether the subject is living or dead) can also be quite helpful. For instance, Hoskins (1992) conducted telephone interviews with many former acquaintances of her subject, Mary Murphy, one of the most prolific female authors in the history of accounting. One of Hoskins' best sources was a mail-questionnaire interview with Australian pioneer Louis Goldberg who had been a mentor to Murphy when she was visiting in Australia in the early 1950s. Goldberg could not only provide memories, but he still had, after 40 years, letters of correspondence with Murphy.

New electronic search tools, such as the Internet and e-mail, are useful for conducting interviews. In fact, interviews can be facilitated by means of e-mail as the subject has the advantage of having sufficient time to look up the answers to the questions asked. However, the back-and-forth dialogue typical of a phone call or in-person interview is lost. A valuable Internet site for biographical researchers is SWITCHBOARD (www.switchboard.com), which provides addresses and phone numbers for almost all individuals and businesses in the U.S., and sometimes e-mail addresses as well. The current authors recently used SWITCHBOARD to get the phone number of 86-year-old, internal-auditing guru Lawrence Sawyer about whom a biography is being written. When researching the background of Henry Harney, the man who wrote the first CPA law, Flesher et al. (1996c) felt they were at a dead end and decided to use SWITCHBOARD to see if there were any namesake descendents of the 1896 Henry Harney. Three names were found; all were called, but none admitted to being a descendent of the esteemed early CPA.

Another good Internet site is www.ancestry.com, which gives birth and death dates, social security numbers, and last-known residence of decedents who had social security (Federal Insurance Contributions Act) numbers. Other information can also sometimes be found at www.ancestry.com, but these additional links can only be accessed for a fee.

Internet home pages of potential subjects, their relatives, colleagues, or organizations may also be another source for would-be biographers, if not now, at least in the future.

USING THE FREEDOM OF INFORMATION ACT

An important source of data may often be eschewed by historical researchers due to the perceived difficulties of dealing with the federal bureaucracy. The Freedom of Information Act (FOIA) provides a vital source of inquiry on many subject areas if the tricks of dealing with the government can be mastered. In this section, we describe the saga of a FOIA search that took 31 months and may still not be complete. The purpose is to guide other historical researchers along this difficult path. A step-by-step description of the procedures used in researching an accounting biography is used as the guide. Sample letters are illustrated (see Appendix 2).

First, the researcher must learn the legal background of the FOIA. Passed in 1966, it was intended to provide access to the records of agencies of the executive branch of the federal government. The Act does not apply to the records of Congress or the judicial branch of the government. The law does grant access to the public records of the executive branch by any person.

There are nine categories of information that may be withheld from the public. FOIA does not apply to matters that are:

(1) kept secret in the interest of national defense or foreign policy under an executive order;
(2) related solely to the internal personnel rules and practices of an agency;
(3) specifically exempted from disclosure by statute;
(4) trade secrets and confidential commercial or financial information;
(5) interagency or intra-agency memoranda or letters that would not be available by law to a party other than an agency in litigation with the agency;
(6) personnel and medical files the disclosure of which would constitute a clearly unwarranted invasion of personal privacy;

(7) investigative records compiled for law-enforcement purposes;
(8) related to a financial institution;
(9) geological and geophysical information and data (5 USC 552b, 1996).

The above nine areas of exemption have been expanded drastically by court interpretations and by precedents set by aggressive citizens and insistent reporters (Archibald, 1977, p. 54).

The FOIA was amended in 1974 to assist researchers further. A federal agency has ten working days to indicate its compliance or non-compliance to an original request for a public record. Further, an agency must respond within 20 days to an appeal of the denial of an original request. The fees charged to conduct a FOIA request are limited to reasonable charges to cover document search and duplication costs. No charge or a reduced charge should be levied if furnishing the information benefits the general public. A request need only reasonably describe the records desired. Government records must be reasonably segregated so that portions of the records may be released after deletion of matters exempt under FOIA.

How to Make an FOIA Request

The procedure to follow in making a request under the FOIA is simply to write a carefully drafted letter. The first step is to determine the agency to which to address the request. A list of executive-branch agencies with addresses is available from several sources, including the *United States Government Manual* and at Internet sites for each agency. The envelope and the letter should be marked as a FOIA request.

Probably the most important part of the letter is the request for records. FOIA asks only for a reasonable description of the records. However, it would seem that a good description would improve the results and reduce the costs of the search. Care should be taken in matching the request to the purpose of the research project.

The letter may also contain a request for a waiver or reduction of the search fees. An academic researcher may make such a request by stating that the general purpose of the research project is for the benefit of the general public. If possible delays are to be avoided when a waiver is requested, the requester should offer to pay the search fee up to a stated limit if the waiver is denied.

Even though the FOIA specifically provides for these rights, the requester may ask to expect a response within ten days and that reasons be provided if the request is denied. As an added precaution, the letter should be sent certified mail with return receipt requested.

If the request is denied, then an appeal can be filed. To appeal, attach a copy of the denial letter to a letter stating the arguments against the denial. As an alternative to an appeal, try to get the agency to help in revising the request or simply wait and write another request letter at a later date. Perhaps the personnel or the policies will have changed. Those with experience with FOIA requests insist that persistence is the key (Archibald, 1977, p. 56).

An FOIA Example

The FOIA appears to be a most valuable source of data for accounting history projects, biographies in particular. To illustrate, the FOIA seemed to have great potential as a source of information in researching the life of T. Coleman Andrews, a former President of the American Institute of Accountants (now AICPA). For much of his career, Andrews was a public servant, and for most of that time he was the center of so much attention or controversy that an abundance of governmental records on him might be expected. After leaving a state-government post, Andrews came to Washington, DC in 1941. He worked in the Office of the Under Secretary of War and the Under Secretary of the Navy and served on the staff of General Eisenhower. He also worked as an accountant for the Department of State. After the war, Andrews became the first Director of the Corporation Audits Division of the General Accounting Office (GAO). (Since the GAO is not an agency of the executive branch, the FOIA would not apply.) Andrews next served on the Hoover Commission. Of primary significance for this study, Andrews assumed the post as Commissioner of Internal Revenue in 1953 and made many controversial recommendations during his 33-month tenure. Therefore, requests were made to the Internal Revenue Service (IRS), the State Department, and the Department of Defense to uncover any documents relating to Andrews' government service during these years.

In 1956, Andrews ran as a presidential candidate on an independent ticket with a platform featuring the abolition of the federal income tax and a general limitation of federal governmental powers. With the support of a large number of conservative splinter groups, Andrews was moderately successful in the election. Although Andrews never again ran for office, he did continue to work for conservative causes. He was a strong supporter of George Wallace. Andrews and 12 others founded the John Birch Society in 1958. Certainly, these political activities should have attracted much attention among federal bureaucrats. A fourth letter to the Federal Bureau of Investigation (FBI) might uncover these records.

The sample research case then was to utilize the FOIA to attempt to gain any public records on T. Coleman Andrews by sending request letters to the IRS, the Department of Defense, the State Department, and the FBI. In addition to obtaining valuable research materials, the researchers hope to share the insights that were gained about the data-gathering process. The lessons gleaned may help other researchers.

Results of the FOIA Requests

Appendix 3 illustrates the time frame for the FOIA data-gathering process. Request letters using an identical format were sent to the four agencies on February 3, 1987. Two of the letters were sent certified mail, while the remaining two were posted in the regular mail. This was done to determine if certifying a request letter as suggested by the literature makes a difference. In fact it did make a difference. The certified letter to the FBI was received by that agency on February 9. However, the official acknowledgment letter received from the FBI arrived on March 2; it was dated February 24, the 11th working day after receipt. Responses were received in reply to the non-certified request letters on March 2 and 3. By March 3, there was still no response to the other certified letter to the IRS, so a tracer was filed with the postal service. Since no response was yet forthcoming by March 20, the postmaster was asked to send a second tracer. Nothing was ever heard from either tracer. However, on March 25, 1987, some information was received from the IRS. Lesson number one is to save money and not to bother with certified mail for request letters.

All of the agencies except the IRS requested additional information regarding date and place of birth, and date and proof of death. One of the offices also requested the consent of T. Coleman Andrews to conduct the search. We have not discovered a way to advise future requesters to simultaneously submit proof of death of an individual and their signed consent! Do include the date and place of birth and the date of death in the request letter, in addition to sending a copy of a newspaper obituary. As this information is sufficient to answer all of an agency's requirements, much time could have been saved by sending it with the initial request. (None of the articles consulted on FOIA requests suggested this procedure.)

The Department of Defense notified us that our request had been forwarded to another office, one that handled civilian records. To our surprise and after some confusion, we eventually obtained information from two offices, Civilian Records and Military Records.

The State Department also requested additional information concerning the fee waiver. We were asked to provide evidence that a waiver would be in the public interest by describing our qualifications, the nature of the research, and the purposes for which the requested materials would be used. Further, we were to show that we had expertise in the subject area and the ability and intention to disseminate the information to the public. Also, the requesters were to have no personal or financial interest in the records. Our reply was a one-paragraph letter in response to the above and a vita, apparently satisfying the criteria for a fee waiver.

The first to reply was the IRS, approximately seven weeks after the certified request letter was mailed. The next reply came from the Military Records Office, after a lapse of over three months. Shortly thereafter, the Civilian Records Office of the Department of Defense replied. On July 20, 1987, the State Department answered that they had no documents pertinent as per our request.

Dealing with the FBI proved to be the most exasperating experience of this search. By late July 1987, all of the other requests had been answered, but nothing had been forthcoming from the FBI except two requests for more time. Over the next two years, the only responses from the FBI were requests for more time and eventually a letter asking us not to write more letters inquiring about the delay. Ultimately, it was necessary to request the help of Senator Trent Lott of Mississippi in inquiring about this lengthy delay. After requesting Senator Lott's aid on July 12, 1989, the information was sent by the FBI on September 5, 1989, 31 months after the initial request. Obviously, gathering data through FOIA requests is not a speedy process. Appendix 3 chronicles the time lapse for the receipt of records.

Results of the Request

In regard to the assistance that was eventually offered, the IRS proved to be the most cooperative, as well as the most prompt. The initial packet of materials received from the IRS contained a copy of the speech given by T. Coleman Andrews on taking the oath of office as Commissioner and a copy of the hearings of the Senate Committee on Finance concerning his nomination. We responded with a letter of gratitude for these materials and a request for a further search for additional records, such as copies of speeches, policies, memoranda, or other internal documents. Very shortly, an IRS official telephoned to inquire more specifically about what we needed. She said that very few documents from the days of Andrews' tenure remained except copies of the annual report of the Commissioner. She sent excerpts from the 1953 report.

The Military Records Office of the Department of Defense provided the official personnel folder for Andrews that contained his life history as written by Andrews, application forms, insurance forms, and payroll records. Also of interest was a brief report of an interview with John Carey, then Secretary of the American Institute of Accountants, conducted in 1947 for the GAO. The stated purpose of the interview was a qualification investigation to confer civil-service status upon Mr. Andrews.

Mr. Carey was quoted as saying that Mr. Andrews "is one of the best men in the accounting field in all respects. He is an outstanding administrator and one of the best accountants that has been produced." The Civilian Records Office forwarded copies of personnel records and the resume of Andrews, as well as a news release covering his appointment as Commissioner of Internal Revenue.

The FBI, by far the slowest to respond, did provide the greatest volume of materials, 120 pages. However, so much of the information had been blacked out that what remained was not of great significance. Essentially, all names of individuals other than Andrews were censored. In some cases entire pages were censored except for the introduction and a concluding remark that Mr. Andrews was a loyal American. A total of 146 pages were reviewed pursuant to our request, but only 120 were released. Several pages were clippings from newspapers or press releases. The most interesting of the materials was an exchange of letters between Andrews and J. Edgar Hoover. The letters from Andrews were full of praise and admiration for Mr. Hoover. The responses from Hoover and other evidence do not point to a similar attitude of respect flowing in the opposite direction. One indication of Andrews' admiration for Mr. Hoover was a note that he had arranged for the Pace College of Accounting in New York to grant him an honorary doctorate. When Hoover could not attend the ceremonies, Andrews accepted the degree on Hoover's behalf, subsequently mailing him the degree and hood.

Several lessons can be learned from this particular experience of gathering data through the FOIA. First, certified request letters do not appear to be necessary. Second, include date and place of birth, date of death, and a newspaper obituary with the request letter if it concerns a deceased individual. In more general terms, provide as much information as possible about the subject of the research request. Finally, allow plenty of time for the completion of the project. If a request is made to the FBI, one should allow at least two years to receive the information. Doctoral students and untenured faculty members should be aware of the hazards that might arise as the result of such a lengthy delay. The researcher should also remember how help from a member of Congress can accelerate the process. If these lessons are heeded, the FOIA may prove a valuable source of material for accounting researchers.

A CAUTION

Biographers must know their subjects before they write their finished product, whether that product be an article or a book. However, just because a biographer knows everything about a subject does not mean that every tidbit has to be included in the final publication. It has been said that research is the opium of biographers;

some writers have apparently believed that any act, no matter how small, must be included just because it is available. There is no truth to this rumor; all facts need not be included if they do not further the story. Indeed, an overabundance of resource materials can actually detract from the quality of a biographical work. Alternatively, the truth must be respected; the author should not use only those facts that support a particular theme if the preponderance of evidence is contrary to that theme (Bowen, 1950, p. 12).

A biographer must be immersed in the subject's life and must feel the personality of the individual. Two goals are paramount: (1) understanding the subject's character and (2) understanding how it felt to be a citizen of the subject's era and to pursue the subject's goals (Buckner, 1984, p. 1). To do so, biographers usually have to work without helpers; graduate research assistants can rarely be used. It is not enough to obtain the facts; the biographer must get inside the skin of the subject.

For examples of other problems that biographers face, a 1970 book, *From Puzzles to Portraits: Problems of a Literary Biographer*, should be consulted. This work, by James Clifford, provides many insights relative to biographical research.

Finally, the question of gaps in the subject's life must be addressed. Of course, the more remote the time since the subject's death, the greater likelihood of lengthy gaps. Kendall (1965) suggested that biographers must use due diligence to fill such gaps. Otherwise the biographer may experience sleepless nights wondering when some new archival discovery will completely destroy the entire theme of the biography. The following anecdote from Judd (1991, B5) underscores the problem:

> Not long after my biography of Ford Madox Ford was published, I had a letter from Mr. Thomas Carter, an American, asking whether I knew that Ford had been engaged to his grandmother, Elizabeth Cheatham, who had died only a month before. The name was unknown to Fordians. There were, wrote Mr. Carter, 'masses' of unpublished letters and poems. Did I want to see them?
>
> There was just time to do a postscript for the British paperback and American hardback editions. Nevertheless, I dithered, Hoaxers are not, apparently, unknown to biographers, exaggeration is common. Perhaps the papers made a fundamental difference to Ford's life. I almost didn't want to know. I went.
>
> There are ten poems and sixty-three letters . . . Thankfully, they make no radical difference, but they do add significantly to knowledge of one period of Ford's life. They provide insights into the dating of some of his works, into his financial affairs, his opinions of other writers, and into his emotional state, temporary and enduring. Most are intimate, hurried, self-revealing; one he wanted burnt. They also constitute a warning to biographers.
>
> The lesson for the biographer is chastening: you do not always know when you do not know. None of Ford's biographers was aware of a gap to be filled in the years 1927–1929; we glided over, unseeing . . . . And if that is so for these years, what of the others? Blessed be the biographers of the long, undocumented dead. I am still uneasy at the postman's knock.

AUTOBIOGRAPHIES AND MEMOIRS

When the discussion of biographies arises, there is often a question relating to autobiographies. Penning one's personal history is not just the domain of presidents and movie stars; accountants can also tell their own stories. Actually, most of what has been said with respect to biographies also applies to autobiographies, but authors (autobiographers) often fail to heed the suggestions. The result is a finished product that is not an autobiography, but a memoir. The difference between an autobiography and a memoir is in the amount of research conducted. A memoir, as the word implies, is simply the author's memory of what happened. That memory is tainted by the passing years and by personal biases. The contents of a memoir are simply the views of the writer; they are perceptions and impressions of events. Regardless of their scholarship, memoirs provide nuggets of information about the way people lived during a certain period of time. In fact, some critics believe that memoirs may be better than scholarly autobiographies because the former speak from the heart rather than the brain; facts alone do not always tell the full story.

There are a number of excellent examples of accounting autobiographies and memoirs. *Thomas G. Higgins, CPA: An Autobiography* (1965), a 347-page volume, is a combination autobiography and memoir of a former Arthur Young partner. Donaldson Brown's *Reminiscences of an Industrialist* (1977) is a thoughtful memoir. Still another excellent memoir is that of Maurice Pelobet, published in 2000 after editing by A. R. Roberts (2000). What might be considered a combination biography-memoir is Edgar Jones' volume, *The Memoirs of Edwin Waterhouse: A Founder of Price Waterhouse*, published in 1988. A self-designated memoir that contains evidence of much research is Maxwell Henderson's *Plain Talk! Memoirs of An Auditor General* (1984). Harvey Wineberg's *Thanks for Your Trust: Memories of an Untamed Accountant* (1998) is a recent example of a well-researched memoir, as is the older Ross T. Warner work, *Oklahoma Boy: An Autobiography*. Warner (1968, p. iii), a former partner with a Big-5 firm, included the following methodological note in the preface:

> The stories and adventures related here are all true. They are based principally on memory, aided by newspaper and magazine clippings, and by letters and other documents passed down from members of my family. Fortunately, my mother and father kept all the letters I wrote them from France during World War I, and from these I was able to recall many incidents long forgotten.

An excellent British example is *Cork on Cork: Sir Kenneth Cork Takes Stock* (1988), while *My Memories: Being the Reminiscences of a Nonagenarian*, by Chartered Accountant Thomas Brentnall (1938), is an old Australian memoir.

Other memoirs have been published in article form over the years, while still others reside as typescripts in library archives.

Like biographies, the writing of autobiographies and memoirs has been simplified by the existence of the Internet. One writing tool that some may find helpful is at www.turningmemories.com/coaching.html. This site outlines the topics that should be included in a well-balanced autobiography.

Finally, it should be noted that memoirs and autobiographies are not typically written by objective authors. These publications are often self-indulgent and concerned less with the relationship between the self and the world, but more with the self as the world. As noted earlier, this comment is not necessarily a criticism. In other words, the content of a memoir or autobiography may not always be true, but it is true from the viewpoint of the author, which is perhaps an important observation of how the subject viewed society.

CONCLUSION

As Thomas Carlyle observed: "Biography is the only true history." Biographies of accounting contributors add much to the understanding of the profession and its development. Lest you think biographies are not important, remember the words of Thomas Macauley:

> Those who take no pride in the accomplishments of remote ancestors are those least likely to do anything that will be viewed with pride by remote descendants (Sawyer, 1989, p. 5).

Max Dimont reputedly stated:

> Those people who left only monuments behind as a record of their existence have vanished with time, whereas those who left ideas have survived. A society without ideas has no history (Sawyer, 1989, p. 12).

The obverse of this statement is evidenced by noted 16th century accounting theoretician Simon Stevin of Bruges. No statutes were erected to honor Stevin, not because he was not deserving of a statue, but because church leaders fought to stop any and all memorials because of their disenchantment with Stevin's treatment of God in his writings. However, Stevin's name has survived to the present day because his ideas were good, and those ideas survived (Flesher, 1989, pp. 45–47).

How much of what we think is history is forgotten; dates and battles are remembered for a while, but when the next battle comes along, history is rewritten. Ideas of individuals, however, last longer. Thus, a meaningful study of history need not be more than a study of ideas, ideas that are the product of the thought processes of individuals. To understand ideas fully requires a feel for the context in which those ideas arose; to understand history fully requires biography. In summary, the great lesson of biography is to show what people can do; a life put on record acts as an inspiration to others. Flowers (1974, p. 22) summed up the area of biographical research in accounting with the following:

> Biography as a type of accounting history is worthy of research effort. However, it is very important that the researcher realize that he is undertaking a formidable task. The biographer should study the basic psychological and behavioral patterns of personalities and become familiar with them. For in shaping a biography the writer has the responsibility of portraying a person for posterity.

REFERENCES

Abraham, A. (2000). *Struggling for accountability: An accounting microhistory*. (Paper presented at the 8th World Congress of Accounting Historians, Madrid).

Archibald, S. J. (1977). The revised F.O.I. law and how to use it. *Columbia Journalism Review* (July/August), 54–56.

Barr, A. (1992). A videotape interview by G. J. Previts and D. L. Flesher, Academy of Accounting Historians Videotape Center, University of Mississippi.

Bowen, C. D. (1950). *The writing of biography*. Boston: The Writer, Inc.

Brentnall, T. (1938). *My memories: Being the reminiscences of a nonagenarian*. Melbourne: Robertson & Mullens.

Brown, D. (1977). *Reminiscences of an industrialist*. Easton, PA: Hive Publishing Company (reprint of 1958 edition).

Buckner, K. C. (1975). *Littleton's contribution to the theory of accountancy*. Ph.D. dissertation, Georgia State University.

Buckner, K. C. (1984). Use of the biographical method for accounting research. *The Accounting Historians Notebook, 7*(1), 1 ff.

Burns, T. J., & Coffman, E. N. (1976). *The accounting hall of fame: Profiles of thirty-six members*. Columbus: Ohio State University.

Burns, T. J., & Coffman, E. N. (1991). *The accounting hall of fame: Profiles of fifty members*. Columbus: Ohio State University.

Carlyle, T. (1832). As quoted in: *Columbia World of Quotations*. New York: Columbia University Press, 1996, No. 19901.

Carnegie, G. D., & Varker, S. A. (1995). Edward Wild: Advocate of simplification and an organized profession in colonial Australia. *Accounting Historians Journal, 22*(2), 132–149.

Clifford, J. L. (1970). *From puzzles to portraits: Problems of a literary biographer*. Chapel Hill: University of North Carolina Press.

Coffman, E. N., & Jensen, D. L. (Eds) (1996). *T. Coleman Andrews: A collection of his writings*. Columbus: Ohio State University.

Coffman, E. N., & Jensen, D. L. (Eds) (2000). *Marquis G. Eaton: A collection of his writings*. Columbus: Ohio State University.

Cooper, W. (1981). Carman G. Blough: A personal profile. *The Accounting Historians Notebook, 4*(2), 4–5.

Cork, K. (1988). *Cork on Cork: Sir Kenneth Cork takes stock*. London: Macmillan.

Flesher, D. L. (1989). Simon Stevin of Bruges. In: A. M. Agami (Ed.), *Biographies of Notable Accountants* (2nd ed., pp. 45–47). New York: Random House.

Flesher, D. L. (1997). *Accountancy at Ole Miss: A sesquicentennial salute*. Oxford, MS: University of Mississippi.

Flesher, D. L., & Flesher, T. K. (1985). James O. McKinsey. *Accounting Historians Journal, 12*(2), 117–128.

Flesher, D. L., & Flesher, T. K. (1986). Ivar Kreuger's contribution to U.S. financial reporting. *Accounting Review, 61*(2), 421–434.

Flesher, D. L., & Flesher, T. K. (1989). T. Coleman Andrews and the GAO Corporation Audits Division. *The Government Accountants Journal, 38*(1), 23–28.

Flesher, D. L., Flesher, T. K., & Previts, G. J. (1996a). Joseph Hardcastle: The first person to pass the CPA exam. *The CPA Journal, 86*(4), 16–17.

Flesher, D. L., Flesher, T. K., & Previts, G. J. (1996b). Turn-of-the-century CPAs and the accounting education movement. In: A. J. Richardson (Ed.), *Disorder and Harmony: 20th Century Perspectives on Accounting History* (pp. 75–90). Vancouver: CGA-Canada Research Foundation.

Flesher, D. L., Miranti, P. J., & Previts, G. J. (1996c). The first century of the CPA. *Journal of Accountancy, 182*(4), 51–57.

Flowers, W. B. (1974). Biography and accounting history. *Accounting Historians Journal, 1*(4), 21–22.

Henderson, M. (1984). *Plain talk! Memoirs of an auditor general*. Toronto: McClelland and Stewart.

Higgins, T. G. (1965). *Thomas G. Higgins, CPA: An autobiography*. New York: Comet Press.

Hoskins, M. A. (1992). *The Murphy models for accounting: A test of relevance*. Ph.D. dissertation, University of Mississippi.

Howlett, M. J. (1969). *History of 23 Illinois auditors of public accounts: by the 24th*. Springfield, IL: State of Illinois.

Jensen, D. L. (1999). Arthur Ramer Wyatt: Citation. *Accounting Historians Journal, 26*(1), 156–158.

Jones, E. (Ed.) (1988). *The memoirs of Edwin Waterhouse: A founder of Price Waterhouse*. London: B. T. Batsford Ltd.

Judd, A. (1991). Biography. *Chronicle of Higher Education* (August 14), B5.

Keats, C. (1964). *Magnificent masquerade: The strange case of Dr. Coster and Mr. Musica*. New York: Funk & Wagnalls Company, Inc.

Kendall, P. M. (1965). *The art of biography*. London: George Allen & Unwin, Ltd.

Kerrigan, H. D. (1985). Accounting greats in their time – A personal diary. *The Accounting Historians Notebook, 12*(2), 1 ff.

McCulloch-Williams, M. (1909). *A land-lover and his land*. Armonk, NY: Elijah W. Sells.

O'Neill, E. H. (1939). *Biography by Americans, 1658–1936: A subject bibliography*. Philadelphia: University of Pennsylvania Press.

Pachter, M. (1979). *Telling lives: The biographer's art*. Washington: New Republic Books.

Parker, R. H. (1977). Research needs in accounting history. *Accounting Historians Journal, 4*(2), 1–28.

Pottle, F. A., & Bennett, C. H. (Eds) (1963). *Boswell's journal of a tour to the Hebrides with Samuel Johnson, LL. D. 1773*. London: William Heinemann.

Previts, G. J., & Flesher, D. L. (1996). Retrospective: Andrew Barr: Longest serving SEC chief accountant. *Accounting Historians Journal, 23*(1), 117–125.

Previts, G. J., Flesher, D. L., & Flesher, T. K. (1997). Charles Waldo Haskins. *The CPA Journal, 67*(5), 46–52.

Previts, G. J., & Taylor, R. F. (1978). *John Raymond Wildman*. Tuscaloosa, AL: Academy of Accounting Historians.

Richardson, A. J. (2000). Building the Canadian chartered accountancy profession: A biography of George Edwards, FCA, CBE, LLD, 1861–1947. *Accounting Historians Journal, 27*(2), 87–116.

Roberts, A. R. (Ed.) (2000). *The story of a fortunate man: Reminiscences and recollections of fifty-three years of professional accounting*. Amsterdam: JAI Elsevier.

Romeo, G. C., & Kyj, L. S. (2000). Anson O. Kittredge: Early accounting pioneer. *Accounting Historians Journal, 27*(2), 117–143.

Sawyer, R. (1989). *How to write biographies and company histories*. Missoula: Mountain Press Publishing Company.

Slocum, E., & Roberts, A. R. (1996). Warren W. Nissley: A crusader for collegiate education. *Accounting Historians Journal, 23*(1), 89–116.

Solomons, D. (1994). Costing pioneers: Some links with the past. *Accounting Historians Journal, 21*(2), 136–149.

Warner, R. T. (1968). *Oklahoma boy: An autobiography*. Tulsa: privately published.

Wineberg, H. S. (1998). *Thanks for your trust: Memories of an untamed accountant*. Chicago: Bonus Books.

Young-Bruehl, E. (1990). Biography should be better appreciated on campuses. *Chronicle of Higher Education* (January 10), B1.

Zeff, S. A. (2000). *Henry Rand Hatfield: Humanist, scholar and accounting educator*. Stamford, CN: JAI Press, Inc.

APPENDIX 1

Examples of Accounting Biographical Dissertations

Bryson, R. E. (1976). *Robert M. Trueblood, CPA, The consummate professional*. Ph.D. dissertation, Georgia State University.

Buckner, K. C. (1975). *Littleton's contribution to the theory of accountancy*. Ph.D. dissertation, Georgia State University.

Cooper, W. D. (1980). *Carman G. Blough: A study of selected contributions to the accounting profession*. Ph.D. dissertation, University of Arkansas.

Fesmire, W. E. (1981). *A comparison of the advocations of Henry Sweeney in Stabilized Accounting to recent price level/replacement cost activity*. Ph.D. dissertation, University of Mississippi.

Flesher, T. K. (1979). *An analysis of the tax opinions of Judge Learned Hand and his contributions to the development of the federal tax system*. Ph.D. dissertation, University of Mississippi.

Fox, J. G. (1974). *A comparative study of selected areas of the accounting thought of William Andrew Paton and prevailing accounting thought 1915 to 1970*. Ph.D. dissertation, George Washington University.

Garner, R. M. (1986). *S. Paul Garner: A study of selected contributions to the accounting profession*. Ph.D. dissertation, University of Arkansas.

Hoskins, M. A. (1992). *The Murphy models for accounting: A test of relevance.* Ph.D. dissertation, University of Mississippi.

Humma, N. K. (1983). *An examination of the role of Eric Louis Kohler in the development of the accounting profession.* Ph.D. dissertation, Georgia State University.

King, T. A. T. (1989). *An analytic study of selected contributions of Paul F. Grady to the development of accountancy.* Ph.D. dissertation, Georgia State University.

Lawrence, H. J. (1972). *William A. Paton: Pioneer accounting theorist.* Ph.D. dissertation, University of Mississippi.

Matika, L. A. (1988). *The contributions of Frederick Albert Cleveland to the development of a system of municipal accounting in the progressive era.* Ph.D. dissertation, Kent State University.

Merino, B. D. (1975). *The professionalization of public accounting in America: A comparative analysis of the contributions of selected practitioners, 1900–1925.* Ph.D. dissertation, University of Alabama.

Roberts, A. R. (1971). *Robert H. Montgomery: A pioneer of American accounting.* Ph.D. dissertation, University of Alabama.

Worrels, C. E. (1974). *An analysis of the published writings of Robert H. Montgomery in relation to selected developments in American public accounting.* Ph.D. dissertation, University of Illinois.

APPENDIX 2

Drafts of Letters Used for Requests

FREEDOM OF INFORMATION ACT REQUEST

Office of the Secretary
Department of Defense
The Pentagon
Washington, DC 20301

Dear Secretary,

Under the provisions of 5 U.S.C. 552, I am requesting access to all records concerning Thomas Coleman Andrews, who would have been an employee on the staff of the Under Secretary of War and Under Secretary of the Navy and in the Marine Corps during World War II. Later, Mr. Andrews served in the Marine Corps Reserve.

This request for records is for the purpose of completing a biography. I am a faculty member at the University of Mississippi and have been awarded a research grant to pursue this historical research project. As this project is in the public interest, I am requesting a waiver of any fees for searching or copying the records requested. If this waiver cannot be granted, please supply the records without informing me if the fees do not exceed $50. If the fees exceed $50, please telephone me in advance at (601) 234–3969 or 232–5147 for agreement to such charges.

If all or any part of this request is denied, please cite the specific law or regulation for the denial, and inform me of the appeal procedures available to me under the law.

I would appreciate your handling this request as quickly as possible, and I look forward to hearing from you within ten days.

The Information and Privacy Staff   March 10, 1987
FAIM/IS
Room 1239
Department of State
2201 C Street, N. W.
Washington, DC 20520

CASE NUMBER 8700558

Enclosed is a copy of a newspaper obituary and the date and place of birth and date of death as requested.

Regarding the additional information requested about the fee waiver, I have submitted a copy of my resume that should indicate educational background and work experience as well as publications and research efforts. The research project on T. Coleman Andrews is sponsored by the University of Mississippi, which has granted me a sabbatical leave to pursue these efforts. The research effort should culminate in the publishing of several scholarly works such as a book, articles in academic journals and presentations at professional conferences. The subject should be of interest to accounting and tax educators, and perhaps, historians. Since no scholarly works have ever appeared on T. Coleman Andrews, these publications should make a contribution to the literature. Since income tax reform is a topic of current controversial ideas, a study of his life and views should add to current debate on these issues. My research efforts have already located all public documents. You will note in my resume that I have published a number of topics of a biographical or historical nature. I feel that with my educational and academic background, I will use and disseminate any information, which your agency can provide to reach the public. I do not have a personal or financial interest in the records.

If the information submitted does not meet the requirements for a fee waiver, I will pay search and production costs up to a limit of $50.

Senator Trent Lott   July 12, 1989
United States Senate
Room 487 Russell Office Building
Washington, DC 20510

Honorable Trent Lott:

It was my pleasure to meet you and Mr. Bolin at the reception for Robert Khayat. I am glad that Dr. Davis had the opportunity to introduce us. At that time, I mentioned that I had been having great difficulty in getting research materials from the FBI under a Freedom of Information request. I hope that you will be able to help speed this process along. My initial request was dated February 3, 1987. I have followed up with numerous inquiries about the status since that time. I received only replies expressing regret over the delay. I had hoped to finish this research project before I retire, but I am now wondering if that is possible since I plan to retire in about thirty years!

The request is for information on Thomas Coleman Andrews and the FOIPA number is 281,105. Thank you for your efforts in expediting this process.

APPENDIX 3

Time Frame of FOIA Data-Gathering Process

IRS
2/3/87	Mailed certified request.
3/3/87	Tracer requested on certified letter.
3/20/87	Another tracer requested.
3/25/87	Received some information.
5/6/87	Requested additional information.
5/14/87	Received telephone call in reply.
5/28/87	Received additional information.

State Department
2/3/87	Mailed request.
3/10/87	Answered request for more information on birth and death of Andrews, plus fee waiver.
6/8/87	Inquired about status.
7/20/87	Received reply that nothing had been found.

Appendix 3 (*Continued*)

Defense Department

2/3/87	Mailed request.
3/3/87	Received notice of forwarding to another office.
3/19/87	Answered request for more information.
3/23/87	Received request for more time.
5/10/87	Received information from first office.
5/11/87	Answered request from 2nd office for more information.
5/23/87	Received information from 2nd office.

FBI

2/3/87	Mailed certified request.
3/2/87	Received and answered request for more information on birth and death.
4/7/87	Received request for more time.
6/8/87	Inquired about status of request.
7/13/87	Received request for more time.
11/2/87	Inquired of status of request.
11/6/87	Received letter stating that documents have been found.
6/23/88	Received letter advising of unavoidable delay.
10/25/88	Received letter about delay and request for patience and urging that we stop writing about delay.
7/12/89	Requested letter from Senator Trent Lott.
8/7/89	Received response from Senator Lott.
8/16/89	Received response from Senator Lott which included a letter from the FBI to Lott.
8/31/89	FBI responds to Senator Lott that materials will be forwarded in the very near future.
9/5/89	Materials sent by FBI (with much of the material censored).

BUSINESS HISTORY AND ITS IMPLICATIONS FOR WRITING ACCOUNTING HISTORY

Paul J. Miranti Jr., Daniel L. Jensen and
Edward N. Coffman

INTRODUCTION

This chapter explores the methodology of business history and its implications for scholars interested in analyzing the contours of accountancy's past. It is written to complement earlier discussions of accounting historiography, notably two papers by Previts et al. (1990a, b), and to focus additional attention on historical case study. The chapter is organized into six sections. The first focuses on the origins of this line of inquiry, identifying the major intellectual developments that initially gave it vibrancy. Second, the authors analyze several conceptual issues that permeate business historiography and explain how these issues have influenced the creation of its predominant methodologies. Third, the authors contrast the perspectives that differentiate business and economic history. The role of evidential matter in forming persuasive inferences about business and economic evolution is discussed in a fourth section. Here are identified the basic analytical constructs that underpin this type of inquiry and the way they have been employed by business historians to form stronger intellectual connections with other modes of scholarship. Next, the authors concentrate on what might be characterized as the workhorse of the business historian's craft, the case study, by describing its potential and examining several classic studies in accounting and business history. The concluding section

Doing Accounting History: Contributions to the Development of Accounting Thought
Studies in the Development of Accounting Thought, Volume 6, 121–145
Copyright © 2003 by Elsevier Science Ltd.
All rights of reproduction in any form reserved
ISSN: 1479-3504/PII: S1479350402060076

identifies challenges inherent in the preparation of certain interpretive syntheses that seek a basis for broader generalizations about the performance of business and accounting organizations and institutions over time.

ORIGINS OF BUSINESS AND ACCOUNTING HISTORY

Business history traces its origins to 19th century institutional economics. Following the example of European universities, nascent doctoral programs in the U.S. placed heavy emphasis on the examination of the factors leading to the rise of capitalist institutions and organizations. One early manifestation of this focus was the prominence in the pre-World War II era of historical studies in a monograph series sponsored by such pioneering research centers as the economics departments at Johns Hopkins University and Harvard University, as well as the Faculty of Political Science at Columbia University.

Business history, however, split from economics in 1926, when *Business History Review* was launched under the editorship of N.S.B. Gras at the Harvard Business School (HBS). This scholarly journal was the first dedicated exclusively to the publication of this type of research. This development was a logical extension of HBS' strong predilection for using historical cases for pedagogical purposes dating back to its founding in 1908. It was an approach encouraged by HBS' first dean, Edmund F. Gay, an economic historian specializing in medieval English institutions, who adopted the historical case study method perfected in the Harvard Law School earlier in the 1870s by Christopher C. Langdell (Heaton, 1952; Reiman, 1992; Stevens, 1983). Central to this perspective was the belief that underlying principles controlling the evolution of social processes, such as law or business, could be discovered through the study of historical precedents.

Business history also found acceptance among scholars because its analytical approaches were consistent with the methodologies of science that had been propounded during the fourth quarter of the 19th century by pragmatic philosophers such as Charles S. Peirce, John Dewey, and William James. Consistent with the methods of pragmatic science, business history placed heavy emphasis on the role of induction in extending the boundaries of understanding (Moore, 1961; Morris, 1970). The process of discovery or inquiry began with an awareness of an insufficiency of knowledge or "irritation of doubt," to use Peirce's term (Peirce, 1955a, b, c, d). This approach, in turn, fostered the positing of explanatory hypotheses whose consequences are elaborated by deductive predictions and by drawing on established bodies of knowledge. Hypotheses are then tested through observation to discover the validity of their deducted consequences. The evaluation of particular cases provides the basis for making more general statements about the central tendency of any phenomenon. This type of scientism was highly consistent with a methodology, supportive of historical research, which broadly involved a complementary process of case explications, followed by the synthesis of common findings. In this way, the basis was formed for the assertion of more general statements (Moore, 1961, pp. 183–212; Morris, 1970, pp. 50–58, 64–68). This pattern was not only thought effective in heightening understanding of past events but also in gaining sharper insight into the temporal dimensions of economic and business developments. It was an approach that eventually became strongly grounded in business education through the adoption of the case-study method of instruction.

These scholarly insights gradually found new outlets in the proliferation of journals and associations dedicated to business, economic, and accounting history. In the U.K., the Economic History Society commenced publication of the *Economic History Review* in 1927, which was followed by the launching of the *Journal of Economic History* 13 years later by the Economic History Association in the U.S. Although many of the studies in these journals had a strong macroeconomic perspective, they did provide an outlet for more narrowly focused research dealing with organizations and institutions. In 1954, a new association, the Business History Conference, began issuing a proceedings volume entitled *Business and Economic History* for papers presented at its annual meeting. In 1958, a research journal, *Business History*, was born at the University of Lancaster. Very recently, the Business History Conference provided yet another venue for such research by cosponsoring with the Oxford University Press a new refereed journal, *Enterprise and Society*.

The success of business history also encouraged the emergence of journals in its kindred discipline of accounting history. The pioneer was the *Accounting Historians Journal*, sponsored in 1973 by the Academy of Accounting Historians, formed under the leadership of S. Paul Garner and Gary J. Previts. This publication was subsequently followed by the appearance of two other specialty journals, *Accounting, Business, and Financial History* in the U.K. and *Accounting History* in Australia.

Accounting historians have also found outlets for their research in publications with a broad interest in the social, cultural, and political dimensions of accounting. These venues include *Accounting, Organizations and Society* (U.K.), edited by Anthony Hopwood; *Accounting, Auditing and Accountability Journal* (Australia), edited by James E. Guthrie and Lee D. Parker; and *Critical Perspectives on Accounting*, edited by David Cooper and Tony Tinker.

CONCEPTUAL FOUNDATIONS OF BUSINESS HISTORY

Another nexus between pragmatism, particularly as espoused by Dewey, and business history is a central concern with the role of ideation in humankind's strong desire to achieve security and order. This notion was eloquently expressed in the Gifford Lectures in 1929 when Dewey called on scholars to examine the history of ideas. From Dewey's perspective, this focus involved the study of cognitive transitions that have shaped the rise of civilization. In his view, the drive to create a more stable environment progressed through three overlapping stages. In the first, primitive peoples practiced magical rites in efforts to control life's vicissitudes. In the second stage, religion, usually heavily rooted in spiritualist belief, was used to explain the cosmological order. In the final stage, science sought through disciplined intellectual processes to protect humanity by gaining objective knowledge of and, thus, power over, the natural and social worlds. In the pragmatists' view, science became the driving force for promoting progress and social uplift (Moore, 1970, pp. 187–190).

This philosophical concern about effects that the pervasive need for security exerted on ideological development had a parallel in business historians' early and abiding search for the factors that explained the great rise in material abundance characteristic of economically advanced societies. Unlike economic history that sought to evaluate this question by analyzing macro-statistics, business history focused instead on the firm and the ways that it created greater surpluses through managerial and technological innovation. Central to this line of inquiry was the completion of a plethora of corporate histories that created the basis for the formation of broader syntheses that explained the rise and role of the modern corporation. One such culmination was the work of Alfred D. Chandler (1963, 1977, 1990), whose scholarship illuminated the vital connections between strategic definition and organizational structure, as well as the effects of scale and scope of operations as determinants of corporate growth. Business historians also extended their analysis beyond the question of economic efficiency and considered the impacts of corporate economic power on the development of social and political institutions. Leaders in this latter school include Louis Galambos and Joseph Pratt (Galambos, 1970, 1982, 1983; Galambos & Pratt, 1987), whose work evaluated the role of corporations in governmental affairs, and Thomas K. McCraw, whose studies evaluated how changing conceptions of business regulation influenced industrial efficiency (McCraw, 1984).

Although business historians' approaches to business history have varied, most have been guided by an identifiable core of conceptual constructs. Specifically, business historians have concentrated their attention on three such constructs as active elements in providing economic and social order – institutions, organizations, and learning.

Institutions represent the rules controlling social interaction broadly defined (North, 1990, p. 3). They may be formal or informal (North, 1990, Chaps. 5–6). Examples of formal institutions include the explicit rules that make up a commercial code or the principles promulgated by an authoritative standards-setting body such as the Financial Accounting Standards Board. Informal institutions, on the other hand, are exemplified by the consensual norms that constrain the action of members of highly cohesive social groups such as floor traders in the 19th century London Stock Exchange (Dickson, 1967, pp. 516–520) or the dealings between 11th century Maghrebi traders (Greif, 1989).

Organizations are social entities that are formed to unify the actions of many individuals to achieve a common goal (North, 1990, p. 5). Both organizations and individuals operate in environments shaped in critical ways by institutional structures. Laws and judicial precedents, for example, regulate the ways that organizations may interact with other social elements. Institutional arrangements may also be internalized to foster the achievement of organizational goals. The definition of procedures, routines, and strategies are but a few of the institutional vehicles that organizations employ to enhance the ability to coordinate and control corporate activities (Chandler, 1992; Nelson & Winter, 1982).

The third component of this conceptual hierarchy is *learning* which is a path-dependent process for identifying both effective and ineffective responses for achieving particular objectives (North, 1990, Chap. 9). Learning involves the assessment of current information in light of knowledge distilled from past experience that may be used in the refinement of new guides for future action. Through learning, knowledge of useful practice in dealing with past circumstances may be preserved to protect society by becoming embedded into controlling institutional and organizational structures.

The nature of the interrelationships among learning, institutions, and organizations have important implications for the structuring of historical inquiries. Path-dependent learning implies that history is not only a vehicle for comprehending and memorializing the past, but also functions as a baseline of understanding that shapes in fundamental ways perceptions of both past and future (Arthur, 1988; David, 1985). Besides explaining our origins, history inevitably explains current conditions and provides indications of the direction of future change.

The concepts of learning, institutions, and organizations are useful intellectual devices for gaining a better understanding of the dynamics of social and economic change. Since learning can be fruitfully applied in comprehending the experiential component of social processes, it becomes a theme for unifying the narrative dedicated to explicating the factors that condition change over time. Institutions and organizations are malleable social artifacts whose dimensions are subject to revision based on the learning that comes about through a consideration of the significance of past events. Through this process, institutions and organizations become vital repositories of specialized knowledge designed to preserve social order and to protect against the vicissitudes of an uncertain nature (Nelson & Winter, 1982; North, 1990, Chap. 11, 1994).

BUSINESS HISTORY AND POSITIVE ECONOMICS

Initially history and statistics were perceived as totally complementary modes of analysis in advancing theory in economics and its allied fields of accounting and finance. This belief was espoused as early as 1890 when John Neville Keynes, a pioneer in the emergent field of professional economics, wrote his classic, *Scope and Method of Economics* (1891). It was a perspective that continued as a norm well into the 1950s and is reflected in the following passage from Schumpeter (1954, pp. 12–13):

> First, the subject matter of economics is essentially a unique process in historic time. Nobody can hope to understand the economic phenomena of any, including the present epoch who has not an adequate command of historical *facts* and an adequate amount of historical *sense* or what can be described as *historical experience*. Second, the historical report can not be purely economic but must inevitably reflect also 'institutional' factors that are not purely economic: therefore it affords the best methods for understanding how economic and non-economic facts *are* related to one another and how the various social sciences *should* be related to one another. Third, it is, I believe, the fact that most of the fundamental errors currently committed in economic analysis are due to the lack of historical experience more often to any shortcoming of the economist's equipment. History must of course be understood to include fields that have acquired different names as a consequence of specialization, such as, prehistoric events and ethnology (anthropology).

This traditional view about the importance of history, however, experienced a major transformation in the 1960s with the rise in popularity among scholars of more positivistic approaches to economic inquiry. Accounting scholars began to search for new paradigms because of the negative assessment of U.S. business education made in studies sponsored by both the Ford and Carnegie Foundations. These reports criticized business studies as lacking intellectual rigor, for being insufficiently analytical and overly descriptive, and for being devoid of well-defined theoretical foundations (Gordon & Howell, 1959; Pierson, 1959; Whitely, 1986).

Although these criticisms sparked many responses to revive the faltering image of business studies, most of the new directions taken shared a strong interest in establishing their intellectual edifices on firm, positivistic foundations. The advance of the new positivism was also strongly encouraged and supported by improvements in computer technology that enhanced capacities for gathering, accessing, and analyzing very large collections of data. Moreover, a greater enthusiasm for formal theory and analysis was fostered by advances in applied mathematics that occurred during World War II and the years leading to the

Sputnik era, advances that were probably strongly tied to the resettlement of German mathematicians in U.S. institutions during the 1930s and 1940s. Following the example of financial economics, business studies, including accounting, sought to become more precise social sciences whose understanding could be expanded by the more intensive use of quantitative methods of analysis (Blaug, 1992; Gray, 1989). This tendency was reinforced by the influential writings of theoreticians of scientific method like Sir Karl Popper who, partly on logical grounds, eschewed inductive reasoning processes, such as historical analysis, in favor of more deductive approaches. In this latter case, researchers would propose hypotheses derived from logico-mathematical processes whose validity was tested by rigorous statistical tests of falsifiability (Ackerman, 1976; Blaug, 1992; Popper, 1957). The goal of the new scientific approach in economics was articulated by one of its most distinguished proponents Milton Friedman (1953, p. 5):

> I venture the judgment, however, that currently in the Western world, and especially in the United States, differences about economic policy among disinterested citizens derive predominantly from different predictions about the economic consequences of taking action – differences that in principle can be eliminated by the progress of positive economics – rather than from fundamental differences in basic values, differences about which men can ultimately only fight.

The new positivism, which was rooted in a much improved ability to handle very large data sets and to fashion more complex mathematical representations, influenced accounting research in several ways. Early work translated traditional accounting measurement concepts into formal mathematical structures to facilitate the analysis of their properties and to serve as a basis for theory development (Demski & Feltham, 1970; Ijiri, 1965, 1967; Kaplan, 1969). Concurrently, research was directed toward assessing how accounting information affected financial market efficiency (Ball & Brown, 1968; Beaver, 1969). Later scholars began applying the same analytical techniques for comprehending the general problems of agency that shape both internal and external corporate relationships (Watts & Zimmerman, 1978, 1986). In more recent years, some scholars have re-established contact with the mainstreams in economics by creating mathematical models for analyzing and simulating accounting and financial processes (Demski, 1994; Holmstrom, 1979; Lambert, 2001; Meckling & Jensen, 1976). Others, on the other hand, who have been guided by developments in psychology, have specialized in designing laboratory experiments to assess behavior in accounting environments (Birnberg & Shields, 1989).

The new interest in positivism had a generally adverse affect on the position of historical studies in accounting research. The new paradigms of the 1960s had radically altered beliefs among many scholars about the relative value of particular lines of inquiry. One stark manifestation was the virtual disappearance of formal historical training in doctoral methodology seminars sponsored by leading universities. Accountancy was in danger of losing its capacity to understand the implications of its own evolutionary experience.

EVIDENCE AND HISTORICAL INFERENCE

Although scholarship has materially benefited from the rise of more positivistic approaches, history still offers unique advantages in extending our comprehension of the accounting phenomenon. As we shall see in this section, history's inherent flexibility provides additional ways for broadening understanding of the organizations and institutions that impinge on accounting not possible through purely statistical studies. Mathematical representations of theory may impose restrictions in giving clear understanding because of the inherent characteristics of the particular metrics employed. If quantitative methodologies "drive the wagon," then either the intractability of some representations or the rigidities of some underlying assumptions may lead research away from treating important entities or relationships. Although advances in simulations and in computer technology have taken the edge off, the problem still remains.

In addition, statistics face limitations in dealing with heterogeneous populations. The degrees of statistical correlation, for example, discovered in the behavioral sciences are generally much weaker than the results achieved in the physical sciences. This reality stems from the fact that the attributes of social and economic populations often lack the homogeneity of populations discoverable in the natural world. This difficultly is partly a function of the hazards of defining categories with uniform characteristics within the social realm and partly a function of the free choice among the members of human populations to modify their behavioral patterns in significant ways across a broad spectrum of alternatives. Thus, the evaluation of the true condition of man requires not only quantitative approaches but also methods that are both sensitive and accommodating to the wide range of behavioral differences that are frequently embedded in seemingly similar social categories.

Historical methods, we argue, offer substantial advantages to researchers in accounting for four types of problems: (1) multi-factorial analyses; (2) multi-period analyses; (3) small or skewed population studies; and (4) tests of falsifiability and theoretical amplifications. Historical narratives, for example, may amplify the discoveries of quantitative analyses because of their capacity for evaluating complex arrays of factors that often extend beyond the narrow boundaries of accounting. History also serves as an ideal medium for incorporating and synthesizing the research derived from interdisciplinary sources. In addition, the ability to accommodate *multi-factorial analyses* helps historical approaches to avoid the problem of reductionism to which quantitative approaches may by subject because of the need to design manageable and efficient algorithmic expressions. Moreover, history provides the potential for deeper contextual analysis than is possible through literature reviews of statistical-based research because of this ability to incorporate findings from interdisciplinary sources that relate to general accounting questions. Generalizations about such broad questions as, for example, how accounting information influenced the establishment of corporate governance structures in U.S. financial markets, exemplify the type of broad, complex questions more readily and convincingly addressed through historical narratives than quantitative modeling.

Because of its inherent ability to accommodate multiple factors, historical case studies can provide more detailed analyses about particular events and circumstances than possible in purely statistical studies. In these instances, the ability to assess a wide range of contextual detail surpasses the analytic scope of statistical studies that necessarily concentrate on only a limited range of explanatory variables. The multi-factorial dimension also helps history avoid the problems of reductionism to which more quantitative methods may be more prone because of the need to design efficient algorithmic expressions. In addition, the flexibility also allows historical studies to draw on the findings of both quantitative and qualitative studies, including scholarship beyond the bounds of business and economic affairs.

In addition, historical analysis is well suited for *multi-period analyses*. Questions relating to how a central phenomenon evolved over time are better handled by the traditional tools of history rather than more temporally restricted empirical methods. The latter, again because of the problems of computational efficiency, remain best suited for either static equilibrium analysis or dynamic analysis restricted to a few periods. Broad questions, like, for example, how did accounting facilitate the rise of Western industrialism, are poorly comprehended by relying exclusively on statistical modes of inquiry. Moreover, the flexibility of historical narratives effectively accommodates the complexities of dialectical analyses that deal with opposing points of view about the significance of aspects of accounting change. Unlike statistical hypotheses testing that culminates in either a reject or an accept decision, dialectical analysis involves the blending of elements derived from competing theses over time. The discovery of truth in such cases is incremental, resulting from debate and consensus formation rather than rigid tests of falsifiability. It is a process that does not reject out-of-hand explanations that are not susceptible to statistical evaluation, but rather seeks to amalgamate new intellectual perspectives by evaluating the temporal interaction of competing systems of thought.

How, then, can history be applied in accounting inquiry? In the following sections, we provide guidance for the conduct of two approaches to the development of historical studies of accounting – *case study*, that serves as a building block for broader statements about how accounting organizations and institutions change over time, and *synthesis*, that distills knowledge of historical cases into an understanding of the larger factors at work.

THE HISTORICAL CASE STUDY

The historical case study provides an effective means for developing and formulating generalizations about socioeconomic environments. Although these generalizations are subject to further verification, they can be robust when the environment is dominated by a few entities. The approach is highly suitable in research because many of the most dynamic sectors of modern industrial economies are dominated by oligopolistic structures that account for a high proportion of economic activity. Oligopolies are important in the industrial sector, for example, because they usually represent the major sources of capital spending, research and development, and other activities that are necessary for economic productivity and growth. These relationships between size and overall levels of activity within a segment are not limited to industry; they also have counterparts in crucial service businesses. Consider, for example, that four service industries that were central in creating the modern U.S. economy – railroads, telecommunications, and electrical and gas utilities – were also characterized by either oligopolistic or monopolistic structures. Business historians, in developing the theory of the firm, have long exploited this fact by developing their models from intensive studies of giant enterprises, particularly in the manufacturing sector (Averitt, 1968, Chaps. 2–4; Baskin & Miranti, 1997, pp. 213–219). Similarly, the efficiency of research and the explanatory power of theory in accounting could be enhanced by focusing on the largest firms whose activities have the greatest economic impacts. Moreover, the advantages accruing from such stratified sampling employing case method is not limited to economic organizations. Political and social organizations tend also to be highly concentrated in modern society, thus providing an additional rationale for evaluating historical questions dealing with these matters in large unit contexts.

Historical case studies can also serve as tests of falsifiability, especially where theory and research design is solely formulated by means of deductive processes. Reference to a more complete representation of experience thus serves as a vital check on reality for generalizations based largely on logical abstractions that assume ideal conditions, such as the existence of market efficiency – an assumption that permeates many studies in both accounting and finance.

Additionally, case studies may amplify theory by illustrating how unique circumstances in particular epochs shaped outcomes that were broadly consistent with the predictions of theory. These differences should be expected because the underlying assumptions of theory incorporate ideal circumstances that frequently do not exist in history. Moreover, theories derived primarily from logico-mathematical processes tend to limit variables to achieve greater precision and, thus, may not be fully reflective of the complexities of real-world contexts.

Approaches to Historical Case Study

What general guidelines then can scholars interested in case studies employ in advancing their research agendas? First, it is necessary to adhere to a standard of relevance in research design. Second, a framework for evaluating the limitations of evidentiary matter developed through case studies is needed. Finally, case findings must be evaluated in order to amplify the broader understanding of related theoretical or historical contexts.

Scholarly Significance

A pitfall in the development of case studies is the danger of creating a work that may be dismissed as lacking scholarly significance on either antiquarian or anecdotal grounds. Antiquarianism results from a short-sighted approach to a research problem that fails to consider adequately the broader implications of its findings to major interpretative themes and theoretical constructs. It is a form of scholarly myopia that results in a detachment between the experience of a case subject and the broader social or economic context in which it operates. Many coffee-table books, for example, that lovingly communicate the details of antique furniture or pottery styles fall into this category because they fail to demonstrate how these artistic expressions relate to broader interpretative themes. While such works often communicate substantial detail of the past, they are incomplete applications of the research paradigm because they fail to establish intellectual bridges to the history of ideas and events.

The second problem, that of anecdotal irrelevance, is the product of inappropriate sampling. It stems from the limited explanatory power of a small sample to explain the central tendencies in phenomena composed of large populations. It is a concept that essentially deals with both the statistical irrelevance of and the biases implicit in particular cases in explaining the behavior of large populations. In these cases, it is difficult to assess the generality of a single case with a high degree of confidence because it represents only a small fraction of a much broader encompassing population of unknown character.

Although large populations diminish the usefulness of cases for many questions, there are many important populations in business and economics where a more intensive analysis of particular circumstances provides distinct advantages. As noted above, one such case involves problems dealing with small populations or skewed populations where much of the phenomenon is explainable by the actions of a small number of dominant component elements. In modern economic settings, the great scale and scope of the operations of a relatively few enterprises frequently are major determinants of the direction of change over time. The understanding of social dynamics may be enhanced through case studies of the policies and actions of leading units that have been key agencies in providing order in highly concentrated segments. This technique has been fruitfully exploited in business history case studies where detailed evaluations of giant enterprises have provided support for the specification of useful explanatory paradigms. Perhaps best known in this regard is Chandler (1963, 1977, 1990) who, in explaining how business organizational structures and strategies intersect to shape the development of modern industrial economies, drew on the findings of a plethora of individual corporate histories.

In other instances, where a researched phenomenon embodies a large, homogeneous population, the best that the case study may render is illustrations of the degree to which particular circumstances tend to conform to the predictions of theories derived from more intensive statistical evaluation. Although the findings of such cases may raise doubt about the validity of a theoretical proposition, its significance in dealing with truly large population phenomena is not great because of the low degree of confidence that must be assigned to its conclusions. In this instance, the case is truly an anecdote whose characteristics may or may not reflect the true characteristics of the broader population from whence it is derived. In the case of gas kinetics, for example, the location of a single molecule is not very significant for comprehending the controlling phenomenon. Rather, kinetic action is comprehended in terms of statistical distributions in relation to area and heat levels.

Focus and Planning
The related problem of case-study scope and design is greatly facilitated in business history by its traditional focus on organizations. This concentration unifies the analysis on a particular entity by placing entity-specific limits on the bounds of time, place, and development. Concentration on the experience of a single entity constrains the horizons of the analysis in ways that are more difficult to achieve in histories dealing with more general or intangible issues that are difficult to associate with strict chronologies or particular events. Compare, for example, the focus of a corporate history with that encountered in many intellectual or social histories. Because of their pervasive and often amorphous nature, the concepts

that permeate the social and intellectual analyses are more difficult to place in tightly specified frames of reference. Selection of an organizational focus, on the other hand, usually enables the research project to be structured around readily identifiable milestones in an entity's evolution. Such a focus is especially helpful in limiting a case study's temporal boundaries and, thus, avoiding the problem of writing the "history of the world" because of a poorly defined, research design.

An organizational emphasis is also advantageous because these units are so central to a broad range of activities in modern social settings. Organizations serve as primary vehicles for concentrating the substantial economic or political power that shapes the dynamics of modern society. Moreover, they may serve as key agencies for allocating scarce resources and for coordinating the many interdependent and specialized elements that make up the modern scene.

The Larger Context

Another feature of case work in business history is that it often provides insight into at least two central questions. First, such studies may provide additional enlightenment about important aspects of the epochs in which the featured activities of a research project occur. In this instance, the new factual information discovered through the case study may facilitate the process of either qualifying or even redefining the interpretation of the significance of major eras such as the Great Depression, World War II, or the Industrial Revolution. Alternatively, such cases may function either as tests of prevailing socioeconomic theories or as building blocks useful in the erection of new theoretical constructs. The focus of analysis in these latter cases, however, is frequently not bounded by the temporal constraints of a particular historical period. Rather, they often reveal evolutionary dynamics by considering how a central phenomenon responds to the differing environmental factors over very broad time horizons; for example, how agency relationships and the nature of agency relationships have changed in business organizations from the medieval to the contemporary era.

This inherent dualism creates a need for the business historian to be conversant with the scholarly literature relating to economic theory and to particular epochs. Without such a background, the broader implications of the findings of a research plan may not be fully realized. Such competency could be achieved through the completion of a doctoral field specializing in business and economic institutional history, grounded in a particular era such as contemporary U.S. or Asia.

Practical Suggestions and Important Preliminaries

Case-study planning may be facilitated by the preparation of a *time line*, one technique for relating both core and peripheral issues and events that impinge on a research topic. It does so by identifying major parallel developments that provide background to the primary events and circumstances foremost in the case analysis. Such parallelism also may reveal opportunities for forming intellectual bridges to external, formative developments that had not been anticipated when initially formulating the research project. The time line is, then, a planning device and not a formal component of the research study. It may be constructed by using a computer spreadsheet that is divided into vertical columns for registering the highlights of parallel lines of activity. The first column identifies the major temporal transitions that affect the primary research issue. Additional columns should be included to identify contemporaneous occurrences in related lines of activity that either provide background or some intellectual connection to the main subject of analysis. For example, a study of the evolution of financial accounting standards setting in the U.S. might have an initial column identifying major turning points in the histories of the Committee on Accounting Procedure, the Accounting Principles Board, and the Financial Accounting Standards Board. Parallel columns could be employed to highlight major developments that formed an important backdrop to the standards-setting process, such as national economic, social, and professional affairs.

A flexible *database of evidence* is an essential element in the process of constructing a case study. Ideally, evidential matter should be recorded in ways that facilitate access to and reorganization of the data as narrative development and revisions progress. The traditional medium has been file cards on which the researcher simply records data that will serve as evidence in support of the study's thesis. The card allows the data to be alternatively arrayed to support changes in the structure of basic arguments as a study progresses. Data may also be marshaled by electronic data processing. Like the cards, electronic data capture is also susceptible to easy manipulation and arraying. Further, either paper cards or electronic entries can be employed to summarize the findings of other scholars as well as to capture factual information. However, electronic notes have an advantage because they are more readily introduced into the narrative, either in the form of footnotes or components of the text.

The reorganization of evidence to support the questions in a study is strongly influenced by case-study type. *Epochal case studies* may be easier to structure because they often embody a clear chronology of events surrounding the evolution of a central phenomenon. The challenge in this case is the identification of significant turning points that may convincingly be related to broader interpretative themes. *Theory-illuminating case studies* present different challenges because they are organized primarily around the analysis of issues rather than of eras. The analyst in this case must address broad issues but must avoid undermining narrative clarity and efficient exposition by chronological back-tracking and the overly frequent revisiting of key events in explaining theoretical developments. Devices like time lines are useful in reducing the potential for narrative confusion. The visualization of the study in this manner may identify the need for restructuring the narrative to avoid distracting the reader with a confusing chronology. The problem may also be avoided by defining a clear chronology of the evolution of scholarship that guides the study.

Another important preliminary step is the development of an *overall outline* of the study that should include three major elements: (1) introduction and statement of problem; (2) data analysis and argument; and (3) conclusion and discussion of findings. The introduction should be brief and should identify the basic problem to be addressed. This section should provide a summarization of the findings of earlier scholarship and the ways that the current study will extend the boundaries of this knowledge. It should discuss any special methodological issues relating to the research project. It should also adumbrate how the paper has been organized.

The largest portion of the case study involves setting forth its basic argument based on the analysis of data. Depending on the scope and complexity of the subject, this element may be composed of a single or several sections. The time line should be especially helpful in developing the outline for this portion of the study. In this section, the evidence summarized on card or electronic media should be tied directly to support the arguments that provide the core of the analysis. The quality of the analysis is primarily the function of two factors – the persuasiveness of the data collected to support the study's assertion and the logic by which evidential matter of differing levels of persuasiveness has been related to support the paper's basic arguments.

The organization of an argument in a case study may take two forms – forward-conclusion and end-conclusion arguments. In *forward-conclusion argument*, findings and conclusions are presented in the introduction of each section with the material following serving as evidential support. This approach is the more readily comprehensible alternative from the perspective of the reader and, thus, should be the predominant mode. Each section of the study begins with an overview paragraph(s) identifying its basic findings. Each paragraph in the study begins with a topic sentence that states its basic conclusions, with subsequent sentences arrayed as evidentiary support. In a well-organized essay, the reader would be able to read the topic sentence and be able to understand the paragraph's basic arguments and conclusions. Such a test should also be performed in conclusion to evaluate the continuity, logic, and completeness of the case.

Although the forward-conclusion method greatly facilitates clear exposition, it requires planning and thought. Its pattern seems counterintuitive in that it embodies a pattern different from the way many learn new information. Individuals frequently consider the consequence of several facts before forming a conclusion. The progression is inductive, moving from facts and observations to overall conclusions. The forward-conclusion form of narrative, however, follows the opposite sequence. It calls for the presentation of conclusions before the citation of supportive evidence. It also indicates the strong need for multiple draft revisions in translating traditional thinking patterns to effective narrative exposition. The initial draft would be expected to follow basic thinking patterns of proceeding from facts to conclusions. The revisions involve reorganizing the essay into conclusions; facts are sequenced to enhance expositional clarity.

End-conclusion arguments should be reserved for the special case of trying to persuade readers of controversial findings. In this case, the writer seeks to convince readers by drawing them deeply into the detailed analysis of the case evidence. Basically, the study's structure is established in a manner that compels the reader to consider the logical analysis of data that support the unusual research result.

The primary objective of the overall conclusion is to explain how the study's findings extend the boundaries of understanding about the research subject. One technique is to contrast the conclusions of the study with the central findings of other scholars who have written on the topic and whose findings are summarized in the introduction. In this way, the study's findings are highlighted in a way that also implicitly addresses the questions of research significance and relevancy. In addition, the writer may also wish to expand the discussion to explain how the study's findings may impinge on questions that were not initially identified as part of the fundamental core of analysis.

FOUR HISTORICAL CASE STUDIES FROM THE ACCOUNTING LITERATURE

Four studies are used below to illustrate important aspects of the historical, case-study methodology. The first two studies, Brief (1965) and Miranti (1989), address aspects of railroad accounting. The third and fourth studies, Fleischman et al. (1991) and Levenstein (1998), explore the relationship between accounting information and the historical development of business enterprise. Readers new to accounting history may wish to follow a reading of these brief analyses with an examination of the four studies in their entirety.

Two Case Studies on Railroad Development in the U.S.

From the standpoint of historical analysis, the development of railroads in the U.S. is important for two reasons. First, railroads were this country's first big business, and they initiated many institutional and organizational practices, including cost and financial accounting methods, that influenced the development of later maturing, industrial giants. Second, it was an industry that has attracted significant attention from both social and political historians seeking to understand better both the rise of the strong, modern executive branch of the federal government (an historical transition that began with the formation of the Interstate Commerce Commission to regulate the railroad industry) and the interrelationship between politics and government, on the one hand, and the new and powerful economic institutions, on the other. The analysis of accounting developments provides useful insights into the nature of both of these important transitions in the U.S.

We begin with Brief's "Nineteenth Century Accounting Error" (1965). Brief argued the relevance of studying 19th century depreciation practices both as a test of rationalistic theories of resource allocation and as a way to understand the role of accounting in economies emerging from the industrial revolution. Noting the heavy reliance on rationality in the influential writings of Weber, Schumpeter, and other social scientists, Brief motivated his study by noting the little recognized possibility that accounting errors "whether due to fraud, speculation, *or* accounting conventions" may be "an important independent 'cause' of economic events" (p. 13).

Brief focused on U.S. and U.K. depreciation accounting during the 19th century as a domain in which accounting conventions could produce large errors as the industrial revolution brought about ever larger concentrations of capital assets. He argued that accounting conventions led to significant, unrecorded, capital-consumption charges that had the potential to influence the allocation of resources in the economy. Citing commentary by 19th century accountants and historians of the period, he noted that replacement accounting, that understates cumulative capital charges by the very nature of the convention, dominated railroad accounting for capital assets during this period. Also, citing contemporary commentary, he found evidence that business entities that did not follow replacement accounting manipulated their depreciation "reserves" to produce favorable income reports during lean years. He also disputed the claim by some accounting historians that 19th century financial reporting had a conservative bias, stating that "the accounting literature does not support the contention . . ." (p. 31).

Thus, the paper provided a framework for the development of a number of hypotheses concerning the interplay between depreciation conventions, management behavior, and economic development during the 19th century. It suggested various ways in which case studies of particular railroads might be framed to bear on this central issue. Brief relied largely on secondary sources and did not engage in inspections of actual records or financial reports, thus inviting case studies of depreciation policy in particular public utilities and industrial enterprises by reference to primary sources.

The second illustration is Miranti's "The Mind's Eye of Reform: The ICC's Bureau of Statistics and Accounts and a Vision of Regulation" (1989), a case study of the Interstate Commerce Commission (ICC) during the period 1887–1940. Miranti argued that the difficulties encountered in developing accurate and relevant railroad statistics often undermined the agency's ability to achieve its regulatory goals. The ICC, from its very beginning, was involved in efforts to compile and analyze data useful in regulating railroads. Through records required or compiled by the ICC, an overabundance of periodic reports and schedules providing detailed summaries of the actions of thousands of workings and the operation of equipment and facilities over a vast continental nation were provided. Through this reporting process, regulators had hoped to obtain more precise information to help enhance their control over the industry. Miranti carefully anchored his study in the extensive literature on the regulation of interstate commerce produced by economists and political scientists. He also explored primary sources including correspondence, statistical reports, and court records to uncover and characterize the accounting and statistical systems put in place to support the Commission's regulatory objectives. His analysis of these systems showed that serious difficulties were encountered in developing reliable, relevant, and objective measures. "Complex economic processes and interrelationships ... often proved difficult to reduce to precise measurement. In addition, changing public policy priorities or economic conditions forced major revisions in the agency's reporting model at critical junctures. These and other factors at times occluded the vision afforded through the mind's eye of regulation" (Miranti, 1989, pp. 470–471). Miranti stated: "The ICC's accounting model was not a magic hat from which one could readily pull algorithms that instantly solved regulatory problems. The application of mea-surement was dogged by serious technical impediments such as the difficulties of estimating marginal costs of service, the current value of assets, and the allocation of joint cost among various classes of freight" (1989, p. 507). In addition, the study illustrated how the accounting controls developed by the ICC responded to the changing economic and political environment, including the development of more effective markets in the transportation sector and shifting public-policy objectives.

Accounting Information and the Historical Development of Business Enterprise

The third and fourth case studies explore the relationship between accounting information, the growth of the firm, and the resulting nexus enhances our understanding of an important transitional period in the historical development of business enterprise. Fleischman et al. (1991) argued that knowledge of accounting, particularly cost accounting, has been overlooked as a factor promoting the rise of business enterprise during the British Industrial Revolution. Earlier studies argued that management of these early enterprises focused on capturing labor efficiencies and assumed that the management of technology was beyond the capacities of then-existing accounting systems. Based on a careful inspection of records and accounts in several British industrial firms, the authors demonstrated that the level of accounting sophistication among industrial leaders was quite high. They also persuasively argued that the lack of accounting knowledge would have retarded the growth of Europe's industrial base during the formative early-modern period. Accounting knowledge, in their view, was as crucial as technological knowledge in fostering the industrial takeoff in 18th century Europe.

Levenstein (1998), on the other hand, focused on Dow Chemical Company during its formative years at the dawn of the 20th century. Based on a careful analysis of company documents, including weekly production reports and financial statements, the author reconstructed Dow's information system and traced its evolution over the period 1891–1914. Using Schumpetrian notions of adaptive and innovative firms, Levenstein showed that changes in corporate organization, strategy, market structure, and technology changed the needs for information, thereby shaping the development of the accounting system at Dow. A relatively simple accounting system sufficed in managing the firm when Dow followed a purely adaptive strategy of conforming to the dictates of the industrial cartel in which it participated. However, the information necessary to pursue its later strategy of product innovation was far more sophisticated.

HISTORICAL SYNTHESIS

The objective of synthesis is to discover through the analysis of case studies the underlying factors that control the operation of a particular phenomenon such as a theory or the significance of an historical era. It is an intellectual distillation of the findings of unifying questions addressed in multiple studies of micro-components of a body of knowledge. As noted above, this approach may be especially effective in enhancing comprehension when subject populations are composed of relatively few elements.

However, the utility of case-driven theory in extending knowledge of the social sciences is circumscribed by limitations, many of which also affect more statistical modes of truth discovery. One limitation is that the persuasiveness of theory is a function of the number and quality of the underlying cases that provide the principal source of supporting evidence. Even in instances where small populations predominate, the number of case studies selected may not capture the full range of significant factors that shape an historical development. New discoveries through casework might cause revision of central findings of prevailing generalizations. Moreover, the quality and significance of data in supporting cases may vary depending on the scope or the scholarly skills of preparers. The usefulness of underlying evidential matter may also be undermined by a lack of congruence between the questions addressed in case studies and those that unify a synthetic effort.

The process of synthesis building is always prone to revision and qualification because of the fundamental dynamism of scholarship. Case-driven theories are subject to modification because of the subsequent extension of knowledge stemming from the findings of new case analyses. Syntheses may also require revision because of the differing perspectives that shape scholarly agendas associated with the emergence of new paradigms for understanding social dynamics.

The problem of historical contingency also raises questions about the comprehensiveness and explanatory power of any theory. The study of social evolutionary processes frequently focuses on the crystallization of specific arrays of institutional arrangements and the rejection or marginalization of alternative forms for governing some aspect of collective activity. Because the predominant emphasis in historical studies has been on the explanation of what has succeeded in the past, the significance of paths not chosen is usually overlooked. However, the discourse that supported abandoned social forms may provide later scholars a rich but overlooked source of propositions and insights that may ultimately be employed to challenge the intellectual foundations of mainstream explanatory constructs. A variant has to do with the limitations imposed by narrative perspective in synthesis building. Frequently, social evolutionary processes are explained primarily from the point of view of one or a few groups whose interests have been positively affected. What is usually not evaluated extensively is the impact of such transitions on groups that did not benefit from such change. This common limitation in explanatory scope encourages the articulation of antithetical responses that seek the revision of accepted generalizations and give vibrancy to scholarly dialectics.

Yet, in spite of the mutable nature of the synthesis, its continued amplification is an important goal for case-based research. It serves as a dark mirror through which our mind's eye comprehends the nature of "institutional." It provides a vital intellectual orientation in identifying where we have come from, where we are, and whence we are headed. For these and other reasons, synthesis building will remain an important goal in business and accounting history.

The scholarly work of Chandler provides an excellent example of how case-study analysis has been used to support the development of more general theoretical statements. In Chandler's case, such research supported the formulation of theory on two fronts. The first focus was economic and dealt with the issues that explain the rise of the modern industrial corporation. The second was social and conceived the factors that explain the rise of an identifiable class of professional managers in modern society. The key insights about these reciprocal questions are embedded in three of Chandler's major works. The first, *Strategy and Structure* (1963), was an exploratory study of the experience of four leading corporations that adumbrated the interplay between planning and organization that facilitated the rise of giant industrial enterprise in the U.S. Subsequently, the more deeply researched *The Visible Hand* (1977) not only established a broader-based model to understand corporate evolution but also the rise of modern professional management. Finally, these scholarly insights into the process of institutional and professional evolution were extended to a global context in *Scale and Scope* (1990) in which Chandler explained how these broad patterns of change accommodated unique international circumstances.

The economic question had to do with the shortcomings of the Neoclassical model of the firm to explain the economics of leading firms in modern oligopolistic settings. In the framework of this traditional analysis inherited from Adam Smith and David Ricardo, business entities were assumed to lack any substantial market power, compelled to compete solely on the basis of price. Under this scenario, price operated as a major dynamic for the market forces, characterized as an "invisible hand" by Smith, in that the efficient production and distribution of goods and services in an economy was assured. Although a reasonable representation of the vast number of small firms that composed pre-industrial economies, it was a model found wanting in analyzing the economics of the giant business enterprises that transformed advanced societies beginning in the last quarter of the 19th century. This question became the focus of the work of many generations of scholars in economics and business, as well as the investigative activities of key governmental agencies with economic oversight responsibilities, such as the U.S. Industrial Commission and the Federal Trade Commission.

In his search for a theoretical framework to explain this transition, Chandler employed a methodology that was primarily informed by the findings of cases rather than by the predictions of other theoretical systems. This method is made especially clear in the introductory chapter to *The Visible Hand* where he sets forth seven questions that guide his analysis of the vast body of sources consisting principally of corporate histories and annual reports, business biographies, and governmental reports. What emerges from Chandler's work is a theory that not only explains why particular industries became oligopolistic and others did not, but also details the precise timing of this transition in both the national and international environments. Chandler's analysis also places in perspective the impacts of technology on economic development, particularly from the development of three new energy sources – coal, electricity, and petroleum. His work makes clear why successful concentration only emerged in a relatively few industries with high fixed-cost structures where unit manufacturing costs could be dramatically reduced by long production throughputs of highly standardized products. This new class of firm was vital to a national economy because it served as the major source of investment in such growth-inducing activities as research and development and capital spending. Moreover, Chandler's theory demonstrates how transaction-cost reductions could be achieved by a successful blending of strategic plans and organizational struc- tures. It also clarified how strategy, innovation, and organization became central elements in the corporate learning processes of giant business enterprises.

What has proved most controversial in the Chandlerian economic theorizing is the great emphasis placed on firm-specific and industry-specific factors and the limited influence of social-political factors in explaining the rise of U.S. big business. Chandler saw little impact on the process of firm development and growth from major national policies articulated to confront the problem of industrial concentration in a democratic society, such as anti-trust legislation.

The second theoretical issue related to the emergence of an identifiable class of professional managers in U.S. society as an adjunct to late 19th century industrialization. This question was motivated by two separate lines of historic in- terpretation. The first was the search for an alternative to the Progressive thesis that developed prior to World War II that identified the rise of a liberal, national state as the defining feature of the new society that emerged in the U.S. during the 20th century. Chandler and other scholars of his generation instead argued that a more fitting symbol of change was the rise of giant organizations, not only in business but also in government and other dimensions of national social life. A second point of departure was with the characterization put forth by New Left historians such as Josephson, who in the 1930s attributed the success of big business to the machina- tions of a corrupt and ruthless class of "robber barons" (Josephson, 1934). Drawing on Weber's works on bureaucracy and Parsons' functionalist theory of professional development, Chandler refuted the robber-baron thesis by arguing that the needs for specialized knowledge to operate successfully enterprises of great scale and scope was the impetus to the emergence of a new and identifiable social class, the professional manager (Chandler, 1977, Chap. 1, passim; Parsons, 1960; Weber, 1964). What emerges from Chandler's synthesis is the image of business leaders and functionaries as economic rationalists, confronted with serious problems of resource coordination and control, who were strongly motivated to maximize returns on invested capital.

CONCLUSION

Historical methodologies hold out the promise to scholars of the discovery of important new knowledge about the evolution of accounting institutions and organizations. The case study and the general synthesis are two predominant forms of inquiry in this field that may be effectively used to evaluate specific questions whose central elements have specific attributes that are difficult to address using purely quantitative techniques. It is a methodology well suited for analyzing dynamic processes over broad time periods. It is also capable of being used for making in-depth, multi-factorial assessments of particular enterprises or processes. Its findings may also be especially robust in examining the properties of populations that are dominated by a relatively few controlling elements as, for example, the large, dominant firms operating in oligopolistic settings that are so common in the modern economic world. And it is a scholarly approach that has been long-recognized as having high value as a complement to more quantitative research techniques. For these and other reasons, well-conceived historical inquiry will continue to inform research and, thus, to extend the horizons of understanding in accounting.

REFERENCES

Ackerman, R. (1976). *The philosophy of Karl Popper*. Amherst: University of Massachusetts Press.

Arthur, W. B. (1988). Self-reinforcing mechanisms in economics. In: P. W. Anderson, K. Arrow & D. Pines (Eds), *The Economy as an Evolving Complex System* (pp. 9–31). Reading, MA: Addison-Wesley.

Averitt, R. T. (1968). *The dual economy: The dynamics of American industry structure*. New York: Norton.

Ball, R., & Brown, P. (1968). An empirical evaluation of accounting numbers. *Journal of Accounting Research, 6*(2), 159–178.

Baskin, J. B., & Miranti, P. J., Jr. (1997). *A history of corporate finance*. New York: Cambridge University Press.

Beaver, W. H. (1969). The information content of annual earnings announcements. In: *Empirical Research in Accounting: Selected Studies, 1968* (pp. 48–53). Chicago: University of Chicago Graduate School of Business.

Birnberg, J. G., & Shields, M. D. (1989). Three decades of behavioral accounting research. *Behavioral Research in Accounting, 1*(1), 23–74.

Blaug, M. (1992). *The methodology of economics: Or how economists explain* (2nd ed.). New York: Cambridge University Press.

Brief, R. (1965). Nineteenth century accounting error. *Journal of Accounting Research, 3*(1), 12–31.

Chandler, A. D., Jr. (1963). *Strategy and structure: Chapters in the history of American industrial enterprise*. Cambridge: MIT Press.

Chandler, A. D., Jr. (1977). *The visible hand: The managerial revolution in American business*. Cambridge: Harvard University Press.

Chandler, A. D., Jr. (1990). *Scale and scope: The dynamics of industrial capitalism*. Cambridge: Harvard University Press.

Chandler, A. D., Jr. (1992). Organizational capabilities and the economic history of the industrial enterprise. *Journal of Economic Perspectives, 6*(3), 79–100.

David, P. (1985). Clio and the economics of QWERTY. *American Economic Review, 75*(2), 332–337.

Demski, J. S. (1994). *Managerial uses of accounting information*. Boston: Kluwer.

Demski, J., & Feltham, G. A. (1970). The use of models in information evaluation. *The Accounting Review, 45*(4), 623–640.

Dickson, P. G. M. (1967). *The financial revolution in England: A study in the development of public credit, 1688–1756*. New York: St. Martin's Press.

Fleischman, R. K., Parker, L. D., & Vamplew, W. (1991). New cost accounting perspectives on technological change in the British industrial revolution. In: O. F. Graves (Ed.), *The Costing Heritage: Studies in Honor of S. Paul Garner* (pp. 11–24). Harrisonburg, VA: Academy of Accounting Historians. Also published in: R. K. Fleischman & L. D. Parker (1997), *What is Past is Prologue: Cost Accounting in the British Industrial Resolution, 1760–1850*. New York: Garland Publishing, Inc.

Friedman, M. (1953). *Essays in positive economics*. Chicago: University of Chicago Press.

Galambos, L. (1970). The emerging organizational synthesis in modern American history. *Business History Review, 44*(3), 279–290.

Galambos, L. (1982). *America at middle age: A new history of the United States in the twentieth century*. New York: McGraw Hill.

Galambos, L. (1983). Technology, political economy and professionalization: Central themes for the organizational synthesis. *Business History Review, 57*(4), 471–493.

Galambos, L., & Pratt, J. (1987). *The rise of the corporate commonwealth: U.S. business and public policy in the twentieth century*. New York: Basic Books.

Gordon, R. A., & Howell, J. E. (1959). *Higher education for business*. New York: Columbia University Press.

Gray, H. P. (1989). Social science or quasi science. *Eastern Economic Journal, 15*(4), 273–286.

Greif, A. (1989). Reputation and coalition in medieval trade: Evidence on the Maghribi traders. *Journal of Economic History, 49*(4), 857–882.

Heaton, H. (1952). *A scholar in action: Edwin F. Gay*. Cambridge: Harvard University Press.

Holmstrom, B. (1979). Moral hazard and observability. *Bell Journal of Economics, 10*(1), 74–91.

Ijiri, Y. (1965). Axioms and structure of conventional accounting measurement. *The Accounting Review, 40*(1), 36–53.

Ijiri, Y. (1967). *The foundations of accounting measurement – A mathematical, economic and behavioral inquiry*. Englewood Cliffs, NJ: Prentice Hall.

Kaplan, R. S. (1969). Optimal investigation strategies with imperfect information. *Journal of Accounting Research, 7*(1), 32–43.

Keynes, J. N. (1891). *Scope and method of political economy*. London: Macmillan.

Josephson, M. (1934). *The robber barons: The great American capitalists, 1861–1901*. New York: Harcourt, Brace.

Lambert, R. A. (2001). Contracting theory and accounting. *Journal of Accounting and Economics, 32*(1), 3–87.

Levenstein, M. (1998). *Accounting for growth: Information systems and the creation of the large corporation*. Stanford: Stanford University Press.

McCraw, T. K. (1984). *Prophets of regulation: Charles Francis Adams, Louis D. Brandeis, James M. Landis, Alfred E. Kahn*. Cambridge: Harvard University Press.

Meckling, W. H., & Jensen, M. C. (1976). The theory of the firm: Managerial behavior, agency costs and ownership structure. *Journal of Financial Economics, 3*(4), 305–360.

Miranti, P. J., Jr. (1989). The mind's eye of reform: The ICC's bureau of statistics and accounts and a vision of regulation, 1887–1940. *Business History Review, 63*(3), 469–509.

Moore, E. C. (1961). *American pragmatism: Peirce, James and Dewey*. New York: Columbia University Press.

Morris, C. (1970). *The pragmatic movement in American philosophy*. New York: George Brazillan.

Nelson, R., & Winter, S. G. (1982). *An evolutionary theory of economic change*. Cambridge: Harvard University Press.

North, D. C. (1990). *Institutions, institutional change and economic performance*. New York: Cambridge University Press.

North, D. C. (1994). Economic performance through time. *American Economic Review, 84*(3), 359–368.

Parsons, T. (1960). *Structure and process in modern society*. Glencoe, IL: Free Press.

Pierson, F. C. (1959). *The education of American businessmen*. New York: McGraw-Hill.

Popper, K. R. (1957). *The poverty of historicism*. Boston: Beacon.

Peirce, C. S. (1955a). The fixation of belief. In: J. Buchler (Ed.), *Philosophical Writings of Peirce* (pp. 5–22). New York: Dover.

Peirce, C. S. (1955b). Abduction and induction. In: J. Buchler (Ed.), *Philosophical Writings of Peirce* (pp. 150–156). New York: Dover.

Peirce, C. S. (1955c). The probability of induction. In: J. Buchler (Ed.), *Philosophical Writings of Peirce* (pp. 174–189). New York: Dover.

Peirce, C. S. (1955d). The architecture of theories. In: J. Buchler (Ed.), *Philosophical Writing of Peirce* (pp. 315–323). New York: Dover.

Previts, G. J., Parker, L. D., & Coffman E. N. (1990a). Accounting history: Definition and relevance. *Abacus, 26*(1), 1–16. Also published in: E. N. Coffman, R. H. Tondkar & G. J. Previts (Eds) (1997), *Historical Perspectives of Selected Financial Accounting Topics* (2nd ed., pp. 328–348). New York: McGraw-Hill.

Previts, G. J., Parker, L. D., & Coffman, E. N. (1990b). An accounting historiography: Subject matter and methodology. *Abacus, 26*(2), 136–158. Also published in: E. N. Coffman, R. H. Tondkar & G. J. Previts (Eds) (1997), *Historical Perspectives of Selected Financial Accounting Topics* (2nd ed., pp. 349–377). New York: McGraw-Hill.

Reiman, M. W. (1992). Holmes's *Common Law* and German legal science. In: R. W. Gordon (Ed.), *The Legacy of Oliver Wendell Holmes, Jr*. (pp. 72–114). Stanford: Stanford University Press.

Schumpeter, J. A. (1954). *History of economic analysis*. New York: Oxford University Press.

Stevens, R. (1983). *Law school: Legal education in America from the 1850s to the 1980s*. Chapel Hill: University of North Carolina Press.

Watts, R. L., & Zimmerman, J. L. (1978). Toward a positive theory of the determination of accounting standards. *The Accounting Review, 53*(1), 112–134.

Watts, R. L., & Zimmerman, J. L. (1986). *Positive accounting theory*. Englewood Cliffs, NJ: Prentice-Hall.

Weber, M. (1964). *The theory of social and economic organization*. A. M. Henderson & T. Parsons (Trans.). New York: Free Press.

Whitely, R. (1986). The transformation of business finance into financial economics: The roles of academic expansion and changes in U.S. capital markets. *Accounting, Organizations and Society, 11*(2), 171–192.

ON INTEGRATING EMPIRICAL AND HISTORICAL ACCOUNTING RESEARCH

Robert J. Bricker and Nandini Chandar

INTRODUCTION

Douglas North (1994, p. 359) wrote:

> Economic history is about the performance of economies through time. The objective of research in the field is not only to shed new light on the economic past, but also to contribute to economic theory by providing an analytical framework that will enable us to understand economic change.

This paper addresses the integration of empirical and historical accounting research through the use of economic models and historical perspectives. It is intended for empiricists interested in conducting research set in historical time periods and for historians interested in incorporating the discipline and rigor of economic theory into their work. We discuss the potential synergies of this integration, approaches towards achieving them, and illustrative literature, focusing on the use of agency models and historical perspectives in empirical and historical accounting research. We particularly focus on two issues. First, we discuss the use by accounting historians of economic, and particularly agency, models and perspectives in their studies. Second, we discuss the incorporation of historical context into empirical, capital-markets research.

Doing Accounting History: Contributions to the Development of Accounting Thought
Studies in the Development of Accounting Thought, Volume 6, 147–162
Copyright © 2003 by Elsevier Science Ltd.
All rights of reproduction in any form reserved
ISSN: 1479-3504/PII: S1479350402060088

CAPITAL MARKETS AND ACCOUNTING HISTORY RESEARCH: TWO SEPARATE PATHS

An Historical Perspective for Capital Markets Research

Empirical, capital-market studies employ a variety of economic models and statistical methods. These studies can be characterized by their use of standardized data that may be derived from Compustat, CRSP, or from a number of other sources, and mathematical/statistical analyses of several sorts, usually related to regression analysis. Accounting history studies, in the narrative/descriptive tradition, apply economic theory far less frequently, commonly use non-standardized data (although there are notable exceptions), and typically employ narration, description, and classical logic as principal methods of analysis.

A large body of empirical, capital-markets research is based on the application of economic models such as the capital-asset pricing model (CAPM), agency theory, and models relating to information economics, game theory, and Marxist economic theory. The CAPM, with its hypothesis of market efficiency, has stimulated a vast empirical literature on the relationship between accounting information and stock prices. The efficient-markets hypothesis has also caused changes in implications and rationales for the regulation of corporate disclosures. With increased access to archival data, accounting researchers are beginning to apply contemporary economic models and methods to historical data.

One benefit of conducting research on historical time periods is the development of perspectives about current problems; that is, simply, to learn about the past as background to present-day issues (Previts & Merino, 1998). The growing availability of archival data sources covering historical periods is attracting new communities of researchers to apply contemporary markets methods to gain perspectives on the operation of securities markets in previous eras. It seems likely that the occurrence of such work will increase.

Consequently, it is not uncommon to find accounting empirical studies that use models, theories, and empirical methods from economics and finance in conjunction with data from historical time periods. Stigler's "Public Regulation of the Securities Markets" (1964) is an historical analysis critiquing the effects of the Securities Acts of 1933–1934, using 1923 to 1955 empirical data of several sorts. Benston (1973) performed a similar analysis that included both an historical description of the period surrounding the enactment of the legislation and an empirical analysis of the effect of the legislation on NYSE securities. Chow (1983) applied contracting theory and capital-markets models to study the effects of the Securities Acts on bondholder and shareholder wealth. Sivakumar and Waymire

(1993, 1994) examined voluntary corporate disclosures by industrial corporations at the turn of the century using contemporary, market-based, valuation models. They concluded that firms did not selectively disclose favorable information. Porter et al. (1995) utilized the CAPM to study the impact of the American Sugar Refining Company's voluntary, secrecy policy reversal in 1908, and found that there were positive abnormal returns surrounding the event. Although these studies have had their critics, they nonetheless represent interesting and thought-provoking examples of the marriage of economics and history through the analysis of empirical markets data from historical time periods.

While such studies have the potential to contribute to a perspective on accounting history, some scholars have criticized these studies for not adequately considering the historical contexts or antecedents that are relevant to the events under investigation. For example, Merino et al. (1987, p. 748) critiqued Chow's study and wrote:

> The primary objective of this study is to convince accounting researchers that an adequate historical inquiry should be considered an integral part of all 'events' studies .... Our examination (of Chow's study) results in three major criticisms ... (1) lack of a control group; (2) an unsubstantiated test period; and (3) apparent misclassification of events ...

Merino et al. concluded that these problems invalidated Chow's conclusions. Similarly, Bricker and Brown (1997) re-examined the historical context surrounding the event analyzed by Porter et al. (1995) and identified potential confounding events that made it questionable to attribute a direct causality between the disclosure policy reversal and the firm's abnormal returns. Previts and Bricker (1994) cautioned against consequent biases related to this "present-mindedness" which Barzun and Graff (1977, p. 43) defined as "the habit of reading into the past our own modern ideas and intentions."

A principal point of this paper is that it may not be appropriate to apply contemporary capital-markets questions and methods to archival data of earlier periods without careful examination of both the environment of that period and the potential for biases related to present-mindedness. We would further assert that it becomes incumbent upon researchers to establish market efficiency prior to conducting studies using data from earlier time periods. If we have fulfilled our objective in this paper, scholars will be aware that employing an "historical approach" is fraught with both potential and difficulties, requiring more than merely employing the archival data of an earlier period. In the final analysis, capital-market studies of earlier eras are warranted when the historical context of the data is fully considered. With such consideration, we believe that research of this type holds promise for illuminating the evolution of the capital markets and their function in different social, political, and economic environments.

A common problem of empirical studies of historical time periods is an insufficient regard to the context of the period(s) under study. For example, some studies aggregate data over lengthy time periods without consideration for changing socioeconomic conditions, including disclosure standards, the regulatory environment, and business practices and conditions. Yet, it seems reasonable to assert that the complexities, dynamics, and dependencies that characterize organizations and their evolution can scarcely be captured by strictly econometric methods. Consequently, empirical, capital-markets research in which historical time periods and associated contexts are studied and analyzed may improve the quality of the research design, as well as the interpretation and conclusions.

These critiques notwithstanding, empirical studies of historical periods hold promise for findings of relevance to current financial reporting and accounting problems. However, it is important that they thoroughly consider the context of each earlier period in designing the research, selecting data (facts), interpreting results, and deriving new theory and policy implications. This attention is particularly important because capital-markets research depends on a set of assumptions related to market efficiency (Dyckman & Morse, 1986). The business/finance environments of prior eras may require, for example, different notions of public information that render current conceptions of market efficiency inappropriate. In short, capital-markets researchers need to avoid the biases of present-mindedness in conducting capital-markets research using archival data from earlier eras.

For empiricists, an important starting point is an acknowledgment that all data, not just historical data, are necessarily selective and, therefore, to some extent interpretive. That is, all study and recounting of history is viewed as inescapably interpretive. This recognition frees the empiricist to gain a rich, intuitive understanding of the context of the period in designing the study. The importance of context when studying historical time periods cannot be overemphasized, particularly in terms of the design of such studies and in the interpretation of results. Differences in agency relationships and the capital-markets environment may well have affected the role of financial reporting and the determinants of security prices and trading volume. Similarly, different trading practices, including stock manipulation, may influence results. The effect of these conditions on security pricing and trading activity should be carefully considered when selecting and interpreting security price and volume data. Also, the effects of existing reporting regulation and regulatory threats should be considered. As a result, entirely different research issues may emerge. For example, instead of examining price and volume responses to information disclosures, researchers may choose to conduct cross-sectional studies of securities pricing and transaction volume comparing companies in which prices were manipulated with those in which prices were not. Other research issues could include differences in disclosure policies between money-trust-controlled companies and other companies, the role of financial reporting for money-trust-controlled companies, the informativeness of dividend versus earnings disclosures among different populations of companies, insider-trading patterns, and the responsiveness of security prices and volumes to broader sets of information disclosures.

Developing an understanding of the context of an historical period is a two-step process that can be organized using the series of steps listed in Table 1. The first step is to ground oneself in the literature, addressing the period in order to gain a general understanding of prevailing socioeconomic conditions and the capital markets of the period. This effort also involves stock-market and financial-reporting practices of the period. Both literature *about* the period and literature *of* the period are pertinent. Literature *about* the period would include historical studies. Literature *of* the period would include both contemporaneous accounts of the period as well as news stories, stock-price listings, and other published materials about companies.

The second stage of this process involves gaining in-depth understandings of the companies to be included in the data sample. Again, this could involve searching for news articles and contemporaneous accounts of the company, as well as subsequent historical studies of the companies in the data sample. It is particularly important to understand an individual company's ownership and control relationships, as well as possible manipulations of the company's securities pricing or information releases that may have occurred. Finally, after using the results of this process in designing the study, it is important, *ex post*, to identify companies whose data influenced the statistical results so as to investigate further these companies with regards to possible causes of the effects found.

In summary, capital-markets researchers need to appreciate that historical business research is distinguishable from business research that merely uses archival data from historical time periods. Research that uncritically applies contemporary methods and hypotheses to archival data of an earlier time period without considering the historical context of those data is apt to incorrectly specify issues, use (at best) noisy data, improperly interpret results, and draw unwarranted conclusions. Historical research requires a careful consideration of contextual factors, the social, economic, and political environments of the period that provide a customary starting point.

Applying Economic Models in Accounting History

In contrast to capital-markets studies in accounting, narrative/descriptive accounting history often focuses on describing sequences of events, conditions, acts,

Table 1. Checklist For Reviewing Data From Historical Time Periods.

I. General background issues
  A. Understanding general socioeconomic conditions
    (1) Review the economic environment, information technologies, and the general state of the
        stock market.
    (2) What role did the stock market play in economic life?
    (3) Who were the participants in the stock market of the period? For example, to what extent
        were small, individual investors participants in the stock market?
    (4) How were companies financed during the period?
    (5) How concentrated or dispersed was company ownership?
    (6) Identify regulatory issues and conditions. How different are they from today?

  B. Understanding stock market trading practices and financial reporting
    (1) How do today's practices differ from those of the period under study?
      (a) What were considered acceptable trading practices?
      (b) To what extent was insider trading allowed?
      (c) To what extent did manipulation of securities trading occur?
      (d) What role did promoters, brokers, investment bankers, pool operators, and insiders take
          in the trading of company securities?
    (2) What were the reporting practices of the period under study?
      (a) What financial information was officially reported and to what extent was it relied upon?
      (b) What types of financial reporting information were relied upon by investors (for example,
          earnings versus dividends)?
      (c) What reliance did investors place on various media reporting company results – for
          example, the company annual report versus news articles preceding the report release,
          or company annual meetings?
    (3) What other methods existed for information dissemination?
      (a) What roles were taken by the popular and financial press?
      (b) What roles were taken by promoters and brokers?
      (c) What roles were taken by investment bankers and similar parties?
      (d) What roles were taken by company managers?
      (e) What sources of information were regarded as credible by investors?
      (f) To what extent were the content and/or timing of company information manufactured
          by parties with economic interests related to the company?

II. Company specific information – applied to companies in the data set
  A. Apply the general issues identified above to specific companies in the data sample.
  B. Review each company's general history, ownership structure, and financing
  C. Search literature to identify known manipulation of company securities trading and/or related
     information dissemination.
  D. Search news reports of the period for items related to the company, paying particular attention
     to unusual events, earnings or operating announcements, or stories about trading in the
     company's securities.
  E. Identify companies whose results are statistically influential and review these companies
     carefully, related to the general issues identified above. Be sure to understand the
     company's history, financing, and controlling interests. Also identify outside parties who
     may have organized trading in the company's securities.

and circumstances without adopting formal models, economic or otherwise. The most visible applications of economic theory in accounting history research have involved applying Marxist or post-Marxist perspectives, which should hardly surprise anyone, as, for example, Tinker and Neimark's (1987) "The Role of Annual Reports in Gender and Class Contradictions at General Motors: 1917–1976." The usefulness of models generally, and economic models specifically, to historians was recognized by Salsbury (1971, p. 38) who wrote:

> ... [a] model is helpful because if it is carefully constructed it allows the historian to focus upon a particular problem and to select out of the past those facts that are relevant to his predetermined interest. At the most advanced level, historians, particularly those who have received their training in a social science such as economics, attempt to use models to test theories about human behavior.

In contrast to accounting history, economic theory is frequently used in economic history. There is an evident recognition of the importance of historical perspectives to economists, the widespread use of economic theories and models in economic history research, and the synergisms of combining historical and economic perspectives. For example, *Approaches to American Economic History* (Taylor & Ellsworth, 1971) contains eight essays, all of which predated Jensen and Meckling (1976). Five are non-quantitative. The first described the use of entrepreneurial economic theory as a decision-maker, risk-taker, and organizer. Even the non-statistical journal, *Economic History*, commonly focuses on some well-known economic model or concept.

On extending this recognition from economic history to business history, Chandler (1977) wrote: "The new (quantitative) economic history has genuine value for business history, as well as broader economic history" (p. 17). Chandler provided an illustration of such a synthesis in institutional history, which he defined as "the study of regularized patterns of action between organizations, and between organizations and individuals ..." (p. 20). Chandler called Weber an institutional history "pioneer" (as well as a founder of modern socialism) and attributed the development of models as an analytical tool in institutional history to him. He further noted the influence of Weber on Schumpeter, who focused on explicit and mathematical models, and on the sociologist Parsons, who "defined and explored the relationships of individual personality to institutions, institutions to larger systems ... and all three to the still broader areas of cultural attitudes and values" (p. 21). All these writers are noteworthy within the context of this paper because they synthesized history and economics.

It is plausible then that economic models and theories may be useful in structuring and conducting some accounting history research.[1] Possible benefits of using economic models and theories to frame accounting history include: a concise, well-understood set of theories and models from which historical studies can organize and address their subject matter; imposition of a discipline related to the identification of pertinent historical events that allows for explanations and interpretations; and a bridging element between studies with differing methods, as, for example, between empirical archival work and historical work, which we specifically address in this paper. In a related way, this bridging role may help scholars transcend intellectual boundaries by addressing research issues using a variety of complementary methods, the results of which can be integrated at more conceptual levels.

There is tremendous potential in accounting history for the integration of historical studies with economic theory. In contrast to statistical approaches that rely on contemporary evidence, historical research provides a panoramic view of markets and institutions that filter out idiosyncrasies and leaves a clearer understanding of the factors that explain institutional survival and change. As an example, an understanding of the impact of information technology on disclosure practices and market efficiency could be greatly enhanced by historical studies such as Yates (1991), who showed how informational technology and organizational change are linked. While statistical approaches typically focus on the (average) strength of relationships among organizational variables, historical studies can provide a clearer picture of the process by which these relationships change. Yates (1991) found that organizational change does not occur smoothly in response to innovations in information technology, but is often made concurrent with other influential factors, frequently to avert crises.

These days, it is sometimes difficult to determine exactly where economic theory ends and that of other disciplines (e.g. psychology) begins. Boundary issues aside, economics provides a particularly good basis for business history research for a variety of reasons,[2] including those described earlier. Economic theory has several practical and valuable attributes in conducting business research, whether it is conducted as empirical markets work, critical theory, business history, or other areas. Most importantly (as described earlier), economics imposes a discipline on research. This rigor occurs because underlying economic assumptions are fairly simple, as well as both widely and well understood, and because economics encourages concise definitions of the objects of inquiry and relationships. Consequently, economics improves the ability to develop parsimonious models from which implications and hypotheses can be derived.

Agency theory and perspectives provide an eminently suitable basis for portraying and studying many relationships in a variety of economic settings. Agency is particularly pertinent because of its elaboration in the form of positive accounting theory (Watts & Zimmerman, 1986). Although extended by Jensen and Meckling (1976) to a capital-markets setting, agency models have much broader applicability and can be usefully employed in evaluating a variety of situations involving principal-agent relationships – contracting, information, and agent choice. Conceived broadly, agency-type perspectives appear pertinent to a large number of issues addressed by accounting historians.

Agency theory has several features commending it for use in accounting history research. Particularly, as related to the development of U.S. capital markets, agency theory emerged (Jensen & Meckling, 1976) from the empirical observations of the separation of ownership from management, commented upon by Veblen (1904), Ripley (1927), the Pujo Committee (1913), and finally Berle and Means (1932) in the early parts of the 20th century. The capital-markets structure of this agency model involves the existence of a shareholder/principal and a manager/agent, who is hired by the shareholder and to whom the manager reports. This application of agency theory to capital-markets settings has long been embraced by empirical and analytical accounting, finance, and economics academics and policy makers.

Because it emerges from economics, agency theory provides a formal, concise, and well-bounded set of tools, assumptions, and perspectives. For the reasons outlined earlier, the use of agency theory in accounting history enhances the ability to accumulate knowledge. For example, the ability to accumulate knowledge is furthered when a common theory is used in conjunction with multiple methods. From this perspective, business history using agency models can advance an already existing body of knowledge.

The basic principal-agent model involves a contractual relationship between a principal and an agent. The principal engages the agent to perform some service on the principal's behalf which requires the agent to exert effort and make decisions (Jensen & Meckling, 1976). The agent has a utility function specified in terms of both pecuniary (monetary) and non-pecuniary (non-monetary) benefits. The utility function enables the construction of a contract offered by the principal to the agent aimed at inducing the agent to act in the interest of the principal. Both the principal and agent's risk preferences may vary, although it is common to model the principal as being risk-averse. The agent is effort-averse, meaning that it is necessary to motivate the agent to act with a contract having incentives aligned with the agent's utility function. The observability of the outcome of the service and the effort of the agent must be specified. Note that in contrast to the common principal-agent setting portrayed in capital markets, it is not necessary that either be unobservable to the principal. Furthermore, monitoring functions, whereby the principal ascertains the truthfulness of the agent's assertions regarding any outcome or act not observable by the principal, need to be identified, if any. Multi-tiered or multi-level principal-agent models can also be constructed. Principal-agent models are often used to address managerial issues (principal and agent settings involving parties *within* a firm), as well as those in the capital-markets setting. They can be used as well to study owner-manager relationships outside of capital-markets settings, and elsewhere.

Extant agency-type, historical studies that also employ agency theory include work such as De Long (1991), who investigated the role of the House of Morgan in corporate America at the turn of the century and applied new models in information economics. He focused on how the need to resolve principal-agent problems engendered by the corporate form of organization results in the creation of institutions that would not exist in a perfectly competitive world. He argued that J. P. Morgan served the interests of individual investors and did not behave in a self-serving way, even with its monopolistic presence, because of its investment in reputational capital. This result of a reputation for skill and honesty can only be acquired over long periods of time, but can be lost quickly. Illustrating positive accounting theory in business history, Watts and Zimmerman (1983) used a principal-agent setting from which to argue that auditors' reputations served as a bond for independence even in early, merchant-guild audits.

Other agency-related work includes Chandler and Tedlow (1985) and Sabel (1991), who used alternative models to explain the role of the "Money Trust," which was argued to have largely controlled corporate finance in the early part of the 20th century. Chandler and Tedlow asserted that technological efficiency was a natural disciplining mechanism containing these powerful economic institutions. Sabel (1991) portrayed Morgan and Company as a maker of market for companies. He contended that this view subsumes De Long's (1991) reputational model, while also addressing the evolutionary pattern of industrial organizations.

Ramirez (1995, p. 677) conducted an empirical evaluation of the proposition that J. P. Morgan and Company resolved the principal-agent problem by alleviating informational asymmetries between investors and managers. Using methodology currently employed in corporate finance, he found that a Morgan affiliation diminished a firm's cost of external finance. He suggested that these results add "more evidence to the growing literature on capital structure and corporate finance." Key to Ramirez's analysis was a careful study of historical context; data gathered and analyzed by Ramirez were premised on this context.

While accounting history studies employing agency theory are few and far between, there are several potential research problems that could benefit from historical research. Some examples are:

(1) How have accounting and business institutions evolved?
(2) Why do we see differential disclosures among firms?
(3) How have accounting and business systems responded to changes in property-rights structures?

(4) What is the relationship between market efficiency and the informativeness of accounting information?

(5) What factors have influenced disclosure-regulation rationales over time?

(6) How do managers make economic and accounting choices?

(7) What is the effect of the Securities Acts on the informativeness of accounting disclosures?

Several of the questions posed above are contemporary accounting research topics. Historical research constructed from an agency perspective could provide new dimensions to our understanding of these issues, complementing those of empirical work.

For interested historians and empiricists, agency models can be used as a framework for studying historical time periods. Primarily non-historical studies are needed that investigate the historical context of capital-markets data so as to properly characterize and portray the relevant agency relationships; for example, the empirical relationships between various firm characteristics or disclosures and security valuation, or the patterns of ownership and control over corporations. These studies would be useful for the design and interpretation of subsequent work; for example, in the identification and portrayal of the underlying economic relationships, the dynamics of security pricing, and corporate governance. From an historical perspective, how have changes in ownership structures and information technologies affected price responses to events prospectively affecting company earnings? In related fashion, primarily historical studies are needed which use historical data or evidence to derive an agency model in particular. Such studies would maintain an underlying assumption that there is *some* set of agency relationships in effect and would focus on explicating in detail the nature of these relationships. Other studies might begin from an historical perspective and use historical data and methods to assess the adequacy of hypothesized agency relationships specified *ex ante*.

Consider a more specific suggestion. One of the implications of agency theory is that manager-agents with earnings-based, incentive bonuses may choose riskier acts than would be preferred by their principals. In *The Great Crash* (1955), Galbraith described in fascinating detail the investment fund practices of the period leading up to and following the stock market crash of 1929 documented in the *Fletcher Report* (U.S. Senate Committee, 1934). Included are descriptions of the profit-sharing contracts for banking-institution managers involved in stock market investing through sponsored investment funds during this period. An agency model of fund investors/depositors and fund managers, as well as the investment acts taken by the fund managers, might be instructively employed to assess relationships between the risk of the investment acts taken by fund

Table 2. Checklist For Modeling Relationships in Historical Time Periods.

A. Identify parties and institutions
   (a) Managers
   (b) Investors (shareholders and creditors)
   (c) Investment bankers and similar parties
   (d) Brokers
   (e) Pool Operators
   (f) Promoters
   (g) Journalists and news sources
   (h) Rival companies
B. Identify parties' incentives
C. Identify the relationships among parties
D. Specify any contractual relationships, their terms and implications
E. Synthesize a model describing the relationships of the parties, the acts they can take, their
   incentives, and the institutional settings within which actions occur.
F. Identify agency issues in terms of information asymmetry, conflicts between incentives and
   contracts, etc. that emerge from this model.
G. Derive behavioral implications for the parties that might be observed in an historical
   context.

managers and their compensation contracts. Premised on the agency model, an increasing relationship might be hypothesized between the proportion of managers' earnings-based, incentive bonuses in their compensation contracts and the risk of their investment acts.

To incorporate agency models, accounting historians should first gain an understanding of basic agency relationships (Jensen & Meckling, 1976) and the application of agency thinking in accounting (Watts & Zimmerman, 1986), as introduced earlier. The modeling exercise requires historians to free themselves from the idea that all facts are unique and incomparable. From this point, historians can use their deep understanding of context to abstract out stylized parties and relationships to provide a model or perspective from which other historical sequences or relationships can be studied, as outlined in Table 2 .

A CASE FOR EPISTEMOLOGICAL PLURALISM

The benefits to be derived by empiricists' use of historical perspectives and historians' use of economic models are premised on the notion of a value to an epistemological pluralism in accounting research. This approach is argued for by writers such as Chua (1986), who echoed the views of many contemporary philosophers who reject the notion that particular approaches to knowing are inherently "better." The synergism of a pluralistic approach also reflects the idea that, at a practical level, the strengths of any particular method of inquiry are also the source of its limitations. For example, while the empirical/statistical methods used in capital-markets studies are rigorous and arguably easier to assess because of their use of a well-understood set of assumptions (from economics), they lose richness by stripping away deep context in order to develop standardized data that are amenable to statistical analysis. Historical studies, by contrast, can suffer from precisely the opposite condition – a tendency towards more ambiguously defined terms and data that render judgments about the study more difficult. From this perspective, the notion of epistemological pluralism is intuitively appealing. The point as it specifically relates to historical research is that history can provide an added dimension to those of the other approach. Writers who have commented on the value of historical research in this regard include Previts et al. (1990a, b), Gordon (1965), Holmstrom (1991), and Fogel (1965), among many. For example, Holmstrom (1991, p. 155), although no historian, wrote:

> Business history can obviously help quench some of our thirst for facts . . . By its very nature, facts about organizations are not easily captured in simple numerical tables to which regressions can be applied in any meaningful sense.

and:

> Historians like to stress idiosyncrasies and path dependence. We are where we are, in part because of historical accident. What I have said above implies that path dependence and other non-economic factors need not conflict with organization theory nor make its optimizing premise irrelevant. Even if economic theory cannot single out the path of development, it can say a lot about comovements along the path. Thus, there is a road we can travel together.

Raff and Temin (1991) echoed the sentiment that pluralistic approaches to knowledge improve synergy:

> Business historians and the new industrial organization theorists are looking – in terms of the old story – at different parts of a common elephant. We believe that the analyses of each would benefit from a view of the animal as a whole.

The epistemological pluralism we espouse implies a value to capital-markets research of incorporating historical perspectives and to accounting history the application use of economic perspectives. Both capital-markets and historical scholars can introduce an element of pluralism to their work. Historians may add economic models to provide perspectives to provide focus and boundaries to their studies. To avoid a "present-mindedness" bias (Barzun & Graff, 1977; Previts & Bricker, 1994), empirical researchers should incorporate historical methods and perspectives when their data are drawn from historical time periods. Furthermore, even when using contemporary data, empirical studies may benefit by more extensive historical considerations of antecedent conditions; that is, as a background to comprehend better present data and issues.

CONCLUDING COMMENTS

This paper discusses the use of explicit economic models in accounting history and the use of historical perspectives in empirical research. Although there is extensive application of economic models in capital-markets research, there has not been much integration of historical perspectives. Historical issues are often addressed by capital-markets researchers through the lenses of contemporary methods, models, perspectives, and circumstances. On the other hand, business history can be conducted without sufficient rigor if careful thought to players, actions, information, strategies, payoffs, outcomes, and equilibriums are not considered, characteristics often ameliorated with the explicit application of a formal economic model. For a number of reasons, however, adding explicit models may be fruitful in many historical exercises. Economic modeling provides a concise, well-understood framework within which historical studies can organize and address their subject matter. Economic models impose a discipline related to the identification of pertinent evidence and allowable explanations and interpretations.

In conclusion, economic theory and history perspectives can usefully complement each other through their application in both capital-markets research and historical inquiry in accounting, thereby promoting synergism in the development of accounting thought and knowledge. The use of economic models and historical perspectives can serve as a bridging element between capital-markets research and accounting history. This integration may help scholars address research issues using a variety of complementary methods, the results of which can be integrated at the modeling/theory level. Romer (1996, p. 202) observed: "Economists who believe that these lines of inquiry (historical and empirical research) can go their separate ways are addressing entirely different kinds of questions or have a different notion of what it means to give a good answer." This perspective is one that both accounting empiricists and historians would do well to remember.

NOTES

1. It is not our argument that all business history should be framed using models and theories from economics or that even explicit modeling and theory development are necessary in historical research. We recognize the ongoing debate regarding the role of theories and models in historical research and certainly do not attempt to add anything to that issue here.

2. Some of these other values include the historical development of accounting as a discipline, which emerged principally from economics as an academic field in the 20th century. Economic theory is also implicitly adopted in accounting practice, including standard-setting bodies such as the FASB and regulatory bodies such as the

SEC. Consequently, it seems reasonable to use economic theory as at least *one* basis of accounting research. This dependence is certainly borne out during the past quarter-century in published accounting research.

REFERENCES

Barzun, J., & Graff, H. F. (1977). *The modern researcher* (3rd ed.). New York: Harcourt Brace.

Benston, G. J. (1973). Required disclosure and the stock market: An evaluation of the Securities Exchange Act of 1934. *American Economic Review, 63*(1), 132–155.

Berle, A. A., Jr., & Means, G. C. (1932). *The modern corporation and private property.* New York: Macmillan.

Bricker, R. J., & Brown, K. (1997). The use of historical data in accounting research: The case of the American sugar refining company. *Accounting Historians Journal, 24*(2), 1–27.

Chandler, A. D. (1977). *The invisible hand.* Cambridge, MA: Harvard University Press.

Chandler, A. D., & Tedlow, R. (1985). *The coming of managerial capitalism: A casebook on the history of American economic institutions.* Homewood, IL: Irwin.

Chow, C. W. (1983). The impact of accounting regulation on bondholder and shareholder wealth: The case of the Securities Act of 1933. *The Accounting Review, 58*(3), 485–520.

Chua, W. F. (1986). Radical developments in accounting thought. *The Accounting Review, 61*(4), 601–632.

De Long, J. B. (1991). Did J. P. Morgan's men add value? An economist's perspective on financial capitalism. In: P. Temin (Ed.), *Inside the Business Enterprise: Historical Perspectives on the Use of Information* (pp. 205–236). Chicago: University of Chicago Press.

Dyckman, T. R., & Morse, D. (1986). *Efficient capital markets and accounting: A critical analysis* (2nd ed.). Englewood Cliffs, NJ: Prentice-Hall.

Fogel, R. W. (1965). The reunification of economic history with economic theory. *AEA Papers and Proceedings, 55*(1), 92–97.

Galbraith, J. K. (1955). *The great crash.* Boston: Houghton Mifflin Company.

Gordon, D. F. (1965). The role of the history of economic thought in the understanding of modern economic theory. *AEA Papers and Proceedings, 55*(1), 119–127.

Holmstrom, B. R. (1991). Comment. In: P. Temin (Ed.), *Inside the Business Enterprise: Historical Perspectives on the Use of Information* (pp. 155–159). Chicago: University of Chicago Press.

Jensen, M. C., & Meckling, W. H. (1976). Theory of the firm: Managerial behavior, agency costs and ownership structure. *Journal of Financial Economics, 3*(4), 305–360.

Merino, B. D., Koch, B. S., & MacRitchie, K. L. (1987). Historical analysis – A diagnostic tool for 'events' studies: The impact of the Securities Act of 1933. *The Accounting Review, 62*(4), 748–762.

North, D. (1994). Economic performance through time. *American Economic Review, 84*(3), 359–368.

Porter, B., Sivakumar, K., & Waymire, G. (1995). Disclosure policies and shareholder wealth in the early twentieth century: The case of the American sugar refining company. *Journal of Accounting, Auditing and Finance, 10*(1), 121–145.

Previts, G. J., & Bricker, R. J. (1994). Fact and theory in accounting history: Presentmindedness and capital markets research. *Contemporary Accounting Research, 10*(2), 625–641.

Previts, G., & Merino, B. (1998). *A history of accounting in the U.S.* Columbus: Ohio State University Press.

Previts, G. J., Parker, L. D., & Coffman, E. N. (1990a). Accounting history: Definition and relevance. *Abacus, 26*(1), 1–16.

Previts, G. J., Parker, L. D., & Coffman, E. N. (1990b). An accounting historiography: Subject matter and methodology. *Abacus, 26*(2), 136–158.

Pujo Committee (1913). *Report of the Committee Appointed Pursuant to House Resolutions 429 and 504 to Investigate the Concentration of Control of Money and Credit,* House Report 1593, 62nd Congress, 3rd session. Washington, DC: Government Printing Office.

Raff, D., & Temin, P. (1991). Business history and recent economic theory: Imperfect information, incentives, and the internal organization of firms. In: P. Temin (Ed.), *Inside The Business Enterprise: Historical Perspectives on the Use of Information* (pp. 7–35). Chicago: University of Chicago Press.

Ramirez, C. D. (1995). Did J. P. Morgan's men add liquidity? Corporate investment, cash flow, and financial structure at the turn of the twentieth century. *Journal of Finance, 50*(2), 661–678.

Ripley, W. (1927). *Main Street and Wall Street.* Boston: Little Brown.

Romer, P. (1996). Shy, indeed, in America? Theory, history, and the origins of modern economic growth. *AEA Papers and Proceedings, 86*(2), 202–206.

Sabel, B. (1991). Comment. In: P. Temin (Ed.), *Inside the Business Enterprise: Historical Perspectives on the Use of Information* (pp. 250–263). Chicago: University of Chicago Press.

Salsbury, S. (1971). The economic interpretation of history: Marx and Beard. In: G. R. Taylor & L. F. Ellsworth (Eds), *Approaches to American Economic History* (pp. 37–49). Charlottesville: The University Press of Virginia.

Sivakumar, K., & Waymire, G. (1993). The information content of earnings in a discretionary environment: Evidence from NYSE industrials – 1905–1910. *Journal of Accounting Research, 31*(1), 62–91.

Sivakumar, K., & Waymire, G. (1994). Voluntary interim disclosure by early 20th century NYSE industrials. *Contemporary Accounting Research, 10*(2), 673–698.

Stigler, G. J. (1994). Public regulation of the securities market. *Journal of Business, 37,* 117–142.

Taylor, G. R., & Ellsworth, L. F. (1971). *Approaches to American economic history.* Charlottesville: The University Press of Virginia.

Tinker, A., & Neimark, M. (1987). The role of annual reports in gender and class contradictions at General Motors: 1917–1976. *Accounting, Organizations and Society, 11*(4/5), 71–88.

U.S. Senate Committee on Banking and Currency (1934). *Stock exchange practices* (the Fletcher Report), Senate Report No. 1455, 73rd Congress, 2nd Session. Washington, DC: U.S. Government Printing Office (reprinted by the Arno Press, New York, 1975).

Veblen, T. (1904). *The theory of business enterprise.* New York: Charles Scribner.

Watts, R. L., & Zimmerman, J. L. (1983). Agency problems, auditing and the theory of the firm: Some evidence. *Journal of Law and Economics, 26,* 613–634.

Watts, R. L., & Zimmerman, J. L. (1986). *Positive accounting theory.* Englewood Cliffs, NJ: Prentice Hall.

Yates, J. (1991). Investing in information: Supply and demand forces in the use of information in American firms, 1850–1920. In: P. Temin (Ed.), *Inside the Business Enterprise: Historical Perspectives on the Use of Information* (pp. 117–154). Chicago: University of Chicago Press.

INVOLVING PRACTITIONERS IN ACCOUNTING HISTORY: AUTOBIOGRAPHICAL VIGNETTES

Richard G. Vangermeersch

EDITOR'S NOTE

Professor Richard Vangermeersch has had a remarkable career, both as an accounting academic and as an accounting practitioner. He has also toiled long and hard on behalf of the Academy of Accounting Historians. He has not only provided service in the traditional sense, but he has also been financially forthcoming with his endowment of the Vangermeersch Manuscript Competition to encourage young scholars in the field. His knowledge of accountancy's history is immense, and he is more than willing to share this expertise with us. His accomplishments range from winning the Academy's most prestigious prize, the President's Hourglass Award, for the "Encyclopedia" to his less than memorable rendition of "Meet me in St. Louie, Louie" in support of the 2004 World Congress, delivered on stage at the Madrid Congress.

Because of this distinguished career, particularly his close association with many practitioner groups, Professor Vangermeersch seemed a natural choice to author this important chapter on relationships with the practice community. Now that the AACSB has strengthened its standard on professional interaction, this aspect of "doing accounting history" will become even more vital than in the past. Professor Vangermeersch was asked to do an autobiographical accounting of his vignettes, experiences, and remembrances. If the result appears to be more personal than the other offerings constituting this book, that was precisely the intent.

Doing Accounting History: Contributions to the Development of Accounting Thought
Studies in the Development of Accounting Thought, Volume 6, 163–184
Copyright © 2003 by Elsevier Science Ltd.
All rights of reproduction in any form reserved
ISSN: 1479-3504/PII: S147935040206009X

INTRODUCTION

Accounting history can have an appeal to accounting practitioners if the accounting historical researcher makes an effort to relate to them during the life of a project. The researcher does need to have a model for a successful relationship with practitioners in an historical project. The researcher also needs to develop logistical support for project success with practitioners in mind, or, alternatively, taking on a practitioner as a coauthor. In this chapter, I will develop an action plan for historical research and will illustrate the approach with various projects I have undertaken. Three types of projects will be described:

(1) ideas from the past with potential for current use in accounting;
(2) historical celebrations of the anniversary of major events and organizations in accounting; and
(3) the processes through which *The History of Accounting: An International Encyclopedia* was completed.

I believe that I have a comparative edge in doing these types of projects, and it is my hope that this chapter will allow me to share that advantage with other researchers in accounting history. A first step in this sharing is the delineation of the research model, followed by a suggested program of action for its use. It is also important to note that findings from practitioner-based, accounting historical study can also be recast in more academic terms for the "more scholarly market." Hence, the accounting historian should view projects as ongoing, with publication possibilities in many different venues.

A MODEL AND A SUGGESTED PLAN OF ACTION

Model

I finally located a description of the model I have used intuitively for years in an 1886 book by John F. Genung entitled *The Practical Elements of Rhetoric with Illustrative Examples*. Genung devoted the second half of his book to "Invention." Since subsequent books on rhetoric I have reviewed did not contain such a section, I searched for explanations.

Genung graduated from Union College in 1870, prepared for the Baptist ministry at the Rochester Theological Seminary, and then took advanced studies in Hebrew and English literature at the University of Leipzig. Genung was an instructor of writing at Amherst College from 1882 to 1889 and a professor of rhetoric there from 1889 to 1906, hired to teach composition to the student body (Whicher, 1919,

p. 658). As this was a new direction for Amherst College, Genung had no suitable text for the course. He proceeded to be involved in developing various types of publications to meet this need (Mathis, 1991, pp. 8–9):

> ...But he had no suitable text for this task so he took it upon himself to write one for this purpose. His text had to address an immediate and pressing need – it had to help him in the classroom. And if one examines all of Genung's texts, not individually but as a progression of the same text, what one sees is not the development of a new rhetorical theory but the struggle of a writing teacher 'groping for method.'

Genung (1886, p. 217) discussed three stages to the inventive process for a literary undertaking: (1) finding; (2) sifting; and (3) ordering the material of discourse. While granting that there is an artistic factor in the invention process, Genung (1886, p. 221) stated:

> ...The inventive mind habitually views facts and ideas as adapted to have power in others. It does not construct for itself alone; it seeks by a natural instinct to conform its thinking to the capacity and standards of the people addressed. The inventive mind has a tact to get into the ways of other minds and direct their thoughts and desires...

Genung considered three habits that promoted invention in the finding and sifting stages. The first was the habit of observation, the keen and intelligent use of eyes and ears (p. 227). He referred to mental alertness as "... simply keeping the mind ready to receive ideas, directed actively to what is around us and before us, in the attitude of constant interrogation" (p. 227). Genung recommended that the author "... approach with interest in a wide and varied range of subjects" (p. 228). Then, common sense must be applied by the rational and sobering palliative of the unruly imagination, not for the sake of less vividness, but for the sake of increased and more solid truth (pp. 231–232).

Genung's second habit for promoting invention was the habit of thought. Clearness must be desired, so the writer must rigorously think the vagueness and obscurity out of the subject and commit him/herself only to what can be made plain. "The sincere writer will move only in the region where his vision is clear" (p. 232). Next, there must be a seeking of order, the foundation of a logical plan (p. 233). The writer then must seek independent conclusions and develop confidence in those judgments and conclusions. Genung (1886, p. 235) stressed:

> ...But there are many things that will not bear to be settled by snap-judgment and dismissed as if the last word were said. They require patience, cautious investigation, stern repression of hasty opinion, determination to be wary of first appearances. It is often a real strength of mind and true moral courage to hold decisions in abeyance, to confess uncertainty, to acknowledge how slender are the grounds for a conclusion.

Genung's third habit was the habit of reading, active or creative reading. "The habit of reading creatively is what distinguishes the scholar from the bookworm, and the thinker from the listless absorber of print" (p. 236). Genung reviewed three types of reading: (1) disciplinary, for some great works of literature to which the reader may give a little thought and minute study every day (p. 239); (2) rapid, for a general survey (p. 240); and (3) topical, for specific purposes (p. 240). Genung (pp. 243–244) ended this section with a plea to read more broadly and deeply than required by the immediate occasion:

> ...It is of great advantage for him to cultivate the ability to keep several definite topics of meditation rounding and ripening in his mind as once. Such ability may easily become a fixed and spontaneous habit, which will endow his whole sphere of observation with greatly increased significance. Whatever he reads, even casually, is almost sure to contain something that either clusters round some nucleus of thought already in his mind or, no less frequently, establishes a new thought center therein.

While Genung devoted 24 pages to the finding and sifting stages, he expended 55 pages on the third stage of ordering in which he developed research and writing strategies that will not be covered here. However, Genung (p. 245) did give an overriding theme for this part:

> The writer's whole quest is to find the simple and natural progress of the thought, from beginning to culmination, to follow that one order which answers best to what has been well called 'the self-movement of the subject.'

Plan for Action

In my view, Genung's model would lead to a more creative writing experience than engendering reactions to a specific text or topic. Here, I wish to share my seeming comparative advantage in practitioner-oriented, accounting historical research to develop a plan of action. There are four parts to this plan employing Genung's models: (1) reading; (2) formal study; (3) practical experience; and (4) interactions with accounting practitioners. I might add a fifth item – teaching a variety of courses allows greater opportunities to develop ideas because of the captive audiences to provide reactions.

For the first part of the plan, as Genung suggested, I stress the "need to read," or, to use Genung's term, "creative reading." Genung (p. 237) defined "creative reading" as:

> ...simply mental alertness applied to books, and set in the direction of invention. It is the scholar's privilege to make this power so thoroughly a second nature that the creative attitude may invigorate all his readings, however rapidly or even cursorily it may be carried on, or for whatever purpose.

There are many accounting history books that lay a good framework for this purpose. Garner's *Evolution of Cost Accounting to 1925* (1954) comes immediately to mind as a good starting point for cost/management accounting.

Other books of similar stature include Chatfield's *A History of Accounting Thought* (1977), Johnson and Kaplan's *Relevance Lost: The Rise and Fall of Management Accounting* (1987), Previts and Merino's *A History of Accountancy in the United States* (1998), and Urwick and Wolf's *The Golden Book of Management* (1984). The latter book is especially useful since it gives brief biographies of more than 100 management pioneers. I have found through the years the many editions of the *Accountants' Handbook* to be worth their weight in gold. These editions are veritable treasure troves of ideas that may need some dusting-off and tweaking, but can be of high interest to practitioners.

It is important to be able to relate accounting to the societal framework of the day. Business and economic histories are excellent in this regard. Chandler offers an array of publications of immense worth. One should be very familiar with the general history of his country when relating findings to practitioners. World, institutional, and critical histories are also of significant merit.

The suggested program for reading would be one or two accounting history books, such as Garner (1954) and Previts and Merino (1998). A perusal of the many editions of the *Accountants' Handbook* and the *Cost Accountants' Handbook* will yield "much bang for the buck." Read Chandler's *The Visible Hand* (1977). Davis' (1986) series of books on Franklin D. Roosevelt, for instance, provides excellent background for placing accounting into perspective during the turbulent thirties.

The second part of the four-step program is a more formal study of accounting, business, economics, and social histories. Although I was an accounting major "all the way" through the Ph.D., I had the opportunity to take a good number of history courses as an undergraduate. The University of Florida's Ph.D. program allowed, in the mid-1960s, studies in both economic history and economic theory. A course in the history of economic thought has proven especially useful. While I have never taken courses in the methodology of historical research, I have read numerous books and have attended many sessions on the subject.

Accounting historical researchers should at least audit a course on the history of economic thought. What a splendid way to broaden the perspectives of accounting history and to relate the rich intellectual history of accounting in a broader context to students and practitioners alike. Accounting historical researchers should also consider taking a course in historical methods.

The third part of the four-step program, practical experience, is, by far, the most difficult to achieve. Genung stressed the need to be able to direct one's findings to the audience. In retrospect, I have been fortunate to have had a variety of accounting jobs, totaling about five years. The two positions that helped the most were my years as both an industrial accountant and a cost-engineering accountant in a medium-sized textile plant with an engineering subsidiary and, later, my 14-month tour of duty with the U.S. General Accounting Office (GAO). The industrial accounting job increased my awareness of the importance of industrial and mechanical engineering to accounting. The GAO job, coupled with my master's thesis on the GAO, has provided me a life-long interest in collecting evidence to weed out poor management practices. Stints as a staff accountant in a medium-sized public accounting firm, as an internal auditor at Ingersoll-Rand, as a systems accountant with NASA, and as an accounting trainer at the American University in Cairo were also helpful.

The suggested program for this third part is to take a sabbatical year to immerse yourself in some aspect of accounting practice. Perhaps an internship or an extended consulting assignment would be possible. As subsequently mentioned, interaction with practitioners at various professional meetings may yield a practitioner coauthor.

The fourth step is interacting with accounting practitioner groups. Genung would say that these groups will provide you with the give-and-take needed both to develop and sell your ideas on the history of accounting and to explore a potential market for doing an institutional history of a more "company history type." My involvement with two local IMA chapters (Bangor-Waterville and Providence) and with the national IMA has yielded high dividends, as will be seen. The Rhode Island Society of CPAs and the AICPA have offered additional opportunities.

The suggested program for the fourth step is easier to attain than the third as there are quite a few accounting practitioner groups to join. The Financial Executives Institute and the Institute of Internal Auditors come quickly to mind. There are many more. Choose at least two of these groups and attend each meeting. Try to attain a leadership position. Network. Exchange ideas. Bring accounting history into the discussions, especially if you have an historical finding to share with members or an organizational anniversary to celebrate.

IDEAS FROM THE PAST WITH POTENTIAL FOR CURRENT USE IN ACCOUNTING

I will now relate some autobiographical vignettes on how I have interested practitioners with ideas from the past that have potential for current use in accounting. The reader is advised that a separate bibliography of my writings appears as Appendix 1 and is presented in the order in which the items are referenced in the text.

Alexander Hamilton Church

A long-time colleague, Henry Schwarzbach, and I agreed to do the last of three presentations on the future of cost/management accounting for our local IMA chapter in Providence in 1982. While attending the first two, I began to think about revising the three product-cost system (direct material, direct labor, and manufacturing overhead) to include a fourth, machine labor. The idea engendered much discussion and led to a pilot study at Foxboro Industries.

This discussion reminded me that perhaps Alexander Hamilton Church had suggested something similar. I perused Church's (1917) book, *Manufacturing Accounting*, that I had purchased for $0.25 years before, thereby inaugurating a continuing research interest in Church's writings and life. The results of the Foxboro study were published in 1983 as "Why We Should Account for the 4th Cost of Manufacturing" [1]. This article was reviewed in a colorful manner in the *Journal of Accountancy* (1983) and has been frequently cited, as noted by Meyers and Koval (1994, p. 90). Schwarzbach and I were a team for a number of years with engineering colleagues, specializing in robotics and presenting the machine-labor system (really Church's with Hans Renold) at many meetings. One of these presentations was published as "Cost Accounting Rethought in the Age of Robotics" [2] at the Robots 9 meeting in Detroit in 1985. I visited the Dearborn headquarters of the Robot Institute of America to sell the officials there on the presentation.

A practitioner-oriented book, *Alexander Hamilton Church: A Man of Ideas for All Seasons* [3], was published in 1988. This work eventually led to two brief pieces dealing with H. L. Gantt [4] and Church [5] respectively on capacity. In addition to these more practitioner-oriented writings, I have done a series of more academic-oriented pieces on Church [6–10].

While there had been significant coverage of Church by Solomons (1952), Brummet (1957), Garner (1954), and Wells (1978), my work on Church was more holistic and came at a time when Kaplan (1983, 1984) published his seminal articles. Johnson and Kaplan (1987) considered Church a key linchpin between engineering and accounting.

Distribution Costing
If my purchase of Church's book for a quarter was a buy, the purchase of Heckert and Miner's *Distribution Costs* (1953) for a dime was a veritable steal. This book, in my view, remains the best ever written on this topic. Heckert and Miner wisely used a "list approach," one of which was a list of 43 items of additional marketing information needed by accountants. I used this list for a brief presentation at a Providence Chapter IMA meeting to see if a practitioner had some cases to contribute to a coauthored article on distribution costs. Bill Brosnan, a cost-consulting CPA, volunteered to add some "hands-on" examples, resulting in the publication of "Enhancing Revenues Via Distribution Cost Control" in 1985 [11].

If I had not been involved with a local IMA chapter, I would not have been able to test Heckert and Miner's list easily. To be sure, the article was not very profound, but the message hit a vital nerve. Deakin et al. (1988) featured it in their bibliography. The article was reprinted in Portuguese in Brazil in 1989.

Conference on Cost Accounting for the 1990s

If a sales pitch was needed to make a presentation at Robots 9, it took a "super pitch" to get into the IMA's (then NAA) "Conference on Cost Accounting for the 1990s: The Challenge of Technological Change" in Boston in 1986. The promotion occurred during a 1985 visit to IMA headquarters to grade the CMA exam. The proceedings of the conference included a verbatim record of "Milestones in the History of Management Accounting" [12], in which I presented the "glob" of overhead and the "death of the last direct labor" routines. There was a very nice comment on the presentation in *Management Accounting* (July 1986, p. 69):

> Reviewing the milestones, in the history of management accounting, Professor Richard Vangermeersch . . . said accountants have lost track of the needs of engineers. 'Over 60 years ago, engineers decided accountants were placing too heavy concentration on financial reporting and not dealing with engineering problems from a realistic standpoint,' said Prof. Vangermeersch. 'Now it is essential to the survival of U.S. manufacturing that production engineers and accountants work together.'

A similar review was published in the *Journal of Accountancy* (August 1986, p. 18). The milestones presented received top billing in an advertisement in *Management Accounting* for the videotape of the conference. The "overhead glob" was included in a book published in the U.K. by Bromwich and Bhimani (1994, p. 86). If I had not been at the IMA to sell the topic to its leadership, there would have been no presentation.

NACA Reviews
The success of "Milestones" led to a research contract to review the first 30 years of the National Association of Cost Accountants (NACA) *Bulletins* and *Yearbooks*. The project was summarized in "Renewing our Heritage" [13] in *Management Accounting* in 1987. The lead caption was: "There is a rich literature base for management accountants and not enough people know about it" (p. 47). Ten reasons were given for this renewal:

(1) the study of this literature leads to ideas that once were quite well developed but are now lost;

(2) . . . gives you the opportunity to support your proposals with past writings;

(3) . . . increases your ability to be verbal in management accounting;

(4) . . . enlarges your pantheon of accounting heroes;

(5) ... leads to an awareness of management accountants in action in a number of case studies;

(6) ... builds your general backgrounds in such areas as management, marketing, wage administration, and economics;

(7) ... shows the professionalism of the NAA and its members and its contributions to this literature;

(8) ... gives an awareness of the controversial topics in the field;

(9) ... should give you an incentive to build your accounting library by including other things than current tax regulations and FASB statements;

(10) ... makes one more flexible, more willing to attempt changes, and more valuable to one's employer – in short, a far stronger management accountant (pp. 47–49).

The three volumes of *Relevance Rediscovered* were published in 1990 [14], 1991 [15], and 1992 [16].

Natural Business Year
While teaching intermediate accounting in 1989 after a 15-year hiatus, I noted no coverage in the text for the topic of the natural business year. I had discussed the importance of that topic with practitioners in 1973 [17,18]. A colleague specializing in taxes, Mark Higgins, agreed to coauthor a piece on why the natural business year had disappeared and why it should be covered. A presentation was made at the 1989 Academy of Accounting Historians' annual meeting [19]. A more academic piece followed in 1990 [20]. I used this research as a basis for a complaint against the AICPA for failing to lobby Congress on the natural business year in a meeting of selected Rhode Island CPAs and AICPA officials. The strong agreements expressed by the practitioners led to a letter to the editor in the *Journal of Accountancy* [21].

It will be recalled that I added one more point to the four from Genung – the importance of teaching different courses through the years. I believe that professors need that change to explore different ideas from accounting history to improve current practice.

Rouse Company
As another example of the value of teaching different courses to generate ideas from accounting history, I used a lecture from a team-taught (with Henry Schwarzbach) graduate course on the use of current value at the Rouse Company. Rouse had started this practice in 1973 and then further amplified it in 1976. I visited Rouse's home office in Columbia, Maryland. Schwarzbach and I then presented a paper on the findings [22] and stressed the history of Rouse's decisions in a 1991 article [23, p. 52]:

The TRC story shows that constructive innovation in financial reporting is not dead. Corporate accountants can initiate new presentations supplementary to GAAP basis statements in order to improve communication with investors and creditors and provide information useful for evaluation and decision making. Such presentations can also receive favorable treatment by auditors and regulators.

Capacity

At the same time as the natural business-year project, I started another venture that was also based on a seemingly downplayed topic in cost/management accounting, ideal capacity. C. J. McNair and I, as colleagues at Rhode Island, became actively involved in exchanging ideas on cost/management accounting. Since McNair seemed very interested in "ideal capacity" specifically and "capacity" in general, we drafted a graduate assistant to prepare a collection of readings noted in the *Accountants' Index* on topics related to capacity. We prepared and submitted to the IMA, as part of a manuscript obligation to the Providence Chapter, an article on the findings. While the article was not chosen for publication, I have kept the file.

While visiting the IMA Research Director, Julian Freedman, I noted a revived IMA interest in capacity. I volunteered to the organization my file of articles on capacity, a submission on the topic, and help in its dealings with CAM-I (Consortium for Advanced Manufacturing–International). McNair and I received an IMA grant to write *Total Capacity Management* [24]. The first part of the book was practice-based; the second featured historical trends in capacity-cost management; and the third part was an annotated bibliography of capacity-cost literature. McNair added in-depth case examples since she had tested "ideal-capacity" models in a number of field studies.

We were also contracted by the Society of Management Accountants of Canada to compile a Management Accounting Guideline [MAG No. 42] on capacity [25], that was later adopted as Statement of Management Accounting 4Y [26] by the IMA. We have also done an academic piece hypothesizing that the National Industrial Recovery Administration was the major reason in 1933 for the switch from a more engineering-based ideal capacity to a lower-volume capacity basis to meet the New Deal goals of high prices, high wages, and low production [27].

This vignette is another illustration of the importance of being near the scene of the action. While McNair was very unsure how the IMA Committee on Research would react to a history-oriented project, I was correct in assuming it would be very interested in a broader-based study of capacity. The members were particularly fascinated by our theory that the New Deal caused the disconnect in management accounting from an engineering-based realism about capacity to a bureaucratic determination of a low-capacity number to minimize idle time.

HISTORICAL CELEBRATIONS OF MAJOR ACCOUNTING ANNIVERSARIES

I have used anniversary celebrations of major events and organizations in accounting as occasions for retrospectives that appeal to practitioners. The purpose of these efforts is not necessarily academic and/or critical in nature, but is somewhat more festive in nature. However, this informality does not prevent these works from being useful in demonstrating the importance of history to accounting practitioners. Certainly, the writer has enjoyed making accounting history alive for many different people.

Rhode Island Society of CPAs

My first effort in this regard was the 75th celebration of the founding of the Rhode Island Society of CPAs (RIS). The first effort for this project was a very detailed review of the minute books of the RIS from 1905 through 1974. I was not successful in convincing the Executive Director of the RIS that the 70th anniversary in 1975 deserved special attention. But two years later, the Executive Director and the Board of Directors showed a great deal more interest in the 75th celebration, and a committee of 25 persons, including myself, was formed. Action and funding soon followed.

The committee decided to do four publications, one for each of the first four dinner meetings during the 1980–1981 fiscal year. The first booklet included the chronology of major RIS events from 1905 to 1930, the first installment of a narrative history, and reproduced pages from the membership signature book from 1905 to 1941 [28]. The second booklet was comprised of the chronology of events for the second 25 years and part two of the narrative history [29]. The third booklet contained the third 25 years, part three of the narrative history, and the membership signature book from 1941 to 1965 [30]. The fourth booklet was the souvenir edition and included everything above plus brief biographies of 14 significant members and my projection of "The Rhode Island Society of CPAs in the Year 2005" [31]. A detailed record of the work was published as "Tips for Writing a History of a State Society of CPAs" (1982) [32]. An update to 1990 of the history of the RIS was published in two 1991 issues of the *Society Report* [33], [34].

The response to the reproduction of the membership signature book was very positive. Members were fascinated by this memorabilia, as they were by the brief biographies of the 14 significant members. These history projects sprang from my being an active member of the RIS and my willingness to push for a major celebration sufficiently early that the logistics were not insurmountable. I persevered after the initial failure.

AICPA Centennial

While Chairman of the Committee on Archives (1978–1980) of the Academy of Accounting Historians, I examined the heralded Robert H. Montgomery Collection in the Rare Book and Manuscript Library at Columbia University. In the process of reviewing the card catalog, I noted that Columbia still had for sale one or two copies of two pamphlets, "The Montgomery Library of Accountancy in Columbia University: A Second Check List" (1930) and the "Exhibition of Selected Books and Manuscripts from the Montgomery Library of Accountancy, October 1937." The second pamphlet was a catalog of the exhibit at Columbia for the 50th anniversary celebration of the AICPA (then the AIA).

As Genung had advised, I did some creative reading and decided that the Academy of Accounting Historians should play a part in the 1987 centennial celebration of the AICPA, with a special effort on using the Montgomery Collection. This collection was noted in the report of the Committee on Archives [35]. I also decided to write a letter to the editor of the *Journal of Accountancy*, that was entitled "Plan Now for Centennial" and was included in the Professional Notes and Letters section [36]. A key sentence in the letter was: "One of the features of the fiftieth anniversary celebration in 1937 was an exhibition of selected books and manuscripts from the Montgomery Library of Accountancy at Columbia University, New York City, which could well be repeated for the centennial."

The publication of the letter inspired me to try to get permission from Columbia to exhibit items from the Montgomery Collection. It was a hard sell, but John C. (Sandy) Burton, the Dean at Columbia, was extremely helpful in arranging for exhibit space for 35 items from the Montgomery Collection in 1987. The next step was the exciting task of selecting the items to be exhibited, leading to the brochure, "The Origins of a Great Profession," published by the Academy of Accounting Historians with a generous gift from Merv Wingfield [37]. This brochure was included in the AICPA package of information for attendees at the centennial.

I contacted Peter McMickle, a noted expert on rare books in accounting, in hopes that he would be involved in the exhibition. McMickle, who was then teaching a doctoral course on accounting history, had his students do reviews for 25 of the 35 items. This work, with a generous donation from Avron and Robert Fogelman, resulted in *The Origins of a Great Profession* [38]. This booklet was distributed to attendees at the AICPA centennial, to viewers at Columbia, and to Academy members.

I described the project in much detail in "A Few Suggestions for Potential Hourglass Awardees" [39]. The last paragraph (p. 7) is apropos for this chapter:

> In addition to my thanking The Academy for the Hourglass, I hope to have inspired some members to do another version of 'Celebration Accounting.' Both accounting practitioners and educators are eager to participate in this form of accounting scholarship aimed at a major accounting historical event. While there are many obstacles to success, it is possible to 'get it all together' because there is a demand for historical output tied into a major event. Our project attracted funding because it was well developed and had a great deal of both administrative work and actual output to sell . . .

IMA 75th Anniversary

The impetus from the AICPA centennial led me to the then-National Association of Accountants for its 75th anniversary in 1994. During stays at the IMA, I spent some time researching its early history. Preliminary findings were submitted to the IMA as a manuscript submission from the Providence Chapter. The IMA published "A Call to Share in NAA's History" in 1989 [40].

I also shared findings, notes, and ideas with Meyers and Koval for their 1994 book on the 75-year history of the IMA. Subsequently, in conjunction with the Northeastern Regional American Accounting Association (NERAAA) meeting in Buffalo, the city where the IMA was founded in 1919, I presented a romanticized script of the founding meeting. The script was performed to music at the NERAAA meeting and was published as "Present at the Creation" in the 75th-anniversary issue of *Management Accounting* [41]. As another part of the 75th celebration, I was instrumental in getting a contract for Pat Romano (1995), a retired IMA research director, to do an annotated bibliography of the IMA's research publications.

It made sense to follow up on the work on the IMA nationally by doing the same for the 75th-anniversary celebration of the Providence Chapter in 1995. This project on the chapter's history was well supported [42].

THE HISTORY OF ACCOUNTING: AN INTERNATIONAL ENCYCLOPEDIA

While there was, perhaps, a limited market of practitioners for *The History of Accounting: An International Encyclopedia*, the editors did aver that it would be useful "for researchers in both public accounting firms and in large corporations" [43, p. viii]. I noted ten items in the encyclopedia that I thought would be of special interest for practitioners:

 (1) "Activity Based Accounting" (pp. 24–26) by Schwarzbach;
 (2) "Breakeven Chart" (pp. 79–81) by Ferrara;
 (3) "Budgeting" (pp. 84–87) by Brownell and Roberts;
 (4) "Common Costs" (pp. 135–136) by Wells;
 (5) "Distribution Costs" (pp. 209–212) by Vangermeersch;
 (6) "Human Resource Accounting" (pp. 303–305) by Flamholtz;
 (7) "Liquidity: Accounting Measurement" (pp. 386–389) by Vangermeersch;
 (8) "Operational (Value for Money) Auditing" (pp. 441–443) by Flesher;
 (9) "Standard Costing" (pp. 550–553) by Vangermeersch; and
(10) "Statistical Sampling" (pp. 557–561) by Tucker.

There were seven milestones marking the encyclopedia's process that I will describe individually.

Milestone 1: The First Attempt or the False Start of 1984–1985: Schumpeter's *History of Economic Analysis* (1954), purchased for a course on the history of economic thought at the University of Florida, added to the intellectual dimension of the course and left me with the idea that the field of accounting needed a similar book. This long-dormant idea was resurrected by the exciting experiences during the Fourth World Congress of Accounting Historians in Pisa (1984) and a 12-week sabbatical stay in Europe.

I solicited helpers for a somewhat ill-defined project in "A Request for Nominees for Contributors to Accounting Thought" in 1985 [44]. While there were three noteworthy responses to the request, I quickly abandoned the project at that point.

Milestone 2: The Successful Start the Second Time Around, 1990: I received an exploratory letter from Garland Publishing in mid-November 1990, about the possibility of editing an encyclopedia on the history of accounting. Gary Previts had recommended me to Garland as possibly interested in doing a one-volume encyclopedia on the history of accounting and accounting thought. Perhaps Previts remembered my abortive plea for help in 1985.

I immediately jumped at the chance to do this project. Garland provided me the carrot to entice others who had not responded to my first effort. It was also a good basis on which to contact Michael Chatfield, a recognized expert in the area of the history of accounting thought. Chatfield had published two editions of *A History of Accounting Thought* in 1974 and in 1977. I could offer a good background in the history of both financial and cost/managerial accounting, as well as extensive administrative experience within the Academy of Accounting Historians. Chatfield clearly had done the classic work in the area and provided both experience and name recognition to the project. Chatfield immediately responded affirmatively. He provided the "vision" for doing the project. He wrote in a December 24 letter:

In my view, there is a gap in the literature between the surveys of accounting history on the one hand, and the detailed bibliographical listings on the other. A ready reference should be immediately useful to anyone doing research. It could be referenced to a bibliography in the same text.

As with a number of examples previously presented, a coauthor and a network of accounting historians enabled me to solicit input in areas apart from my expertise. Also, Chatfield added a broad perspective and experience, both of which I needed. Hence, the invention stage was achieved.

Milestone 3: Research to Select Topics: There were a series of wide sweeps of different materials to "net" possible topics. I chose the "3 by 5" index-card approach to collect data. This method yields the greatest number of ideas that can be viewed in one spot on a desk or floor, no matter how time consuming. I started first with Leinicke and Flesher's, "The Leading Contributors to Accounting" (1983). They listed 93 names, for which 93 index cards were opened. One notation was put on each card, so that when all done, the writer could view the importance of a potential topic by the number of its index cards. The writer then plodded through every issue of the *Accounting Historians Journal* and *The Accounting Historians Notebook*. A few years before, I had prepared a list of key books in my library. I then transferred that list to index cards. Chatfield's book was examined as well. By far the most helpful step for this milestone was the responses to the request for topics sent to every member on the 1991 roster of the Academy of Accounting Historians. There were 111 respondents to this request.

Milestone 4: Meeting with Chatfield, May 1991: With a briefcase jammed with index cards and a list of them separated into three topical tiers, I arrived in Ashland, Oregon for an intensive few days of work with Chatfield, who added a number more from the index to his book. We also worked on the instructions to the contributors. We then culled the list to 456 items, classifying them by estimated words required. We agreed on edit responsibility for each item.

Looking back on the first master control worksheets (done painfully on 13-column paper), I noted the fact that the coeditors added just a few more to the original list and did drop about 60 from it. Many of those dropped were well covered in other items. A few were judged upon closer examination to be immaterial. The work done at the Ashland meeting allowed me to prepare a formal proposal to Garland on May 30, 1991 (ahead of the June deadline) and to have a contract issued on July 1, 1991.

Milestone 5: Dealing with Contributors: It took a great deal of time in August 1991 to get together a package of seven items for each prospective contributor. These were:

(1) a formal request form;
(2) excerpts from the proposal;
(3) editor's comments on the content for the contribution;
(4) instructions for the cover sheet;
(5) a style sheet;
(6) tips for authors submitting computer disks; and
(7) a sample entry, "Edward Thomas Jones (1767–1833)," prepared by Chatfield.

Fortunately, I had a full-year sabbatical for the 1991–1992 academic year and could devote much time to this part of the work.

I used the master worksheet to post the names of the potential contributors solicited in early September 1991. I met many of them at the 1991 AAA annual meeting, so some additional personal contact occurred there. I also opened a file folder on each of the items for which I was responsible. By mid-October, there were some positive responses to the mailing, but fewer than anticipated. If the potential contributor did not choose to do the proposed entry, another one was solicited or I chose to do it myself. I had originally planned to do 13 entries, but this grew to 25 after this stage. Nonrespondents were also called and formally urged to respond. All correspondence was then filed in the respective folders.

As the entries and disks were received, they were reviewed and placed in the file folders. Notations were made on the master worksheet. The editors at Garland reviewed the first five batches of ten entries received and gave a very positive clearance. Still, the progress was somewhat slower then I had hoped. On September 21, 1992, I subtly hinted by letter to those who still had not finished. When the completed manuscript went to Garland in February 1994, another update was sent to contributors. On September 12, 1995, the contributors were informed of the planned publication date in October.

As Chatfield was doing his items, the editors agreed to delete about 60 of the original items since they were either immaterial or included in other entries. A few entries were added. Chatfield also transferred 45 items to me. That meant I had 70 items to author or coauthor.

Milestone 6: Delivery of the First Draft, 1994: This stage was the most tedious and mechanical of the eight milestones. It involved transferring the entries from old disks onto new disks where items now appeared in alphabetical order, with ten entries per disk. Each entry had to be run and photocopied. Backup disks were produced. The completed first draft and accompanying disks were delivered to Garland in New York City in late February, just before the deadline date. It is important to note the contribution of Rhode Island's Accounting Department's secretary, Lois Pazienza, to this milestone. While I had kept the folders in good order and had "cleaned-up" some obvious problems, I did not have the patience and the training to do this job. "Pazienza" means "patience" in Italian, an accurate surname for Lois. Without adequate machinery and talented personnel, this project would have been much more difficult, if not nearly impossible, to achieve.

It was a long wait from late February to the date I collected the copy-edited entries, July 26, 1994. Both editors had hoped to receive the copy-edited manuscript by middle or late May, so that we could devote our summers to answering the queries raised by the copy editor. Hence, the lost time until July 26 was a major setback for us. I made the wise decision to put the entries on my desk and go home to regroup. Garland had changed the title from *An Encyclopedia of the History of Accounting and Accounting Thought* to *The History of Accounting: An Encyclopedia*. Subsequently, Garland added the word "International."

Chatfield was sent the entries that he had written for responses to the copy editors. I was able to deliver by hand some of the issues raised to the contributors at the annual meeting of the AAA in August. By November 9, most of the remaining entries were fairly much under control, as were the last 24 entries kept by Garland for further review. By January 5, 1995, the task was finished.

Milestone 7: Corrections to the Cold-Read Copy and the Index: Garland did not finish the "cold-read" process until late July 1995, so, once again, the editors lost the prime work months of May, June, and July. Garland, however, did prepare completed copies with page numbers for both editors. We plodded through the process of reading, rereading, and then rereading. Chatfield agreed to do the index since he had a clear vision of what that should be.

I, with my coauthor, brought fruition to the original "invention." My decision to have Chatfield as coeditor was a correct one. However, it took the "Global Village of Accounting Historians" to do an encyclopedia like this. The fact that there is an institutional body focusing on accounting history makes this type of networking possible. It is this networking potential that readers of this book really need to appreciate and to develop. There are some accounting practitioners in this network. They are available both for ideas about and a potential market for topics in accounting history.

CONCLUSIONS

I would like to offer brief paragraphs to underscore topics of particular importance to me.

The Genung Model: Genung's invention stage allows rhetoric to play a role in the selection of a topic. The invention is, therefore, immediately involved with the practicality of the topic. As Genung was developing an academic program to attain success in composition with his students writing themes in a rhetorical manner, his model was much more creative than a program in which students were assigned a topic to be debated. Researchers in accounting history have to "invent" a topic that accounting practitioners will find useful. Once this invention has happened, the researcher has a very important message to relate to practitioners.

Plan to Achieve Success: Much time must be spent in "creative reading." "Aha! experiences" come much later, after much reading. Many meetings with practitioners are required to build the base for suggestions from past works in accounting and for celebrations of key accounting events. Perhaps an accounting historical researcher will be frustrated by the significant investment of time required to yield an invention. I hope that my examples will give these researchers a signal that this hard, time-consuming work does have a payoff.

Obviously, the invention must be sold to accounting practitioners. The accounting history researcher must then be willing and able to promote his/her invention. The stronger the networking with accounting practitioners, the less difficulty the accounting historical researcher has in completing the effort.

Words like "work," "plan," "read," "relate," "test," network," "lead," and "sell" are all important to the accounting historical researcher to be successful. I have been frustrated at times by the notion that accounting history is what you can do if all else fails in other research areas in accounting, as if accounting history can just be done with little background at all. Accounting historical researchers are scholars with a bent for relating accounting history to accounting practitioners. There is no shortcut to success.

Marketing the Products of a Given Study: I believe that accounting historical researchers can relate to accounting practitioners with a "hands-on" idea, which is not to suggest that the accounting historical researcher cannot also frame his/her efforts in a more scholarly fashion for an academic journal article, monograph, or book. The immense time and effort discussed here can be maximized by recognizing that different markets require different tacts. I find that accounting historical researchers are too cautious in adapting their efforts to different markets, and I hope that my examples illustrate an ability to relate a given invention to different markets.

Network of Accounting Historians: There is a very strong and very helpful band of accounting historians quite willing to help the readers of this monograph. The Academy of Accounting Historians has helped provide institutional help since 1973. There are very active accounting history organizations in such countries as Italy, Spain, France, Australia/New Zealand, Japan, the People's Republic of China, and others. There are some accounting practitioners in these organizations. There are many outlets for paper presentations and publications. *The History of Accounting: An International Encyclopedia* is a good example of a project made possible by that network.

Suggestions for Future Work: I have not been successful in my attempt to develop a "Great Books in Accounting Series" for both academics and for practitioners, using the carrot of continuing professional education credits. However, I have not yet "thrown in the towel" on this issue or I would not have raised it here.

Celebrations of key accounting events, firms, and people are always a possibility. I will strive mightily to have the RIS celebrate its centennial in 2005. I have just been relatively unsuccessful with the Massachusetts Society of CPAs centennial in 2000. Again, success does not come easily in accounting historical research, but it can be attained using the buzzwords mentioned above. Genung's model for invention should prove helpful in these tasks in accounting historical research.

REFERENCES

Bromwich, M., & Bhimani, A. (1994). *Management accounting: Pathways to progress*. London: Chartered Institute of Management Accountants.

Brummet, R. L. (1957). *Overhead costing: The costing of manufactured products*. Ann Arbor: Bureau of Business Research.

Chandler, A. D. (1977). *The visible hand: The managerial revolution in American business*. Cambridge: Harvard University Press.

Chatfield, M. (1977). *A history of accounting thought* (2nd ed.). Huntington, NY: Kreiger.

Church, A. H. (1917). *Manufacturing accounting*. New York: McGraw-Hill.

Davis, K. S. (1986). *FDR: The new deal years, 1933–1937*. New York: Random House.

Deakin, E. B., Maher, M. W., & Cappel, J. J. (1988). *Contemporary literature in cost accounting: A bibliography with selected annotations*. Homewood, IL: Richard D. Irwin, Inc.

Garner, S. P. (1954). *Evolution of cost accounting to 1925*. University, AL: University of Alabama Press.

Genung, J. F. (1886). *The practical elements of rhetoric with illustrative examples*. Boston: Ginn & Company.

Heckert, J. B., & Miner, R. B. (1953). *Distribution costs* (2nd ed.). New York: Ronald Press.

Johnson, H. T., & Kaplan, R. S. (1987). *Relevance lost: The rise and fall of management accounting*. Boston: Harvard Business School Press.

Journal of Accountancy (1983). Cost accounting: Does it need updating? (Vol. 156, No. 5, p. 138).

Journal of Accountancy (1986). Accounting changes key to manufacturing's survival, NAA is told (Vol. 162, No. 2, pp. 16–20).

Kaplan, R. S. (1983). Measuring manufacturing performance: A new challenge for managerial accounting research. *Accounting Review, 58*(2), 686–705.

Kaplan, R. S. (1984). The evolution of management accounting. *Accounting Review, 59*(3), 390–418.

Leinicke, L. M., & Flesher, D. L. (1983). The leading contributors to accountancy. *The Accounting Historians Notebook, 6*(2), 7–11.

Management Accounting (1986). Cost accounting for the 1990s (Vol. 68, No. 1, p. 69).

Mathis, S. (1991). *The womb of the future: John F. Genung and the foundations of the current-traditional rhetoric* (Master of Arts thesis). University of Rhode Island.

Meyers, G. U., & Koval, E. S. (1994). *Proud of the past: 75 Years of excellence through leadership, 1919–1994*. Montvale, NJ: IMA.

Previts, G. J., & Merino, B. D. (1998). *A history of accountancy in the United States: The cultural significance of accounting* (2nd ed.). Columbus, OH: Ohio State University Press.

Romano, P. (1995). *IMA's legacy: Creating value through research, a window to the future*. Montvale, NJ: IMA Foundation for Applied Research.

Schumpeter, J. A. (1954). *History of economic analysis*. New York: Oxford University Press.

Solomons, D. (1952). The historical development of cost accounting. In: D. Solomons (Ed.), *Studies in Costing* (pp. 1–52). London: Sweet and Maxwell.

Urwick, L. F., & Wolf, W. B. (1984). *The golden book of management* (2nd ed.). New York: Amacom.

Wells, M. C. (1978). *Accounting for common costs*. Champaign-Urbana, IL: Center of International Education and Research in Accounting.

Whicher, G. F. (1919). Genung's rhetoric. *The Nation* (November 22), 658.

APPENDIX A

Vangermeersch References

[1]   Why we should account for the 4th cost of manufacturing (with H. R. Schwarzbach). *Management Accounting* (July 1983), 24–28.

[2]   Cost accounting rethought in the age of robotics (with H. R. Schwarzbach). *Robots 9 Conference Proceedings: Current Issues, Future Concerns, 2* (June 2–6, 1985), 17–41.

[3]   *Alexander Hamilton Church: A man of ideas for all seasons*. New York: Garland Press (1998).

[4]   Introduction to H. L. Gantt and the reprint of his 1915 presentation. *Journal of Cost Management* (Spring 1994), 4.

[5]   Comment and selection of 'classics of cost management – overhead: The cost of production preparedness, A. H. Church.' *Journal of Cost Management* (Summer 1995), 66.

[6]   Comment on some remarks by historians of cost accounting on engineering contributions to the subject. *Accounting Historians Journal* (Spring 1989), 135–140.

[7]   The wisdom of Alexander Hamilton Church (Working Paper No. 63). The Academy of Accounting Historians (1985).

[8]   *The contribution of Alexander Hamilton Church to accounting and management*. New York: Garland Press (1986).

[9]   Alexander Hamilton Church, 1866–1936: A man of ideas for all seasons. In: H. R. Givens (Ed.), *Biographies of Notable Accountants* (pp. 1–3). New York: Random House (1986).

[10]   The diagram of the cost system of Hans Renold Limited: A blueprint for accounting for robots. *Accounting Historians Journal* (August 1985), 27–31.

Appendix 1 (*Continued*)

[11]   Enhancing revenues via distribution cost control (with W. T.
         Brosnan). *Management Accounting* (August 1985), 56–60.
[12]   Milestones in the history of management accounting. *Cost
         Accounting for the 1990s. The Challenge of Technological Change:
         Proceedings*. Montvale, NJ: National Association of Accountants
         (1986).
[13]   Renewing our heritage: Ten reasons why management accountants
         should study the classic cost accounting articles. *Management
         Accounting* (July 1987), 47–49.
[14]   *Relevance rediscovered: An anthology of 25 significant articles
         from the NACA bulletins and yearbooks 1919–1929*. Montvale, NJ:
         NAA (1991).
[15]   *Relevance rediscovered: An anthology of 25 significant articles
         from the NACA bulletins and yearbooks 1929–1939*. Montvale, NJ:
         NAA (1991).
[16]   *Relevance rediscovered: An anthology of 25 significant articles
         from the NACA bulletins and yearbooks 1939–1949*. Montvale, NJ:
         NAA (1992).
[17]   Accounting, a hindrance to planning and control. *Management
         Planning* (July/August 1973), 101–103.
[18]   Can accounting be a hindrance to planning and control? *Newspaper
         Controller* (May 1974), 6–9.
[19]   The natural business year: A review of accounting literature from
         1915 through 1985 shows a shift of proactive to reactive behavior
         by accountants (with M. Higgins). *The Accounting Historians
         Notebook* (Spring 1990), 42–43.
[20]   The natural business year: A shift from proactive to reactive
         behavior by accountants. *Accounting Historians Journal*
         (December 1990), 37–56.
[21]   Natural business year (with M. Higgins). *Journal of Accountancy*
         (November 1990), 5.
[22]   The current value experiences of The Rouse Company, 1973–1989
         (with H. Schwarzbach). *Collected Abstracts*, HERAAA Annual
         Conference (1990), 59.
[23]   The current value experiences of The Rouse Company, 1973–1989
         (with H. Schwarzbach). *Accounting Horizons*, 5(2) (1991), 45–54.
[24]   *Total capacity management: Optimizing at the operational, tactical,
         and strategic levels* (with C. J. McNair). Boca Raton, FL: FAR and
         St. Lucie Press (1998).

Appendix 1 (*Continued*)

[25]   *Measuring the cost of capacity* (with C. J. McNair). Management
          Accounting Guideline No. 42, Hamilton, Ontario, Canada (1996).
[26]   *Measuring the cost of capacity* (with C. J. McNair). Statement of
          Management Accounting 4Y. Montvale, NJ: IMA (1996).
[27]   The fall of management accounting: The NIRA and the
          homogenization of cost practices in the United States (with C. J.
          McNair). In: A. J. Richardson (Ed.), *Disorder and Harmony: 20th
          Century Perspectives on Accounting History: Selected Papers from
          the 7th World Congress of Accounting Historians.* Vancouver, BC:
          Canada, CGA-Canada Research Foundation (1996).
[28–31]   *75th Anniversary: Rhode Island Society of CPAs, founded 1905,
          1980,* Parts 1, 2, 3, and 4, 1980–1981.
[32]   Tips for writing a history of a state society of CPAs. *The Accounting
          Historians Notebook* (Spring 1982), 1, 16.
[33–34]   Rhode Island Society's 85th Anniversary 1905 to 1990. *Society
          Report* (January 1991), 1–2; (March 1991), 8–9.
[35]   Ideas from the archives committee. *The Accounting Historians
          Notebook, 3*(2) (1980), 7.
[36]   Plan now for centennial. *Journal of Accountancy* (April 1981), 31.
[37]   The origins of a great profession. Academy of Accounting
          Historians (1987).
[38]   *The origins of a great profession* (with P. L. McMickle). Memphis:
          The Academy of Accounting Historians (1987).
[39]   A few suggestions for potential hourglass awardees. *The
          Accounting Historians Notebook* (Fall 1988), 6–7.
[40]   A call to share in NAA's history. *Association Leader* (May 15,
          1989), 3, 11.
[41]   Present at the creation: It's 1919 and you're in Buffalo witnessing
          the birth of a new accounting group. *Management Accounting* (June
          1994), 38–41.
[42]   *History of the Providence chapter of the Institute of Management
          Accountants, 1920–1995.* Providence, Providence Chapter of IMA
          (1995).
[43]   *The history of accounting: An international encyclopedia* (with M.
          Chatfield). New York: Garland Publishing, Inc. (1996).
[44]   A request for nominees for contributors to accounting thought. *The
          Accounting Historians Notebook* (Spring 1985), 7.

THE USE OF THE INTERNET IN ACCOUNTING HISTORY RESEARCH

Leonard Goodman and Dan Palmon

INTRODUCTION

This article examines innovations in information technology that have changed the way accounting historians collect information. The following section describes how accounting historians can locate information such as books, journal articles, newspaper pieces, and encyclopedia entries on-line. Next, we consider the use of proprietary and public-access databases to obtain financial reporting information that may be valuable to accounting historians, followed by a description of how search engines and accounting-based websites can simplify the search for information. Subsequently, we explore the use of web-based newsgroups as a tool for a discussion and evaluation of research findings. Discussed next is the increasingly important role that "electronic agents" are likely to play in making it easier for accounting historians and others to collect information. We also examine the limitations and access difficulties associated with archival webpages. We then consider the risks associated with relying upon information received from the Internet and safeguards that assure that the information is sent by the party whom the researcher believes sent it. The last topic before the conclusion is the advantages of on-line access to primary source documents and the difficulties associated with becoming too comfortable with the Internet.

Doing Accounting History: Contributions to the Development of Accounting Thought
Studies in the Development of Accounting Thought, Volume 6, 185–202
Copyright © 2003 by Elsevier Science Ltd.
All rights of reproduction in any form reserved
ISSN: 1479-3504/PII: S1479350402060106

FINDING MATERIALS ON-LINE

Books

Prior to the advent of computer technology, a researcher interested in an accounting history topic would usually begin with a search of a library's card catalog to determine if any books had been written on that topic. Using a book title, an author's name, or a subject heading, the researcher could find a call number for the appropriate book. Commonalities in the cataloguing systems used by research libraries would lead the accounting historian to a specific shelf location in the general area of the library where the likely books were located.

Computer technology has greatly simplified the task of finding the right book, while perhaps removing some of the joy of strolling through a library's open shelves. Although the same shelves are probably still open as in the past, more people than ever before are making this journey in an almost always-open "on-line library."

On-line, public-access catalogs (OPACs) now serve the same function that printed cards, physically contained in alphabetical drawers in a library's reference section, did in the past. OPACs allow researchers who are connected via the Internet to access the card catalogs of a number of universities as well as some highly respected public libraries, such as the U.K.'s National Library (www.bl.uk), the U.S.'s Library of Congress (www.loc.gov) and the National Library of Australia (www.nla.gov.au).

While the term OPAC is generally used to describe the on-line version of a library's card catalog, libraries tend to have proprietary systems with their own name. For example, at Oxford University a system known as OLIS is used, while at Stanford University, the system is called Socrates. These systems perform similar tasks; that is, they allow users to determine if the library has a particular book. These systems typically use the same information – the author's name, book title, or subject area that would help find a book on a particular topic in a traditional, printed version of a library's card catalog. However, in contrast to old-fashioned, card-catalog systems, OPACs with their on-line capabilities can also inform the user if a book is on the shelf, missing, or otherwise unavailable. OPAC systems are also able to link directly to on-line resources, such as indices and journals.

Research libraries, at least for now, may still be the best source for out-of-print and difficult-to-find scholarly titles because of their interlibrary loan capabilities. However, on-line booksellers such as Amazon.com (www.amazon.com) and Barnes and Noble (www.barnesandnoble.com) have made it easier for researchers to locate and purchase books that may be difficult to find either because they had small production runs or were published years ago and have not been reprinted. In contrast to commercial booksellers, research libraries usually do not charge a fee for those who use their interlibrary loan. This free service, however, is beginning to change as many research libraries are attempting to reduce their own costs by adopting an activity-based costing approach to their interlibrary loan services.

Although OPACs have many common features, there are differences that are likely to slow down those unfamiliar with a particular system. Moreover, while catalogs for all academic libraries are freely searchable, access to some databases may be restricted, and a researcher unable to produce the appropriate password or other valid identification may be turned away. These databases contain information that the library has purchased from outside vendors under terms that restrict access to authorized users.

Gaining access to a university's OPAC can be done by typing in a direct Internet address. For example, typing www.library.hbs.edu as an Internet address will directly access the Baker Library at the Harvard Business School. If the Library's Internet address is not known, access can usually be achieved, first by locating Harvard's home page on the Internet, and then by searching for an entry for its library system.

Search engines such as Yahoo and Google provide links to OPACs worldwide. For example, entering the words "Danish Libraries" in a Yahoo search provides a link that leads to the Copenhagen Business School where access could be obtained to the School's OPAC system (www.cbs.dk/library/indexuk.html) and its accounting resources. An on-line search of OPACs can be frustrated if the researcher cannot read the primary language of the host country. While some of these links may indicate that information is available in English, it was our experience that it is often difficult to advance past the first screen to access the English language information.

The technology in this area is changing in a way that allows easy retrieval of specific information. Net Libraries, Inc. has developed a system that converts scholarly books into an electronic format that can be read on-line. The system permits a user who enters a particular topic or keyword from a web-based browser to obtain a listing of books in which this word or topic appears. Clicking on the title of a selected book leads to each of the locations in the book in which the item of interest appears.

Although the researcher may miss the opportunity to find interesting items by physically "browsing" the library, browsing in the digital era is much more efficient because it requires less time and is not restricted by the hours that the library is open. The use of specific keywords or topics reduces the need to read a longer selection of a work to find a specific reference to an item of interest.

Net Library, which can be found at www.netlibrary.com, was the early and presumed dominant player in this market since it quickly placed a substantial number of scholarly books in its database. However, newer entries with deeper pockets, such as Ebrary.com and Questia Media, have created a much larger database of scholarly books.

Like NetLibrary, some OPACs offer electronic books. However, as of now, they are mostly for out-of-copyright books in fields such as literature rather than accounting history. The Academy of Accounting Historians has to a degree helped fill this void by including landmark books such as Garner's *Evolution of Cost Accounting to 1925* (1954) on its website. This book can be accessed at http://weatherhead.cwru.edu/Accounting/old/pub/garner/. An advantage of accessing books through the Academy's website or through OPACs is that there is no user fee.

Articles

Electronic access to articles about business and accounting publications can be obtained by subscription through ABI/INFORM, the largest purveyor of electronically produced abstracts and articles about business. In contrast to other services that have currently both on-line and in-print services, ABI/INFORM is strictly an on-line service. When ABI/INFORM was started in 1971, few people could visualize what was to come. Even by the late 1970s and early 1980s, relatively few librarians knew how to perform an electronic search. Librarians with this specialized skill would type arcane computer commands into a device that resembled an oversized electronic typewriter that, in turn, transmitted the requested data to a mainframe computer via the handset of a telephone placed into an acoustic coupler. Later companies like LEXIS-NEXIS would establish their own niche with small monochrome monitors and dedicated terminals from which authorized users could perform electronic searches for articles.

There are three versions of ABI/INFORM – Global, Research, and Select. Albeit the most expensive, the broadest in terms of its likelihood to satisfy the research needs of the largest group of business researchers is ABI/INFORM Global, which contains more than 1,300 sources, including hundreds of English-language titles from outside the U.S. ABI/INFORM Research has relatively few English-language titles from outside the U.S. and has far fewer total sources than ABI/INFORM Global. ABI/INFORM Select offers less than a third of the sources available on ABI/INFORM Global. ABI/INFORM now provides the entire text of articles on-line for the most frequently requested publications.

Some well-known indices of business and accounting articles that were available for so many years only in print form are now available on-line. Consider in this regard the *Accountants' Index*, published in print form by the AICPA from 1920 until 1991. Beginning in 1992, responsibility for publishing the *Accountants' Index* was assumed by University Microforms, Inc. (UMI) (www.umi.com). Renaming this source the *Accounting and Tax Index*, UMI now has both a print version and an on-line one that can be accessed through many university library systems.

Similarly, H. W. Wilson's *Reader's Guide to Business Periodicals*, with print volumes dating back to the beginning of the 20th century, has an on-line version renamed H. W. Wilson's *Business Databases* (www.hwwilson.com). It covers over 500 English-language business titles with full-text coverage available for over 250 English-language business publications going back to January 1995. Abstracts from more than 500 English-language titles have been available from June 1990, with indexing available from July 1982.

LEXIS-NEXIS offers access to an extensive number of up-to-date business, finance, tax, legal, and political documents through its interactive service, accessible only with its own special, user-friendly software or on web-based LEXIS-NEXIS Global Advantage. Subscribers to LEXIS-NEXIS can either pay for the actual amount of time spent on the system or an unlimited access fee.

Dow Jones Interactive (DJIA) has some similar features and can search for articles that mention a company's name. This aid can be a tremendous help to accounting historians who want to obtain information about companies over a period of time.

Publishers such as Academic Press, Elsevier, Oxford, Cambridge, Wiley, and others offer packages of on-line journals, including many that can be viewed on-line. These include many high-quality, peer-reviewed journals. Libraries will, of course, vary in terms of their willingness and ability to pay for these on-line journals. Such packaging may be an incentive for libraries to acquire through on-line access many lesser-known journals that it might not otherwise acquire.

Some libraries purchase access to on-line systems, such as Ingenta (www.ingenta.com), that offer summaries of thousands of publications with links to full texts of many of them. Access to full text is available to individual subscribers of Ingenta and to authorized users of institutional subscribers. Non-subscribers can pay per selected title and have the requested item e-mailed or faxed.

Accounting historians in search of sources of information should also consider performing a search of ABC-CLIO (http://sb2.abc-clio.com), an excellent, on-line, subscription-based, historical database for indexed abstracts of articles. The ABC-CLIO website is divided into two parts. The first part, "America: History and Life," provides historical coverage of the U.S. and Canada from prehistory to the present. The second part, "Historical Abstracts," is a complete reference guide to the history of the world (excluding the U.S. and Canada) from 1450 to the present. Abstracts from over 2,000 journals published throughout the world are covered in its database, including abstracts from two highly respected journals in accounting history – *Accounting, Business, and Financial History* (abstracts from 1997-present) and the *Accounting Historians Journal* (abstracts from 1989-present).

ABC-CLIO also has abstracts covering many journals in economics and related disciplines. EconLit (www.econlit.org), however, an expanded version of the *Journal of Economic Literature*, is a more likely first thought as a source of information for scholarly works in the economics field.

Microfiche, Microfilm, and On-line Newspapers

The Internet has not eliminated the need to go to libraries to use equipment that few people will have at home. Libraries have machines that researchers need to use to view documents that may only be available on either microfiche or microfilm. Indeed, these machines are important tools for accounting history researchers. Reports such as old copies of the SEC's Annual Report that might otherwise take up many library shelves are often stored only on microfiche.

Microfilm may be the only way, at least for now, to read a very old newspaper article from the *Financial Times, New York Times,* or *Wall Street Journal. Financial Times* articles for up to three years back are available through the on-line systems of many university libraries. The *New York Times* is available through LEXIS-NEXIS from 1980 in full text (abstracts to 1969) and through DJIA from 1980 in abstract only. DJIA has full text *New York Times* articles for the last 90 days. The *Wall Street Journal* is available through DJIA from 1984 in full text. Most out-of-print newspapers (e.g. the *New York Observer*) are not available on-line.

It can soon be expected, however, that older issues of the *New York Times* and the *Wall Street Journal* will be available on-line. Bell and Howell ProQuest on-line information service (www.proquest.com) has recently signed agreements with both newspapers that will bring to the Internet the full text of both papers, including photos, graphics, and advertisements. In contrast to the limitations associated with searching the microfilmed versions of the digitized versions of these newspapers (with the microfilm sometimes "flying" off the spool when one has spun the spool too far), on-line searching will be available via keywords and Boolean operators. ProQuest's agreement with the *New York Times* will bring prior issues of the paper dating all the way back to its first issue in 1851. Its agreement with the *Wall Street Journal* will provide on-line issues of the paper from 1899. It is expected that these projects will be completed relatively quickly. ProQuest anticipates digitizing back issues of the *New York Times* in just 15 months, with electronic files covering ten-year segments released every month beginning March 2001. The digitization of the *Wall Street Journal* is expected over the same 15-month time frame.

It can be presumed that older copies of these two newspapers are becoming available on-line because there is sufficient demand for them among those who prefer the convenience of Internet access. While the benefits of having these newspapers available on the Internet may justify the costs involved in making them accessible in this manner, this economy is unlikely to exist for many documents that may be of interest to accounting historians but are only available on microfiche or microfilm. Consider, in this regard, that the National Archives of the U.S. has available in either microfiche or microfilm form such voluminous government records as the Interstate Commerce Commission (ICC) Annual Reports from 1888 to 1914, the General Records of the Department of the Treasury, and the records of the Internal Revenue Service from 1862 to 1866. The ICC reports alone consist of 1,348 rolls of 16 mm microfilm. Having these documents available in microfiche or microfilm is a positive in terms of the likelihood of future access since documents preserved in these media are expected to last hundreds of years if properly maintained.

Encyclopedia Entries

Articles of possible interest to accounting historians can also be found in on-line encyclopedias. While there are a number of accounting encyclopedias and hand-books, none are published on-line.[1] Some encyclopedias in general use, however, are offered on-line and may provide researchers interested in accounting history with useful information. As an example, *Encyclopedia Britannica*, which for so many years had only been produced in printed form and which was somewhat slowly adapted to computer technology, in recent years has adopted three versions – hardcopy, one on CD-ROM, and an on-line, web-based version. More recently, *Encyclopedia Britannica* decided to allow free access via the Internet, www.britannica.com. In doing so, *Britannica*, which for so many years had set the standard by which other encyclopedias are measured, opened for general use a resource of tremendous benefit to all types of researchers.

Other encyclopedias that may be of use to accounting historians are beginning to appear in on-line versions. For example, the Encyclopedia of Cleveland History (http://ech.cwru.edu) has been opened for general use, as has the handbook for the State of Texas (www.tsha.utexas.edu). Another electronic encyclopedia that may contain information valuable to accounting historians is Microsoft's Encarta.

ON-LINE FINANCIAL INFORMATION ABOUT BUSINESSES

Accounting historians often need to know all sorts of information before a research project is completed. Information about officers of a corporation, business events, and the assessments of trends, particularly in the area of financial reporting, are often needed prior to drawing conclusions. Annual reports are often good sources for this type of information.

Company annual reports are available on microfiche through UMI. UMI's collection covers annual reports of large companies from 1891 to 1987, with a complete chronology of annual reports available for some companies beginning with their first annual report (e.g. General Motors, 1911 and Coca-Cola, 1920). Recent annual reports of publicly traded companies are usually included in on-line websites such as those maintained by the companies themselves and in websites of government agencies that regulate security filings.

The time period associated with the earliest available on-line financial data that deal with security prices predates by just a few years the U.S. Securities and Exchange Act of 1934, the U.S. law that first required publicly traded companies to provide continuous information about their financial position and result of operations. Thus, accounting historians will find information included in even the oldest on-line sources of financial information to be relatively recent.

Proprietary databases such as CRSP, Compustat, and Research Insight provide a wealth of information about security prices and financial statements. CRSP provides security prices for publicly traded companies whose securities are listed on the New York Stock Exchange. This information is available on a monthly basis since 1925 and on a daily basis since 1962. For American Stock Exchange companies, information is available on both a daily and monthly basis from 1962. Data for companies listed on the NASDAQ are available on a monthly and daily basis from December 1972. CRSP also includes daily and monthly price data on U.S. government bonds from 1961.

Compustat, issued by Standard & Poor's (S&P) Corporation, is the primary source for financial statement information. It provides annual and quarterly financial data for companies required to file with the SEC. Compustat also provides specialized industry-specific data. Compustat's ExecuComp has compiled information on executive compensation, including stock options, for approximately 2,000 firms. These data, beginning in 1992, were taken from the firms' proxy statements.

While databases such as CRSP and Compustat are powerful in manipulating data, they can require considerable expertise simply to view information that may be relatively easy to access in print and/or other formats. For example, a researcher wanting to know daily stock prices may, depending upon circumstances, find it easier to access this information from a library's printed copy of Moody's or S&P than from CRSP.

Research Insight, another S&P product, which is similar to Compustat, has more of an international focus. It contains extensive financial statement data for companies with securities listed on stock exchanges in foreign countries with well-developed financial markets. The database DataStream (www.datastream. com) provides comprehensive historical coverage of more than 140,000 securities and instruments from markets worldwide. In some cases, information is available for companies for more than 25 years.

For those doing research on earnings forecasts, I/B/E/S has quarterly and annual earnings forecast data for approximately 6,000 U.S. firms starting in 1976, as well as similar data for over 11,000 international firms starting in 1987. The forecast data include both consensus forecasts for each firm and specific predictions by each analyst who supplies information to I/B/E/S. The forecasts are often used to proxy for the market's expectation of earnings in earnings/returns studies.

Other proprietary systems that provide financial information include Bloomberg, DJIA, Geoinvestor, and LEXIS-NEXIS. LEXIS-NEXIS financial databases include SEC filings, business journals, and news services. Its annual reports go back as far as 1973, while its 10-K and proxy statements cover 1987 to the present. The LEXIS-NEXIS services contain a vast array of news and business information from around the world, including documents and databases in German, Dutch, French, Italian, and Spanish. These databases and documents are constantly updated from thousands of sources of information. Historical researchers who have access to LEXIS-NEXIS will find it to be a powerful research tool. DJIA has similar features plus historical market data. Geoinvestor (www.geoinvestor.com/countryindex.htm) is another source of broad-based, international financial data. It provides more than 20,000 links to English-language webpages in 41 countries plus Hong Kong. Each country's webpage has a navigation bar, listing six categories of data and information – Financial, News, Economic, Monetary, Fiscal, and Research. Another major source of financial news and information is Bloomberg (www.bloomberg.com). It covers the U.S. and many international sites, primarily for more-developed countries.

Other websites also contain important historical financial information. For example, the Federal Deposit Insurance Corporation offers a significant amount of information about the U.S. banking industry through its website, www.fdic.gov. This site provides recent financial information about banking institutions, as well as historical information beginning in 1934 for commercial banks and in 1984 for savings banks and other financial institutions.

A massive, public-access database, the Electronic Data Gathering Archival Research (EDGAR) project of the SEC, located at www.sec.gov/edgarhp.htm, provides a wealth of current financial information about companies that have registered with the SEC so that their securities can be traded on a U.S. stock exchange.

In some countries, stock exchanges are the primary market regulators. The International Federation of Stock Exchanges (www.fibv.com), an organization of the world's stock exchanges, provides links to member exchanges and, in some cases, to on-line financial information required of listed companies. However, the on-line accessibility of data from these sources may vary both in regard to required disclosures and user-friendliness.

Structured databases such as CRSP, Compustat, and Research Insight, in contrast to what might be considered a nonstructured agglomeration of financial databases (e.g. on-line filings that a company may be required to make on EDGAR), are more systematic and standardized across companies. While the more structured approach of proprietary databases is important to the empirical researcher needing to manipulate data in a market study, some accounting historians may find it easier to find needed financial information about companies in on-line financial (non-database) sources such as EDGAR or through links of the International Federation of Stock Exchanges. While these financial, non-database sources are sometimes less user-friendly (i.e. finding and printing specific financial information from EDGAR is sometimes difficult), they do not require the access to more expensive proprietary databases which, while available at many research libraries, often require specialized training to use.

SEARCH ENGINES AND ACCOUNTING-BASED WEBSITES

Search engines have the potential to simplify the search for information that may be of interest to the accounting historian. The Internet provides all-purpose directories such as Yahoo where one can search within a given category. The researcher cannot add categories, and there is none for accounting history. Accounting resources on these sites are poorly organized because they are typically spread over a broad range of categories. The way to pick up this information is by searching with keywords. This technique, however, is time consuming and often yields poor results.

If the search is too general, the researcher ends up with too many "hits," whereas if the search is too specific, the result is too few. Search engines such as Google (www.google.com) use unique algorithms to determine the relevance and importance of various webpages to the specified search. Taking advantage of advances in artificial intelligence, Google is able to produce more efficient searches (Mossberg, 2000). In the future, intelligent agents and other advanced technologies are expected to produce search results instantly with a very high degree of accuracy.

In the interim, accounting historians trying to find information using these search engines can locate an extraordinary amount of potentially useful information with some of it specific to accounting history. For example, a Google search performed by entering Pacioli's name provided a reasonable selection of web links relating to Pacioli's seminal contribution to accounting. Performing a Google search by entering FASB and also IASB led almost immediately to the official website of these organizations, as well as to some reasonably related ones.

However, only a few successful "hits" were found when performing a Google search for information about less well-remembered accounting pioneers and for organizations that may have had a significant impact but may no longer exist. For example, a researcher who wants information on the *American Society of Public Accountants*, a predecessor organization of the AICPA, or on Robert Montgomery, cofounder of what became one of the largest accounting firms in the world, would have been better served using a printed copy of Chatfield and Vangermeersch (1996) or Previts and Merino (1998).

A number of accounting Internet sites exist. The Rutgers Accounting Web (RAW) is one of the oldest. Located at www.accounting.rutgers.edu, RAW organizes and disseminates accounting resources on the Internet, providing links to important sources of accounting information. The website of important accounting organizations, such as the Financial Accounting Standards Board and the American Accounting Association, are hosted on the RAW. Similarly, the website of the Institute of Chartered Accountants in England and Wales, located at http://www.icaew.co.uk, provides many valuable links of interest to accounting academics and professionals.

For a while, only large accounting firms and professional accounting organizations with many members, such as the AICPA, IMA, AGA, and state CPA societies, could afford and felt the need to have their own websites. The growth of the Internet, along with the availability of inexpensive and easy-to-use, web-design software has led to a business environment in which much smaller accounting firms and organizations have felt a need to develop their own websites.

The Academy of Accounting Historians website, formerly maintained by Case Western Reserve University and now found at www.accounting.rutgers.edu/raw/aah/, provides information about forthcoming meetings of accounting historians and brief summaries about the Academy's research centers and committees.

The Academy's website has links to individual histories of companies, technology, money, railroads, petroleum marketing, and other informational sources, such as the papers of Frederick W. Taylor (http://attila.stevens-tech.edu/~rdowns/). It also has links to accounting and business history groups located in England, Spain, and Germany. It provides links to a French site that focuses on the history of aluminum and another one devoted to Japanese railways. While association websites are typically written in the language of the applicable country, there is often some material in English and in some cases a bilingual web service, such as the Spanish Railway Foundation.

NEWSGROUPS

Accounting historians might participate in web-based newsgroups in search of specific information. Newsgroups serve as an on-line medium of expression for individuals interested in a specific topic. These individuals might submit messages in expectation that another interested party might assist them with a problem. While newsgroup discussions may contain information that may be valuable to accounting historians, finding this information can be frustrating. Google, which recently acquired the Usenet Discussion Service of deja.com, has indicated that it intends to integrate Deja's full archive of more than 500 million archived messages into Google's other search capabilities so that users will be able to search and browse these millions of messages with the same speed as with Google's primary searches.

Participation in newsgroup discussion is available to anyone with on-line access. An individual participating in a newsgroup discussion can begin a discussion or write a response to what others have written. Responses to an initiated discussion become part of a "thread," a threaded discussion that others may wish to join. If a new, "threaded" discussion diverges from its original initiated topic, new threads may be created. Unmoderated discussion groups may lack focus because there is no screening of messages before they appear on the monitors of those participating in the discussion.

Some groups, such as Economic History Net (www://eh.net), use moderated discussion groups to ensure that contributions are relevant to the topic being discussed. In the case of Economic History Net, those with a scholarly interest in a topic may request to have their name placed on a list-serve (a computerized e-mail list). The list's moderator e-mails relevant information to individuals having a scholarly interest in the area for which the list's coordinator has assumed responsibility. Both newsgroups and list-serves may be restricted to those whom the designated moderator feels should be on the list.

Working in this manner, Economic History Net provides a forum for asking and answering questions relating to economic history. It hosts discussions in which researchers can discuss and evaluate recent research findings in their field, as well as consider the relevance of their work to contemporary economic problems and to work in related fields.

It would appear, at least to the authors, that this type of approach to creating an on-line, threaded discussion would also work well for accounting historians. One of the major accounting historians' groups, such as the Academy of Accounting Historians or the Accounting History Special Interest Group of the Accounting Association of Australia and New Zealand, would seem a logical choice for coordinating this type of activity. An accounting historian with a broad knowledge of accounting history, working with increasingly user-friendly software, could coordinate controlled, threaded, newsgroup discussions in which researchers could share information, not only about the findings of their research but also about the challenges of obtaining data, assessing its validity, and interpreting its meaning.

"EXTENSIBLE BUSINESS REPORTING LANGUAGE" (XBRL): IMPROVING THE EFFICIENCY OF DATA COLLECTION AND RETRIEVAL

The nature of accounting reporting and data acquisition is likely to change dramatically over the next few years. Intelligent (electronic) agents are likely to play an increasingly important role in data collection and retrieval of future digital filings. An electronic agent is a computer program that is used independently to initiate an action or respond to electronic records or performances, in whole or in part, without review or action by an individual. For example, electronic agents can look at earnings reported on-line via EDGAR and prices reflected on the applicable stock exchange and, automatically, without human intervention, calculate price-earnings ratios in all the places it needs to be done. While this example is highly simplified, it illustrates the basic concept of how electronic agents operate.

Currently, intelligent agents have to extract, categorize, and analyze data displayed in HTML (Hypertext Markup Language), the standard formatting computer language designed mainly for presentations. HTML limits the ability of intelligent agents to perform complex tasks. Difficulties in using HTML are likely to be overcome by Extensible Business Reporting Language (XBRL), a new proposed standard for business reports. XBRL permits the automatic exchange and reliable extraction of financial information. The endorsement of XBRL by a broad range of accounting groups offers the financial community a standards-based method to prepare, publish, exchange, and analyze financial reports and the information they contain. XBRL will transform company financial reporting into a continuous, on-demand process. XBRL is the business version of extended markup language (XML).

In so doing, XBRL has the potential to transform the web into a virtual financial database. In other words, using electronic-retrieval agents, accounting historians and other researchers will be able to extract any type of information from multiple sources in real-time. XBRL will allow financial reporting to move away from the old model of "one size fits all" because every user will have the ability to order a report especially created for his/her specifications.

ARCHIVAL WEBPAGES

Only a few years ago, it was only economical for a limited number of enterprises to establish a professional-looking website. Now, software such as Dreamweaver and Fireworks make it easy to create professional-looking sites. Moreover, the information reported on these sites can be easily and quickly updated.

With more information being generated in digital form, archival storage of webpages is beginning to provide researchers with the most important documentation of the digital age. Due to information overflow, and the frequency with which digital data is being updated and modified, accounting historians are soon to face the great challenge of extracting specific web-based data from deleted webpages. For example, FASB exposure drafts are available on the web before the final statement is issued. At this point, the exposure draft is deleted from the web because it is of little interest to anyone except historians.

Currently, there is an effort beginning to collect and store archival webpages. There are basically two main sources for accessing archival webpages, namely www.alexa.com and www.archive.org. Alexa.com's electronic robots are continuously crawling the Internet to collect data for the purpose of archiving the web. The archive currently has 18 terabytes of data from approximately five million websites and two billion pages. A copy of the collected data is donated to the Internet Archive Organization (Archive.org), which is endowed to help preserve the data as part of a collective digital heritage. Alexa.com provides users with a limited access to archival data in the form of the most recent version of the archived page. This service can be obtained by downloading the software, that has other functions, from Alexa's corporate website.

A more suitable service for accounting researchers is provided by the Internet Archive Organization. This organization provides researchers with the ability to access all the stored data for the purpose of research and scholarly work. At present, using collections of this size requires programming skills. However, in the future, with the development of more sophisticated tools and methods, every researcher will have an easy and meaningful access to the collective history.

The Internet Archive Organization collects all publicly available information on the Internet that is posted as static HTML files. With the advent of Internet technology, however, less and less data will be posted as simple HTML files to the web and more and more information will be provided dynamically. While existing pages impose a relatively easy task for intelligent agents, dynamic webpages are a different story. Dynamic webpages are pages that are created on the fly, the actual data being stored and updated in a database physically located on the server. There is no representation in a webpage form except when a webpage has an embedded code that retrieves this specific data from a database via a query.

The efficient retrieval of deleted webpages is hard to achieve without a sophisti-cated data categorization method. Currently, there is no unique address for deleted webpages. Pages are referenced to the Uniform Resource Locator (URL) to which they are linked. The only way to uniquely identify a deleted webpage is by the orig-inal date shown on it. Even if you have a deleted webpage with a date, you still do not know how many times it was updated and if it was subsequently deleted. This problem is analogous to an historian coming across a dated, hardcopy document but not knowing if it is an update of an earlier version and/or if it was subsequently replaced by a later edition.

Other related issues are data storage and data extraction. Given the size and the growth of the World Wide Web, one of the most challenging tasks is to be able to store all the existing information. An efficient indexing technique has to be incorporated into the database schema so that data retrieval is efficient. Another important task, related to storage, is storage preservation, which involves backups of huge datasets, migration to new media, and data formats.

With respect to data extraction, it is expected in the future that we will be able to search multiperiod archival data using highly sophisticated algorithms and receive a formatted result more relevant to our search in seconds. It may behoove historians to develop their own version of XML to facilitate research of web-based information of historical relevance.

IN THE AGE OF THE INTERNET KNOWING WHOSE INFORMATION TO TRUST

Accounting historians face challenges when using the Internet as a source of in-formation. Accounting historians need to be assured that the information used in their research is accurate and provided by a reliable source. A crude proxy for the reliability of information is familiarity with the individual or organization that provides the information. When extracting information from a well-known source, such as the *Financial Times* or the *Wall Street Journal*, most researchers would rely on both the accuracy and the integrity of that information. However, when we find relevant data, for example, on "anybody.com," our initial level of confidence is likely to be low if we are unfamiliar with the information source.

Even with informational sources we feel reliable, the risk of having on-line digital data tampered with is a concern of which accounting historians should be aware. Intruders can maliciously change data (files) on on-line webpages and public databases or engage in "session hijacking" where surfers are redirected to an alternative webpage without their knowledge. Assurance that information is being sent by who the researcher believes is sending it can be achieved by having a trusted third party attest to the practices of the entity and various information items. Researchers and historians should search for a third party's seal of assurance on websites from which they extract information. WebTrust, TRUSTe, and BBBOnline are some of the providers of these seals.

WebTrust is a seal developed by the AICPA/CICA to attest on several different principles – privacy, security, availability, business practices/transaction integrity, confidentiality, and nonrepudiation. A party who sends a message cannot later deny sending this message. It is more likely that the WebTrust seal will be most effective when researchers retrieve information from unknown sources, or from small companies and individuals. The seal in the case of WebTrust, while primarily developed to protect those engaged in e-commerce, can provide an assurance to the accounting historian that the information being received was sent by the intended sender without alteration.

Researchers should also be concerned with tampered data. Reporting inaccurate data by reliable sources is an uncommon phenomenon, but can similarly occur in any reporting media, digital or non-digital. Whether inaccurate data are more likely to occur in a digitized media than in a non-digitized one is an unanswered question as digitized information is still very young.

PRIMARY SOURCE INFORMATION IN
THE DIGITAL AGE

The researcher who personally examines primary source documents, such as letters, memoranda, notes, account books, and other relevant records, is in a better position to perform successful, groundbreaking historical research than someone who relies mainly on secondary sources that are typically of secondary importance.

Some important primary source documents are linked to web-related technologies. For example, the Library of Congress' five-part CD-ROM product, "Birth of a Nation," successfully integrates primary source documents, including photographs with links to the Library of Congress' American Memory Web Site, allowing instant access to related historical documents. Similarly, Encarta's Africana, 2000 CD-ROM, a visually stunning and fascinating work that contains more than 3,000 articles and panoramic images of African and African-American locations, is linked to hundreds of related websites.

The Research Libraries Group (RLG), an international organization devoted to improving access to information that supports research, is involved with the archival community in making it easier to find primary source documents through its "archival resources service" (www.rlg.org/arr/index.html). Searches performed using this service often lead to "findings aids" that contain detailed information about individuals and/or organizations that may be of interest to historical researchers.

While RLG's "archival resources service" offers the advantage of a single point of entry and a uniform presentation for worldwide archival holdings, a researcher can often use a search engine such as Google to access the same information. For example, entering the name of Andrew Barr, Jr. in both a Google search and in RLG's "archival resources service" leads to the same URL (www.library.uiuc.edu/ahx/ead/ua/262 0058/2620058b.html) at the University of Illinois Archives that provides a finding aid for the papers of this former SEC Chief Accountant. While some on-line findings aids are linked to full text and images of related primary source material, most appear to be limited to an overview of the collection, a somewhat more detailed description of the boxes and folders listing where the papers can be found, and information about restrictions on access and use.

It is conjectured that much of the full text and images of primary source documents in finding aids are not yet available on-line because it is difficult to justify the time and effort involved in making decisions as to which specific documents should be made available in this manner. Since digitization of noncomputer-generated documents require scanning of documents, the cost of this scanning and publishing these documents on-line is also an important factor.

A major reason that primary source information is not available on-line is that it is important only to a small group of researchers. One way to deal with the problem, at least for now, is to make a finding aid available on-line but to release the entire text of requested information only when asked to do so. Another possible factor slowing down the pace of placing full text and images on line is the fact that those entrusted with the care of primary source documents may be concerned about the disclosure of information that might prove to be embarrassing.

The lack of convenience in terms of quick Internet access for primary source documents may contain a silver lining. Lack of on-line access may encourage the researcher to travel to a location where important primary source documents are physically located. This physical presence provides an opportunity for the researcher to examine actual source documents personally and, in a sense, to authenticate information that the research relies upon. Also, the researcher may discover at the same location, often through serendipity, other important primary source information.

CONCLUSIONS

This paper has shown how innovations in information technology have made electronic sources of information easily available for research in accounting history.

The major categories that were covered include primary and secondary sources of information and financial data, including financial reporting information. It is shown that while financial databases and secondary sources of information such as books, journal articles, newspaper pieces, and encyclopedia entries are becoming widely available on-line, the availability of primary sources of information is progressing at a much slower pace. The paper also shows how and where to search and find on-line information relevant for researchers in accounting history and points out important factors regarding the reliability of the information retrieved.

Given the rapid speed with which information technology is changing, the paper points out that the financial community has increasingly begun to embrace Extensible Business Reporting Language. The anticipated, broad adoption of this intelligent-agent-based computer language is expected to improve the efficiency of data collection and retrieval greatly.

The digital revolution unfolding before our eyes is still evolving. Creative yet careful use of the new technology may well make this generation of accounting historians the most productive and innovative.

NOTE

1. The Internet provides a means to improve the value of scholarly works such as encyclopedic and bibliographic works that with the passage of time need new entries and/or modifications of earlier ones. In this respect, the authors believe that a continuing update and placement on the Internet of *The History of Accounting: An International Encyclopedia*, edited by Michael Chatfield and Richard Vangermeersch (Chatfield & Vangermeersch, 1996), would provide a valuable service to accounting historians. Similarly, an updating and placement on the Internet of bibliographic works such as R. H. Parker's *Selected Bibliography of Works on the History of Accounting 1981–1987* (Parker, 1988) would also provide a valuable service to accounting historians.

REFERENCES

Chatfield, M., & Vangermeersch, R. (Eds) (1996). *The history of accounting, an international encyclopedia*. New York: Garland Publishing.
Garner, P. S. (1954). *Evolution of cost accounting to 1925*. Tuscaloosa: University of Alabama Press.
Mossberg, W. H. (2000). Google is smart, fast, honest and may be the best sleuth on the Web. *Wall Street Journal* (March 1), B1.
Parker, R. H. (1988). Select bibliography of works on the history of accounting, 1981–1987. *Accounting Historians Journal, 15*(2), 1–81.
Previts, G. J., & Merino, B. D. (1998). *A history of accountancy in the United States*. Columbus: Ohio State University Press.

THE *ACCOUNTING HISTORIANS JOURNAL* INDEX: EMPLOYING THE *ACCOUNTING RESEARCH DATABASE* TO PROFILE AND SUPPORT RESEARCH

Francisco A. Badua, Gary J. Previts and
Miklos A. Vasarhelyi

INTRODUCTION

The *Accounting Historians Journal (AHJ)* database is a comprehensive listing of all the major research papers published in *AHJ*. Apart from enumerating the papers and the associated bibliographic information (author, pages, volume, number, etc.), the database also provides citation counts and taxonomic classifications for each paper. Consequently, a wide range of aggregate and longitudinal statistics as well as citation analysis can be performed. This very rich set of data and statistics raises a number of research issues and opportunities. The database was developed as part of the effort to update and expand the *Accounting Research Database (ARD)*, which is available online at http://rarc.rutgers.edu/publication/default.htm (see Appendix B). The *ARD* was created to facilitate the research of accounting academics and practitioners. It lists and taxonomically categorizes the major papers published from 1963 (the year of the first volume of the *Journal of*

Doing Accounting History: Contributions to the Development of Accounting Thought
Studies in the Development of Accounting Thought, Volume 6, 203–216
Copyright © 2003 by Elsevier Science Ltd.
All rights of reproduction in any form reserved
ISSN: 1479-3504/PII: S1479350402060118

Accounting Research) to 1997 in leading accounting journals. These journals include the *Journal of Accounting Research*; *The Accounting Review*; *Accounting, Organizations and Society*; *Journal of Accounting, Auditing and Finance*; *Journal of Accounting and Economics*; *Auditing: A Journal of Practice and Theory*; and *Contemporary Accounting Research*. As part of an effort to update and expand the *ARD*, *AHJ* was added to the directory in January 2002. The inclusion of *AHJ* starts in 1974, its first year of publication.

Our paper is organized as follows. We begin by establishing the relevance of the web-based dataset which provides utility to a variety of users. In succeeding sections, we discuss the scope of the *AHJ* database, the various taxonomic classifications, and citational analysis approaches. We further examine statistics related to these classifications and approaches. We conclude by identifying issues which differentiate various classifications of historical subject matter. Further, we endorse projects such as the planned digitization of the contents of *AHJ*, which will facilitate access to content identified in the *AHJ* database.

RELEVANCE

In general, the writing of accounting history has served the divergent needs of accounting academics and educators, policy makers, and practitioners. For the first group, academe, accounting history has provided, at one level, a store of pedagogical aids, whether illustrative anecdotes to support a classroom lecture or a rough, narrative framework that helps contextualize the development of the profession for young students. At another level, it has, or should have, provided researchers the background necessary to carry forward the development of accounting thought. By affording a broader perspective on any number of accounting research issues, historical research provides theoretical bases or points of critical attack, depending on the researcher's bent. For the second group, policy makers, accounting history communicates a necessary perspective about contemporary matters by explaining the broad tendencies and intentions behind past policy, thereby informing the decisions of current policy makers. It also guides them by exposing the political and economic effects of past policy decisions. Conversely, accounting history also illustrates how broad socio-political movements may have helped create policy. Finally, for the last group, practitioners, accounting history constitutes a set of narratives about past accounting methods and practices that serve as benchmarks or springboards to help with the development of new techniques to meet present and anticipated future needs (Previts et al., 1990a).

However, the specific form of historical writing at hand, that of the compilation of an accounting history database of the major research papers of the *AHJ*, has characteristics unique to historical databases (Previts et al., 1990b). The fact that the ultimate purpose of the database is its on-line format adds another dimension of relevance. Historical databases differ from other forms of history (e.g. biographies, historiographies, general histories, critical histories, development of thought frameworks) in that databases do not reveal either an extensive level of social and economic background or the intense interpretive and expository endeavors characteristic of other historical writings. However, an index database must provide the user a broad, organized, and manifestly simple user interface to access bibliographic and taxonomic information about relevant publications. In fact, to the extent that the database references all other types of histories, it may be the most fundamental of all sources. While it does not explicitly include the depth of material of other historical genres, it does provide a framework for organizing, understanding, and accessing others in all their richness of detail. The on-line accessibility of the *AHJ* database as part of the *ARD* is intended to enhance this particular advantage. The flexibility of the *ARD*'s search methodologies, as discussed later, provides a more desirable framework for selection of relevant papers by the researcher and practitioner.

SCOPE

The database covers all the major research papers from the inception of *AHJ* in 1974 through to its latest issue. The identification of *AHJ* articles as major research papers was made on the basis of two criteria – length and judgment. Length was the initial criterion as only papers minimally five pages in length were deemed major research papers and included in the database. Subsequently, a former editor of *AHJ* reviewed the remaining papers (those shorter than five pages) and decided that some were of sufficient academic importance to be considered major research papers and therefore included in the database. This approach resulted in a total population of 350 papers as of December 2001.

Taxonomic Classification

The papers included in the *AHJ* database were analyzed according to several taxonomic classification schemata adapted from Brown et al. (1994) (see Table 1 for a list of classifications and Appendix A for full details).

Citation Analysis of Ten Leading Journals

The *AHJ* database also includes a section wherein the citations of *AHJ* authors to research papers in other major accounting journals or to other *AHJ* papers are tallied. The 350 *AHJ* research articles generated a total of 1,413 citations. Highly cited

Table 1.   ARD Taxa.

A. Research Method
B. Inference Style
C. Mode of Reasoning
D. Mode of Analysis
E. School of Thought
F. Information
G. Treatments
H. Accounting Area
I. Geography
J. Objective
K. Applicability
L. Foundation Discipline

---

journals included *The Accounting Review*; *Journal of Accounting Research*; *Contemporary Accounting Research*; *Journal of Accounting and Economics*; *Journal of Accounting and Public Policy*; *Journal of Accounting and Finance*; *Accounting, Organizations and Society*; *Journal of Information Systems*; *Auditing: A Journal of Practice and Theory*; and *Accounting Historians Journal*. Appendix C contains a table detailing statistical findings relevant to the citation analysis.

Aggregate Statistics
Statistics aggregated on the 350 research papers reveal the relative predominance of certain classifications within the taxonomic areas. The dominant classifications in the various *ARD* taxa include mode of reasoning, school of thought, objective, and foundation discipline as documented in Table 2 .

Table 2.   Profile of AHJ Papers.

ARD Taxa	Dominant Category per ARD Taxa
A. Research Method	Internal Logic (35%)
B. Inference Style	Vague Taxon
C. Mode of Reasoning	Qualitative (94%)
D. Mode of Analysis	Not Treated
E. School of Thought	Accounting History (100%)
F. Information	Other (34%)
G. Treatments	Other (24%)
H. Accounting Area	Financial (42%)
I. Geography	U.S. (48%)
J. Objective	For Profit (73%)
K. Applicability	Vague Taxon
L. Foundation Discipline	Humanities-Sociology, Political Science, History, etc. (100%)

Table 3. Parker's Accounting History Taxonomy.

An early version of the following alpha-taxon set was first employed by R. H. Parker (1965) in a bibliography of accounting historical work. It represents a broad classificatory schema useful for *AHJ* papers. At various times up to 1988, Parker updated the bibliography employing elements of the taxonomy below.

    A. General
    B. Ancient Accounting
    C. Early Italian Accounting
    D. Early Netherlands Accounting
    E. Early French Accounting
    F. Early English and Scottish Accounting
        (1) Manorial, household, and parochial accounts
        (2) Mercantile accounts
        (3) Government accounts
    G. Early Irish Accounting
    H. Early German and Austrian Accounting
    I. Early American Accounting
    J. Early Australian Accounting
    K. Early Japanese Accounting
    L. Early Indian Accounting
    M. Professional Accountancy
    N. Auditing
    O. Cost and Management Accounting
    P. Corporate Accounting
    Q. Mechanized Accounting and Computers
    R. Executorship Accounting
    S. Financial Accounting Theory
    T. Education
    U. Terminology
    V. Bibliographies, Biographies, and Chronologies
    W. Bank Accounting
    X. Miscellaneous
    Y. Fund Accounting

The aggregate statistics regarding the topical taxa "information" and "treatment" (taxa F and G) are important because the dominant information and treatment sub-taxa were designated "Other." This finding strongly suggests that topics of interest and associated treatments of historical papers are significantly different from those found in other academic accounting literature. Thus, additional classificatory schema would be warranted. A model for the development of specific historical topical taxa would be those employed by Parker (1988). Table 3 contains alphabetic designations and topic taxa variously employed by Parker as early as 1965.

Statistics relevant to the citational analysis show a pattern wherein *The Accounting Review* (*TAR*), which to date still has the greatest number of cited papers in *AHJ*, has slowly given ground to other journals as a source of citations over the years. Aggregate statistics show that of the 1,413 papers cited in the 350 major research pieces in *AHJ*, 672 came from *TAR*, 338 came from *AHJ*, and 231 came from *Accounting, Organizations and Society* (*AOS*). However, longitudinal statistics belie the apparent overwhelming citation dominance of *TAR*. *TAR* had been the most cited journal in the first decade or so of *AHJ* (with the exception of 1988, when Parker's catalog of historical research papers, with a disproportionately large number of *AOS* and *AHJ* citations, appeared in *AHJ*). In recent years, this pattern has changed. *AHJ* achieved citational dominance in 1999, 2000, and 2001, while *AOS* took the lead in 1994, 1995, and 1998. Thus, the trend appears to be that *TAR*, a "general topics" publication, is giving ground to *AHJ* and *AOS*, implying that there now exists a critical mass of papers in historically oriented journals like *AOS* and *AHJ*. Accounting historians may have a propensity toward such outlets, avoiding more general topic journals such as *TAR*. It may also be the case that *TAR* has become less "general topics" oriented as reflected by its hesitancy to publish accounting history. This situation potentially creates a concern as to whether or not historical work will be appreciated and accepted in traditional outlets.

Vague Taxa

The *ARD* employs two taxa that do not appear to be readily amenable to *AHJ*. These are the applicability (taxon K) and inference style (taxon B) taxa. Further, we did not treat mode of analysis (taxon D) because of its similarity to taxon B. Applicability indicates whether a paper is of immediate, medium-term, or long-term relevance to accounting research. In the *ARD*, research papers relating to the accounting history school of thought are regarded as relevant only in the academic realm, unless there is an infrequent, crisis requirement. For example, contemporary journalists in the business press have found accounting history to be of interest for purposes of contrasting 21st century business failures with those which have occurred previously. Therefore, within the body of accounting history literature, it is useful to begin to distinguish differential degrees of contemporary research relevance. Inference style refers to whether a paper has or has not a hypothesis to be tested. Those pieces with testable hypotheses are classified as normative; those that do not, descriptive. The difference in classification results from the fact that the dominant mode of reasoning is qualitative. In more quantitative studies that abound in the body of general accounting literature, hypotheses are explicitly stated (particularly in papers that employ regressions). In the qualitative methodology that dominates in the accounting historical research literature, one does not generally encounter explicit hypotheses. Thus, a protocol for identifying implicit (unstated) hypotheses needs to be established in order to properly classify *AHJ* papers under the inference style taxon. While outcomes reported from the classification of *AHJ* papers are themselves informative and interesting in so far as they quantitatively illustrate patterns, changes, and dominance in *AHJ* content, a practical purpose of adding *AHJ* to the *ARD* is to better represent the diversity of literature and methodology in our discipline.

THE *ACCOUNTING RESEARCH DATABASE*: ACCESS AND REGISTRATION

The *ARD* is available as hardcopy or on-line. The on-line version of the *ARD* is accessible at http://rarc.rutgers.edu/publication/default.htm. Hardcopy editions of *ARD* include the most recently published as the third edition in 1994. The remainder of this paper will be devoted to the description of the various functionalities of the on-line *ARD*.

Although access to the on-line *ARD* requires registration, this registration is free of charge. After entering some identifying information such as first name, last name, and e-mail address, all one need do is to specify a user name and corresponding password to enter. This access pair is valid for 15 sessions, after which one may re-register at no cost.

ARD On-line: Search Methods

The *ARD* on-line allows the user to search for relevant papers in a variety of ways, including searching by author name, by key words in the title, by journal title, and by taxonomic classification. Searching by author name or by journal title is straightforward. The search by words from the title combines two search methods common to many other academic databases, search by key word and search by title. This search method would be useful if the user knows only a few key words in the title or efficiently chooses to include only a few key words so that the *ARD* might yield a variety of matches on the topic of interest. Alternatively, if a person is interested in a specific paper, one could include the complete title in the same search to access the desired paper.

However, perhaps the most interesting aspect of the search methodology in the *ARD* is the search by classification. This sort of query may be unique among academic research databases in that the *ARD* allows the user to search explicitly by research methodology, school of thought, information topic, and mode of reasoning. A useful functionality resulting from this search methodology is that the user might systematically structure searches to yield specific papers at various stages of the development of a particular accounting concept. Perhaps one might start with the topic of interest selected from the information field, under the appropriate school of thought. Initially the user might seek to read papers prepared with statistical methods that show a mere association of variables, such as non-parametric statistics. Later, one might query for theoretical works that would provide the formal framework of the relationship between these variables by searching under the internal logic mode-of-reasoning rubric. As a final step, the user might review formal tests of causation between the variables of interest by searching for papers written with the regression technique as its main mode of reasoning. Thus, the user might very deliberately trace the development of academic thinking on a particular accounting topic, always being alert for gaps, inconsistencies, omissions, or any other development that would provide a research opportunity.

CONCLUSION

The addition of the *AHJ* database to the *ARD*, which has been the topic of this paper, provides a comprehensive compilation of bibliographic and taxonomic information about the major research papers of *AHJ*. Access to the *ARD* per se is global and instantaneous, providing a valuable, flexible resource to students, academics, and practitioners at no cost. The *ARD*, like many other literature databases, provides fundamental and keyword searches (author, title, and so forth). More importantly, the *ARD* provides a unique set of classificatory schema (Table 1) to assist in more advanced and subtle inquiries of its content. While these added classifying features contain some subjective properties; namely, coding bias in taxa C (mode of reasoning), F (information), and G (treatment), this "hazard" is a negligible concern provided the person conducting the inquiry is not naïve as to its existence. Our analyses of *AHJ* paper properties have the potential value of applying supplemental topical taxa for historical classification under information (F) and treatment (G). Table 3 identifies the Parker taxonomy for this purpose.

Vague taxa regarding inference style (B) and applicability (K) are a further opportunity for research. Our findings suggest there is a need to develop a protocol to "unpack" the implicit hypotheses which appear in historical papers as classified under taxon B. As to applicability (taxon K), fewer ready responses seem to be available. Our citational analyses point to a growing reliance on history-oriented journals among historical scholars that hitherto has not existed. Yet, there remains a concern that U.S.-educated scholars view their work in an ahistorical context. Until a greater appreciation of historical perspective is achieved, there is a risk that their work will be seen as technical or methods-driven and, thus, less likely to draw on applicable historical work (taxon K).

During the next few years as digitized versions of *AHJ* become available through the Gale History Resource Center (http://www.galegroup.com/modernworld/about.htm) and through the digitization project of the AICPA National Library at the University of Mississippi, more access and ease of use will be supported. This facilitation of access by indexing in the *ARD* and digitization of the content of *AHJ* should be an important part of expanding the potential for use of historical materials by students and scholars, policy makers, and practitioners.

REFERENCES

Brown, L. D., Gardner, J. C., & Vasarhelyi, M. A. (1994). *Accounting research directory* (3rd ed.). Princeton: Markus Wiener Publishers.

Parker, R. H. (1965). Accounting history: A select bibliography. *Abacus, 1*(1), 62–84.

Parker, R. H. (1988). Select bibliography of works on the history of accounting 1981–1987. *Accounting Historians Journal, 15*(2), 1–81.

Previts, G. J., Parker, L. D., & Coffman, E. N. (1990a). Accounting history: Definition and relevance. *Abacus, 26*(1), 1–13.

Previts, G. J., Parker, L. D., & Coffman, E. N. (1990b). An accounting historiography: Subject matter and methodology. *Abacus, 26*(2), 136–158.

APPENDIX A

Taxonomic Classifications

A. *Research Method (analyzes which type of study underlies the research paper):*

Analytical Internal Logic	Empirical Field Studies
Analytical Simulation	Empirical Lab
Archival Primary	Survey
Archival Secondary	Mixed
Empirical Case Studies	

B. *Inference Style (refers to whether a paper has or has not a hypothesis to be tested):*
Inductive (no hypotheses)
Deductive (with hypotheses)

Appendix A (*Continued*)

C. *Mode of Reasoning (intended to identify which type of quantitative or qualitative analysis technique was used to formally arrive at the conclusions of the paper):*

Descriptive Statistics	Non-Parametric
Regression	Correlation
ANOVA	Analytical
Factor Analysis, MDS, Probit, DISCR	Mixed
Markov	Qualitative

D. *Mode of Analysis (refers to whether a paper has or has not a model that predicts the behavior of phenomena of interest; highly correlated with Mode of Reasoning [taxon C] because papers with models very frequently have formally tested hypotheses):*

Normative (with model)
Descriptive (no model)

E. *School of Thought (identifies to which major area of accounting research the paper contributes):*

Behavioral HIPS	Stat. Model Other
Behavioral Other	Accounting Theory
Stat. Model Efficient Market Hypothesis	Accounting History
Stat. Model Time Series	Institutional
Stat. Model Information Economics	Others
Stat. Model Mathematical Programming	Agency Theory
	Expert Systems

F. *Information (identifies the phenomenon of interest in the study):*

Financial Statement	Costs
Net Income or EPS	Budgets
Income Statement	Group Behavior
Balance Sheet	Pricing
Cash Flows	Compensation
Other Financial Statement	External Information
Financial Ratios	Footnotes
Combination of Above	SEC Information (10K, etc.)
Quarterly Report	Forecasts
Foreign Currency	Bond Rating
Pension Audit Opinion	Other
Inflation	Market-Based Information
Debt Covenants	Risk

Appendix A (*Continued*)

Internal Information
Performance Measures
Auditor Behavior
Manager Behavior
Decision Making
Internal Controls

Security Prices or Returns
Security Trading
Options
All of the Above
Mixed

G. *Treatments (identifies which major factor or other phenomenon is seen to cause, be associated with, or otherwise contextualize the phenomenon identified in the information taxon):*

Financial Accounting Methods
Cash
Inventory
Other Current Assets
Property, Plant, and Equipment/
Depreciation
Other Non-Current Assets
Accounting Changes
Business Combinations
Interim Reporting
Amortization/Depletion
Segment Reports
Foreign Currency
Errors
Trail
Judgment
Planning
Efficiency Operational
Audit Theory
Confirmations
Managerial
Transfer Pricing
Breakeven CVPA
Budgeting/Planning
Relevant Costs
Responsibility Accounting
Cost Allocations
Tax Planning

Leases
Long Term Debt
Taxes
Other Liabilities
Valuation
Special Items
Revenue Recognition
Variances
Executive Compensation
Dividends (Cash)
Dividends (Stock)
Pension (Funds)
Other Financial Accounting
Financial Statement Timing
R&D
Oil and Gas
Auditing
Opinion
Sampling
Liability
Risk
Independence
Analytical Review
Internal Control
Timing
Materiality
EDP Audit
Organization

Appendix A (*Continued*)

Overhead Allocations	Internal Audit
Capital Budgeting	Other
HRA Social Accounting	Submission to FASB
Manager Decision Characteristics	Business Failure
Information Structures	Education
Auditor Training	Professional Responsibilities
Insider Training	Forecasts
Probability Elicitation	Decision Aids
International Differences	Organization and Environment
Forms of Organization (e.g. partnership)	Litigation
Auditor Behavior	Mixed
Methodology	

H. *Accounting Area (identifies the major accounting field to which the paper belongs):*

Tax	Audit
Financial	Information Systems
Managerial	Mixed

I. *Geography (geographic context of the paper):*
Non-U.S.
U.S.
Both

J. *Objective (type of entity or entities studied in the paper):*

For-Profit	Regulated
Not-for-Profit	All

K. *Applicability (assesses relevance of the paper):*
Immediate
Medium Term
Long Term

L. *Foundation Discipline (states which academic area informs the paper):*
Psychology
Sociology, Political Science, History, Philosophy, etc.
Economic and Finance
Engineering, Communications, Computer
Science

Appendix A (*Continued*)

Math, Decision Theory, Game Theory
Statistics
Law
Other/Mixed
Accounting
Management

APPENDIX B

The Online Accounting Research Directory (ARD)

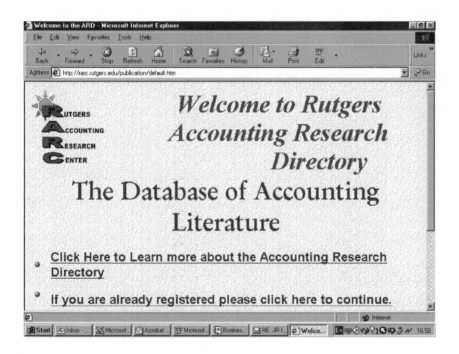

APPENDIX C

Statistics Related to the Citation Analysis of AHJ

Frequency of Citations in *AHJ* from Various Journals

	AHJ	AOS	AUD	CAR	JAAF	JAE	JAPP	JAR	JIS	TAR	Total
1974											0
1975										1	1
1976								1		7	8
1977								1		2	3
1978										6	6
1979										8	8
1980										15	15
1981	1							3		3	7
1982	4				1			1		5	11
1983	2							9		44	55
1984	4	1						1		10	16
1985	5							1		27	33
1986	6	2						1		8	17
1987	3							3		6	12
1988	147	15		1		1	3	9		26	202
1989	6	13					1	19	1	37	77
1990	1	1			1			2		13	18
1991	11	10	1		1		3	8		43	77
1992	10	5		2		1		17		25	60
1993	16	29			1		1	11	1	45	104
1994	14	22	6					5		13	60
1995	11	27				1		7		215	261
1996	12	25					2			28	67
1997	10	21		3	3		3	14		31	85
1998	14	23			1			2		14	54
1999	16	14			2	1		3		7	43
2000	22	3		1				2		16	44
2001	23	20	1	1			1	6		17	69
Total	338	231	8	8	10	4	14	126	2	672	1413

SUBJECT INDEX